"Come into My Time"

"Come into My Time"

Lithuania in Prose Fiction, 1970–90

EDITED AND WITH AN INTRODUCTION BY
Violeta Kelertas

UNIVERSITY OF ILLINOIS PRESS
Urbana and Chicago

© 1992 by the Board of Trustees of the University of Illinois
Manufactured in the United States of America
1 2 3 4 5 C P 5 4 3 2 1

This book is printed on acid-free paper.

Library of Congress Cataloging-in-Publication Data

Come into my time : Lithuania in prose fiction : 1970-90
  / edited and with an introduction by Violeta Kelertas.
      p.   cm.
  A collection of short stories translated from Lithuanian.
  ISBN 0-252-01881-8. — ISBN 0-252-06237-X (pbk.)
  1. Short stories, Lithuanian—Translations into English.
  2. Lithuanian fiction—20th century—History and criticism.
  I. Kelertas, Violeta, 1942–
  PG8771.E8C6   1992
  891'.923010803—dc20
                                                91-37437
                                                CIP

Contents

Acknowledgments

I would like to thank the International Research and Exchanges Board for the grant that allowed me to "come into the time" of the authors of these stories and of the Lithuanian people. 1986–87 saw the beginning of the political activity that culminated in the establishment of Sąjūdis, the national democratic front. The IREX grant put me in the right place at the right time in an eventful year.

I am grateful to the translators, almost all of whom have been my students at one time or another, for devoting to the project the enormous amounts of time and patience that good translation requires. My greatest debt is to Gregory M. Grazevich, without whose dedicated efforts the translations in this book could not have been of the quality that we hope they are.

Thanks are also due to the journal *Lituanus* for permission to reprint four of the translations that have been revised for this collection. Romualdas Granauskas's "The Red Forest," translated by Mirga Girniuvienė, appeared in the winter 1977 issue of *Lituanus*; Juozas Aputis's "The Flying Apple Trees," translated by Violeta Kelertas, in the fall 1980 issue; Ramūnas Klimas's "What I Thought about on the Bus Ride to See My Former Classmate," translated by Rita Dapkus, in spring 1988; and Aputis's "The Author Looks for a Way Out," translation by Rasa S. Avižienis, previously appeared in the fall 1988 issue.

"Come into My Time"

Violeta Kelertas

Introduction

Once almost forgotten by the West, Lithuania is at this writing in the center of the world stage, a position it has not had for nearly fifty years, since it was swallowed up as a result of secret clauses in the Molotov-Ribbentrop pact of 1939, which divided Eastern Europe into Soviet and Nazi spheres of influence. After World War II and the final Soviet invasion in 1944 Lithuania effectively disappeared from the map. A small country of about 3 million inhabitants, it languished as an exploited colony of the Soviet empire, one of the fifteen republics in the USSR. Because of Mikhail Gorbachev's attempts to rejuvenate the economy, however, as well as his much vaunted policies of *perestroika* (restructuring) and *glasnost* (openness), Lithuania has reawakened to new life. Together with the other Balts, the Lithuanians used the instability and disarray in the Soviet Union to their advantage, pushing for not just a new economic system but also a reestablishment of their democratic political structures and independent statehood. Taking Gorbachev at his word when he voiced support for democratization, the Lithuanians held free elections in February 1990; a few weeks later, on 11 March 1990, the newly elected Parliament under President Vytautas Landsbergis declared that it was reestablishing the country's independence. As soon became clear, Gorbachev was not yet ready to disband the empire. Of course, Gorbachev hoped then to use political freedoms merely to secure and stabilize the Soviet Union economically and at that time had no intention of yielding up the supremacy of Russia. From the first he spoke out against the new Lithuanian state, which had no military power of its own and was trying to stage a "singing revolution." On

18 April 1990 Gorbachev imposed an economic blockade against Lithuania, a country dependent on Moscow for almost all its energy and raw materials. But if Gorbachev hoped for a quick solution to his problems with the republic that was the first to attempt to secede from the USSR, he was badly mistaken. The Lithuanians did not collapse and surrender; they only dug in their heels and did without. They knew that they wouldn't starve—their agricultural country could feed them—and as for gasoline, they could take the bus or walk. Gorbachev was counting on the Slavic immigrants (including the Soviet Army) and other nonnative nationalities in Lithuania to foment a revolt from inside the country, but even tanks crushing unarmed civilians on what came to be known as Bloody Sunday (13 January 1991) did not mobilize the populace, nor did economic hardship, unemployment, and a restricted lifestyle. The world watched little Lithuania's struggle against the giant Soviet Union with bated breath, and perhaps with some disbelief that a nation could love its freedom so much that it was willing to suffer for it, suffering for one's convictions and ideals having become almost passé in the West.

The interest of outsiders in Lithuania in the 1990s revolves around several questions. What is the source of the Lithuanians' strength, especially in view of the isolation and repression they suffered over decades? What constitutes the Lithuanian "soul," the people's perception of themselves and reality? How do they view their relationship with Russia and the West? Even before the dramatic events of the Vilnius Spring, however, Lithuania and the Lithuanians would have held an intrinsic interest because of their remarkable medieval past, democratic traditions, and complex recent attempts to deal with their colonial position in the Soviet Empire. This anthology is a compendium of contemporary prose fiction—the genre that is always most enlightening about a people. It describes and explains the processes by which they threw off their shackles and sought independence, but in an indirect way it also relates how they came to be the way they are in a fuller sense. It exposes larger, more universal issues: How does a country whose natural discourse has been obliterated by the Soviet brand of newspeak even begin to speak of itself and what it has experienced? How does it name the unnameable—its past, its history, its suffering—which was denied it for so long? How does it give voice to that which no one except its own inner heart recognizes?

Because it is experience transposed into artistic form, literature can speak even under conditions of censorship. Thus, the stories in this anthology are a part of the collective memory of the cruel and inhuman suffering that began with the Nazi years and runs through

Soviet rule in all its guises, from Stalinism to the relative freedom of the Gorbachev era, which first allowed Stalin's crimes to be voiced out loud (Baltrušaitytė, Gavelis in "Handless," Aputis in some of his work). They also examine societal changes that collectivization of the farms has wrought (Granauskas, Aputis, Ignatavičius). The youngest, urban generation of writers (Klimas, Gavelis, Kondrotas), cognizant of what has now become an international prose style, have different concerns—guilt and soul-searching, the humiliations and disempowerment of fifty years of colonization. They reinterpret the past mythically and allegorically, attempting to give their concerns a viable shape and a form that can encompass them. Thus, it is clear that while freedom of speech was denied and experience negated, the writers still managed to record and indirectly debate the most important cultural and social questions for their society. The literature presented here all appeared in print, with the official blessings of the Bureau of Censorship (Glavlit). Nevertheless, in Russia proper much subject matter like this could be published only in *samizdat* (clandestine underground self-publication). There, at the center, some of it had to wait for the years of *glasnost*.[1] Why the difference? The answer lies in Soviet politics of control: Moscow allowed more freeedom on the peripheries of its empire in hopes of keeping the native populations satisfied. Lithuania produced no literary *samizdat* to speak of, but what it officially published was heavily coded and self-censored—the writers had internalized the rules of the allowable while constantly testing and trying to extend its limits, if only inch by inch.

The Historical and Political Context

Soviet Lithuanian prose fiction needs to be understood in the context of its historical situation and its literary tradition, because history and culture there necessarily have been more intertwined than they normally are elsewhere. The very development of Lithuanian literature was historically conditioned and artificially delayed by geopolitical realities. Lithuania has shared the fate of other small nations in Central and Eastern Europe. As one of the authors in this anthology puts it, Lithuania has always been a "well-traveled highway," a crossroads for invaders from the Teutonic knights to Napoleon. In this century the competing interests of Nazi Germany and Soviet Russia have brought untold suffering and tragedy to hundreds of thousands. Lithuania's history is not well known in the West; therefore, a brief survey of it is relevant, especially as it bears on the writing of literature.

From the thirteenth to the sixteenth century the Grand Duchy of Lithuania existed as a powerful state, even an empire in the medieval sense of the word, but it survived into more modern times only as the weaker partner in the Commonwealth of Poland and Lithuania or as a remote and repressed province of tsarist Russia. Exploited under a severe system of serfdom, its upper classes lacking in national consciousness and hence Polonized, Lithuania did produce writers, some of them of the caliber of Adam Mickiewicz; they contributed mainly to Polish literature, however, even though thematically some of the ideas and sentiments they expressed favored the Lithuanian part of their heritage and could have served to nurture Lithuanian culture. The genesis of prose fiction in Lithuanian was also retarded by the aftermaths of the 1863 rebellion. An attempt by Lithuania to free itself from serfdom, the revolt was brutally suppressed by the Russian Mikhail Muravjov, popularly known as the Hangman, who decimated the idealistic but underequipped progressive forces in the country by mass slaughter on the battlefield, hanging, and Siberian exile. Because it had joined forces with Poland in instigating the rebellion, Lithuania was additionally punished by a prohibition on the press (1864–1904). Russia believed that by forbidding the Latin alphabet and enforcing the Cyrillic one it could woo Lithuania from Polish influence and the Roman Catholicism that bound the two neighboring countries. In spite of these draconian measures, publication of newspapers and books in Lithuanian began in East Prussia. Intensive book-smuggling operations helped raise national consciousness and bring about a national reawakening, making independence possible in 1918. Significantly, this happened only when the country's two rapacious neighbors were weak and preoccupied with their own internal matters: Germany lay defeated after World War I, and Russia had just undergone its communist revolution and had not yet consolidated its power.

During the period of independence, which was to last a brief but fruitful twenty-two years, the Lithuanian literary language was standardized. Finally, Lithuanian culture could enjoy unimpeded development. Stability and freedom, however, came to an abrupt end with World War II. Lithuania suffered especially heavily in the 1940–41 Soviet occupation, which terminated with Stalin's massive deportations of the Lithuanian intelligentsia in the two nights before the Nazi takeover; 60,000 people were deported to Siberia under the most inhumane conditions imaginable.[2] Nazi rule was imposed on the country and lasted until 1944, when the Soviets returned to stay. The Lithuanian underground was initially organized to fight the Nazis, but because of the cruel treatment experienced in 1940 it now directed its energies against the Soviets. The Lithuanians formed military detachments in the forests and countryside and initiated a protracted guerrilla war that involved more than 40,000 men and was ardently supported by the populace; it finally ended only around 1952. At this point the people made a conscious decision that enough blood had been shed and stopped fighting the Russians openly, retreating into an uneasy truce and covert resistance on a much smaller scale.

During Stalin's reign of terror over 300,000 of Lithuania's inhabitants were deported to Siberia.[3] Since about 1987 Gorbachev's policy of openness, or *glasnost*, has allowed honest discussion of this period for the first time. The Lithuanians have labeled the deportations genocide because the manner in which they were carried out makes it obvious that Stalin's goal was to expose the victims to a slow and cruel death by cold and starvation. Men, women, and children, old people and infants, all were transferred to the Arctic by rail (babies born on the way were simply tossed out of the boxcars). Many died en route; others survived to endure ten to twenty-five years of exile and hard labor, starting out without warm clothing, shelter, or the most rudimentary of tools. Only 30,000 (10%) of the victims survived to return to their homeland. This period of bloody repression by the Soviets has branded itself into the national memory and together with the idea of an independent Lithuania formed the basis of survival and enduring—the only alternative to becoming extinct.[4] Since 1990 a daring drive for Lithuanian independence from the Russians and from communism has been taking place with consequences that still cannot be foreseen.

The Literary Context

During the two Soviet occupations Lithuanian writers have had to sing paeans to the invader, laud Stalin as the great liberator and "bringer of the sun," and officially support the policy of socialist realism, in which ideology penetrates all forms of art. In Lithuania, as in Estonia, Latvia, or any other country where the Soviets had installed communism by military force, socialist realism was an ironic mockery of reality, for any pretense of revolutionary romanticism that it might originally have had in Russia proper had been replaced by coercion and force. Only a few Lithuanian writers showed enthusiasm for socialist realism; most of them saw only the blatant deceit and propaganda at the center of the policy.[5] Locally, it was perceived to be an instrument for communist indoctrination and Russification; whenever possible, therefore, nonconformist writers treated it as an alien force to be avoided, subverted, and exploited for their own ends.[6] The post-Stalinist thaw effectively reached Lithuania rather late, only about 1966, producing a slogan in literary criticism that hailed "the return of man to our literature." Man had not really disappeared (how could he have?), but the individual with all the complexities of an inner world had been removed from the foreground of concern. At this point Lithuanian prose writers distinguished themselves in the writing of stream-of-consciousness fiction and were emulated all over the Soviet Union. Nevertheless, the literature of the 1960s contained a fatal contradiction: it was impossible to write about individuals and their motivations when censorship would not allow psychological complexity to be portrayed and when many aspects of social relationships and political conditions could not be mentioned, let alone analyzed with the subtlety and conviction that portrayal from the inner, associative point of view requires. The fiction of this time had moved beyond the stereotypical situations and the strange mix of realism and romanticism usually associated with hard-core socialist realism; however, it often sounded like diluted early Joyce or warmed over Robbe-Grillet. Nevertheless, it did open up new prose techniques, allowing a writer to expose characters' inner worlds. The accomplishments of 1960s prose fiction, then, were mainly on the formal level rather than on the thematic one. For reasons of censorship (quite often self-censorship, where the writers conformed of their own accord and took few risks), literature did not come to grips with the recent uniquely Lithuanian experience, nor did it build on the Lithuanian literary tradition. In light of these shortcomings, this anthology does not include examples of prose fiction of the 1960s, even though this was certainly a better decade for literature than the wasted 1940s or 1950s had been.

It was not until the 1970s and the arrival of a younger generation of writers that Soviet Lithuanian prose fiction began to participate in modern discourse. In my view, this was brought about by the convergence of two tendencies that in the long run proved to be beneficial for the further development of prose: first, a growing familiarity with Western literary trends, avidly followed through translations, primarily from the Polish,[7] and second, the desire to modernize the genre within the context of the literary tradition. It was here that the lessons learned through even limited exposure to writing from outside the Soviet bloc came in handy and were adapted to local conditions by some of the more avant-garde writers.

Since 1945 prose fiction in the West has gone from late modernism to postmodernism. Both these currents presuppose a reader more sophisticated and more adept at interpretation than realism had ever required, because these kinds of texts are much more heavily coded, more dependent on intricate temporal shifts and hidden layers of meaning.[8] This program of concealment and obscuration in the modern narrative happened to coincide very nicely with the nonconformist Lithuanian writer's desire to communicate information that, though it might be dangerous to the state, was true to the reader and the reader's perception of an unfalsified reality. Allegory, magical realism, alternate versions of reality, elaborate subtexts, Aesopian language, irony—all these literary techniques found their way into Lithuanian prose fiction as it attempted to break out of socialist realism in the last two decades. By writing in this modern fashion, writers hoped to evade the censor, who was notoriously obtuse and not up to deciphering the meanings of strange, convoluted texts whose point usually required that the reader work to see it.[9] In the relevant criticism this phenomenon was referred to as "the author's growing confidence in his reader," but in essence it had less to do with confidence than with an increasingly educated and sophisticated audience.

Life under the Soviets also contributed toward training the reader to be perceptive of the slightest verbal nuance and to speak in code. I remember observing two local people meeting for the first time in Vilnius. Within a few minutes one of them remarked to the other, "I have traveled around the [Soviet] Union a good bit." They understood each other perfectly, but it took me, a visitor from faraway lands, some time to realize that this was a coded way of saying that the speaker had been deported to Siberia and seen the Soviet Union without having invested in a ticket. This is an example of how the populace learned to communicate in ways that were not so easily detectable by the network of KGB informers and the listening devices that were a daily fact of life from Stalin on.

The Western reader will notice the frequent occurrence of ellipsis in the translated texts. Although Lithuanian does use this feature more often than English does, Soviet Lithuanian writers tend to depend on the meaningful pause as a cypher, letting the readers fill in the blanks as a means of involving them in decoding and even elaborating the text. There is confidence in the reader to the extent that author and reader are allied against the censor. This would not have been possible under the canons of realism, where everything had to be more or less explicit. Modernization, then, was sought both for its own sake, as a natural maturation process in literary development, and as a means of expression to be exploited in circumventing the harsh realities of publication in a totalitarian society.

Soviet Lithuanian literature shares another feature with most East European fiction written under conditions of media control, that of overwhelming emphasis on moral questions. Actually, this has always formed a part of the literary tradition since Lithuanian statehood was first lost at the turn of the eighteenth century. Therefore, when prose fiction in Lithuanian began to be written around 1890 it labored under the weight of a heritage of didactic religious literature, but at the same time it felt the duty to serve national aims by raising the consciousness of the people and enlightening them, literally bringing them out of their backwardness to a higher level of humanity. Entertainment value was a luxury literature could not afford. Much of the prose fiction of writers like Žemaitė, Jonas Biliūnas, Antanas Vienuolis, Šatrijos Ragana, Juozas Grušas, Vincas Mykolaitis-Putinas, and Antanas Vaičiulaitis shared a scrupulous moral sensitivity, an emphasis on human values and empathy for the downtrodden, be they the poor, women, children, the handicapped, or animals.[10] Many of them were victims of the patriarchal system: women forced into arranged marriages; unwed women, abandoned when they became pregnant, who committed suicide or raised bastard children in a society in which the term *bastard* was a curse even unto the second generation; or women trapped in unequal marriages and exploited. Men wrote about women's problems as much as women did. The emphasis on "the insulted and the injured," of which women were just the most visible layer, became an integral part of the literature.

In the Soviet period human values, being contingent on religion and national tradition, continued to be threatened, this time by urbanization, the devaluation of human life, alienation from traditional social patterns, escape into alcoholism, and other social ills that had been foreign to the traditional Lithuanian way of life. The country became polarized into opportunists (those who supported the communist system and the Russians for reasons of personal gain) and various degrees of dissidents (those who opposed the system and the invaders for moral and national reasons).[11] Moral sensitivity and integrity were the only weapons that a human being could retain in the sea of conformity and control that was imposed from Moscow on all aspects of life. They were the source of self-respect and pride. For East Europeans democracy and freedom mean a return to truth and morality as much as they mean political systems and social or economic structures. People have been ready to die for these values that were denied them for so long. The Baltic Spring and subsequent events demonstrated that people were prepared to suffer and perhaps even die not only for their nations and the reestablishment and safeguarding of their language and culture but also for even more abstract human values.

All these political and sociological factors, together with their psychological consequences for the individual, resonate throughout the stories in this anthology, either overtly or covertly, depending on the date of writing and the political conditions operative at the time (i.e., the level of control from Moscow). The historical and political context, especially the guerrilla war; forced collectivization of the private farms, which had been sacrosanct to the Lithuanian way of life; and, since *glasnost*, a recovery and reevaluation of the Siberian deportations and the entire postwar period—all these have figured prominently in recent literature.

The Stories: A "Native" Interpretation

This section analyzes and attempts to interpret the stories in this anthology as literature, but literature whose meaning may be hidden, enclosed in elaborate code, or allegorically stated. Cesare Segre, for one, has pointed out that a reader needs to know "the codes of custom, of society, and of conceptions of the world" to make sense of a text (he also says that the reader has to know the code language, but the translations take care of that).[12] The analysis of the stories presented here attempts to provide some of these "codes" for readers from other cultures, especially those who have not lived under totalitarianism and who may be unfamiliar with the subterfuges that authors were forced to devise to criticize their society and political system. It is not meant to suggest that the works can have only the meaning elaborated here. Quite the contrary—good literature is always multivalent, allowing for multiple interpretations among individual readers, who bring their individual experiences to bear on a text. In this case, it is possible that I became especially conscious of the political meanings behind the narratives because to me they were suggestive, powerful, yet mysterious texts that I had to decipher to my satisfaction. And I admit that I stumbled on the pattern and design in the stories quite intuitively. Once the hidden organization was revealed to me, however—that is, when my subconscious let my conscious know what project it was that we were engaged in—I abandoned my original, essentially pre-*glasnost*, intention of presenting the stories chronologically according to the author's birthdate and began to order them according to the meaning they had together rather than in isolation. Juxtaposed, the texts amplify and expand each other's themes; confronting the same monster of censorship, they build allegorical models of their situation, argue and debate with each other, and find new, previously unexposed terrains to reveal the pain and frustration of being "minds against the wall." This process may even be imitative of how the authors themselves hit on their taboo subjects and innovative techniques. Their searchings may have been just as haphazard as mine in bringing the pieces together and presenting them to view in this new way (some of them may even deny the validity of these critical interpretations just as authors have done since time immemorial). It seems to me, however, that this particular aspect of the stories is the most interesting today just because the critics inside the country were either too involved in personalities and events to be objective about the tradition taking shape before their eyes, or, as was more likely, they simply did not feel free to join the game of looking for political and revealing subtexts. Thus, I want to caution the reader that there is no one "right" way of reading the stories, that in a different context the reader's interpretation may be just as valid as mine, or more so, and that the reading presented here is only one of many possible ones that I myself could produce at another time and another place. Nevertheless, I feel that this time of emerging freedom in the Baltics and this distanced place, the American academic setting, provide a unique perspective for glimpsing some meanings and details of local color that both enrich the texts and reveal the trajectory of collective consciousness behind them: writers desperately wanting to communicate their experience and, like Handless, to find meaning in it.

"The Red Forest" (1975) combines a universal existentialist point of view, exalting man over God, with a description of the tragic human condition. At the same time, it is a history of humankind, or more specifically, an overview of Lithuanian history from the Stone Age to the warfare of modern times. Because of its love for hand-carved wooden crosses and wayside chapels, Lithuania is known as the Land of Crosses; thus, the image of the red forest of crosses is especially fitting. The author, Romualdas Granauskas, succeeds in finding a visual symbol to synthesize the Lithuanian historical experience: woman raised to the level of Christ, crucified on the cross of human suffering, a veritable *mater dolorosa*. As I previously said, the Lithuanian woman already exists in the literary tradition as victim and as mother-figure; therefore, it is not surprising that woman, rather than man, receives the focus of attention. Men have always gone off to war (in the story, man's role is only that of warrior and son); women have stayed home to spin, worry, pray, and mourn the dead. Their fate is less dramatic, perhaps, but just as full of anguish and torment. Granauskas emphasizes the continuity of the female line. The setting is a land that gets only "half the sun and half the moon, the other half shines for those living peacefully beyond the hills." Taken together with the blood-red forest, the land is recognizably Lithuania, whose history is one of war, invasion, rape (according to folklore, the "floating wreaths of rue" are symbols of lost virginity), murder, and endless and inevitable suffering ("will they nail me to a cross, too?").

The author seems to see a cross-section of the land caught in a time warp in which all historical periods coexist and testify to the brutality and pain that have been Lithuania's fate. Or perhaps the surreal red forest of crosses is superimposed on the realistic landscape of cows to be milked and the world of everyday objects, such as milk pails and prayerbooks, that constitute the farm person's reality. This appearance of the abnormal within the normal corresponds not only to a tragic vision of life but also to the hidden tragedy of Soviet Lithuanian life, the litany of variations of possible deaths figuring as comments on the everyday reality that people had to ignore. For example, "still others disappeared without a trace, and on their crosses hung just a mother's heartache" can be seen as referring to the Siberian exiles—under normal circumstances, people die and are buried, and their relatives can visit their graves. At the end of the story the crippled goose "is not doing anything to anybody," just as the little girl is only "leafing through an old prayerbook," and yet they will both be sacrificed. A commentary on war and human suffering, the story also offers a good introduction on what it means to be Lithuanian. For Romualdas Granauskas, Lithuania is a nation on which the sun does not shine and for which peace is always out of reach. In early 1991 he is still waiting to be proven wrong. The existentialist notions latent in the story (the inevitability of war and death, the fragility of "bones that had been so long in growing") are exploited by the author to present a summary of the Lithuanian sensibility, which has been "crippled" by history and taught to be pessimistically inclined and accepting of fate.

The selections from *Under the Southwestern Sky* refer to the earliest historical period in the collection, examining ethnic problems in the Klaipėda region, which Lithuania had to cede to Hitler in 1939 but

whose Lithuanian population had always fought to resist Germaniza-
tion. These stories by Birutė Baltrušaitytė mainly illustrate this period, although "Gypsy Running with All His Might" goes back to a
still earlier time, reinterpreting the very old Lithuanian literary
theme of the arranged marriage and the negative feelings of the
bride. Traditionally, even in men's texts, the sympathy usually goes
to the woman. Here, however, the interethnic angle adds a new
twist, commenting on the country's current situation: many foreigners, mainly Russians, have been artificially transplanted to Soviet
Lithuania, and the temptation to marry outside the "tribe" is greater
than ever before, yet it is disapproved of by parents and community.
Just as in turn-of-the-century stories from the literary canon, freely
chosen love is the ultimate virtue. Nevertheless, in the next two fragments ("Hands on Starched Apron" and "By This Window") about
the Lithuanian Marta's love for the Nazi Hans this value is questioned as an elaboration of Baltrušaitytė's initial them—that intermarriage means tainting your tribe's blood. Never, never choose
from the enemy in your midst, no matter how attractive he or she
might be, because this means betrayal. Gruesome enough as a love
story in which Marta is made love to by Hans in her father's bed the
night of the father's arrest (could Hans have plotted this to have
Marta alone to himself, making her doubly guilty of betraying her father?), Baltrušaitytė's text fragments further transform themselves
into an even more horrible war story, treating the relationship between the invader and the invaded, prefiguring the inhuman events
of World War II and the moral choices that they were to impose on
the Lithuanian people.

In ". . . And His Very Own Home . . ." and "The Butcher" the
focus shifts from woman's role and her guilt in complying with the
invader to the responsibility and moral choices that men face. Jurgis,
the widowed father of three little girls, wants only to live in peace
and do well by them, taking his role of father and provider seriously.
However, the escape of a man from one of the Nazi concentration
camps forces him to choose between his desire to live a calm, normal
life and to act like a human being, with all that this implies, when
someone else is in danger. While he hesitates, fate decides, and "it's
amen to the shadow—Russian or Pole"—and to Einikis, who brought
him here, and to Jurgis, too. His girls will have to fend for themselves. Baltrušaitytė's entrance into her main characters' innermost
emotions and the headlong pace of events that engulf them help
stress the poignancy of their conflicts and choices.

"The Butcher" is even more grisly than the story of young Marta's infatuation and surrender to Hans. Like Jurgis, Jeronimas

Rupšas, the butcher, is faced with a moral choice that means either death or yielding to the plans of the invading Germans. Rupšas, whose name sounds like the Lithuanian word for toad—one of the worst curses the language possesses—chooses to look the other way and conform to pressure. He tries to run away from his conscience by marrying a young woman and not asking any questions, but the invader has no mercy and violently destroys him and the cosy life he has set up for himself. Obedience is no guarantee of security, because the invader has his own motives and will trample you, whether you comply or not. You are reviled as a traitor by your own kind while losing your life in any case. In re-creating a painful period of the past, *Under the Southwestern Sky* uses a technique well known in censored literatures, the events or atrocities of one period indirectly referring to contemporary atrocities and situations that cannot be named. Thus, Nazi violence and horror are written about directly because this is allowed, but other (Soviet) violence and horror are also invoked for the reader who has had recent experience of it. Contemporary problems that Baltrušaitytė bravely addresses include tangled national relations, prejudice, intermarriage as betrayal, conformity and opportunism, and the moral choices that historical necessity forces on humanity in its state of unpreparedness. The lessons that her work teaches serve for all time, not just for some isolated case, because they are based on tolerance and the ethical imperative.

Romualdas Granauskas and the next author, Juozas Aputis, are known for their commitment to the old village way of life and the values that had been engendered over centuries. The work ethic, the extended family, closeness to nature and mythological beliefs, and the home and the hearth as the center of a decent life have all disappeared with the simultaneous urbanization (which would have come anyway) and Sovietization (which is always perceived as foreign domination) in Lithuanian life.

In "The Bread Eaters" Granauskas uses a polyphonic narrative structure to give all his characters equal time to present their views. The older generation, the Rimkuses', retain the ritual, celebratory way of life and once a year bake their own bread from rye they themselves have grown and harvested. They are attuned to nature and to each other. The old woman milks her cow joyfully, knows how to read nature in the mythological way (the black raven predicting calamity or death), wants everyone to be together, and looks forward to grandchildren. Old man Rimkus wakes up listening for natural signs of the weather, he shows his affection for his wife by fondly noticing her miserable little braid (all that is left of her no doubt once magnificent hair), and he looks forward to his daily chores and the visit by old friends. White butterflies encircle his head like a halo when he walks in the fields. They are his companions in a way that his son-in-law who follows him across the fields is not. The communication gap between the generations yawns wide.

On the other hand, Marytė, the Rimkuses' daughter, and the son-in-law are products of the Soviet way of life. Marytė still retains some affection for her parents—for instance, she worries about their aging and honors her father's decency and goodness when she compares him to her husband—but even she has no sense of roots: she is eager to leave the family and is able to refer to the house she was born in, the traditional idealized mainstay of Lithuanian connectedness, as a "shack." At age twenty-seven she realizes that her life might as well be over because there is no foundation on which to build.

Meanwhile, her husband is even more alienated. He has made a mess of his life by marrying the wrong woman (as illustrated by his encounter with the saleslady Vanda), and he places no value on the old village life based on the community, seeing it only as the quagmire that it has become under the Soviet system. He is an example of the rootless and shiftless generation of rural workers who have lost the old traditions (for example, he knows only a few lines of the folksong that sadly comments on him being the old goat sitting on the pile of woodchips who belongs to no one and nothing). The opening lines of his monologue show that he takes work and tradition to be nonsense. Granauskas integrates ideas about the work ethic by cleverly focusing in the early sequences of the story on the pails—empty or full—and what they are used for, even on how and where the characters relieve themselves:[13] the mother is returning with her pail of milk, while the daughter is just heading toward the barn; the father carries clay to mend the bread oven in his pail, while the son-in-law relieves himself in his. Worse than the disappearance of the work ethic, however, is the son-in-law's dependence on drink. The prevalence of alcoholism will become a major refrain in Soviet Lithuanian prose fiction, reflecting tragic everyday reality. Rimkus's son-in-law articulates very clearly why there is so much drinking when he reveals his thoughts: "got to have something to drink, otherwise I'll go crazy . . . should he catch up and kick [the guy] or should he punch the other one in the mouth? Keep smashing the bastards' faces. And feel the old guilt become smaller and disappear as the new one grows." The explanation he provides here points to alcohol as an escape from Soviet reality and the guilt and dissatisfaction with life that he has caused himself. There is even a nuance of political criticism intended in "They don't even have anything to make vodka with anymore," which refers to the economic decline in recent years, "they" being the Soviet powers that controlled the economy from the center and left the individual totally frustrated and helpless.

The value of bread for the Lithuanians becomes the main symbol used in the story from the title on. Everyone is a "bread eater," but the new way of life has replaced bread baked in your own bread oven, a fixture of the traditional village, with the tasteless manufactured product, and a generation that does not know the flavor of homemade bread is growing up (also, it might be mentioned, one that does not know how to stack and carry wood in the old way, using a rope to tie the bundle together). But for the old Rimkuses, bread and milk (as opposed to the omnipresent vodka) are not just staples of their diet; they have a variety of positive connotations and embody their value system: "the desire to live a long and righteous life" and "the longing to die a beautiful and peaceful death."

Whereas "The Bread Eaters" describes a situation endemic to an entire society, "Wild Boars Run on the Horizon" by Aputis delves into the more individually tragic, elaborating what could be a classic newspaper item. The tractor driver Petras Gvildys communes with nature from a hill top, realizing the divine creative potential of human life and the irony of man's mortality. His contradictory feelings are perhaps stimulated by the bottle he has drunk.[14] He comes home only to be attacked by his wife, who without any warning tries to poke out his eyes with a broom. All she can say by way of explanation is, "That's for your drinking, that's for your bottle, you don't care about your home, nothing here makes any difference to you." When we become privy to her thoughts, we find out that nothing matters to her, either: "not the forest, not the fields, not the animals and—a terrible thing to say—not even the children." Husband and wife, the center of the Lithuanian household, which has remained essentially patriarchal, are both "dehumanized" to the point that the values traditional to an agricultural society (nature, livestock, family) become irrelevant.[15] The wife can only guess at what kept her own mother going in such hours of despair; of course, socialist realism tolerates existentialism better than it does religion, so her question—"what was it?"—goes unanswered. Though religion might pop into the reader's head, the author cannot invoke it, even if he wanted to, because of the canons of socialist realism.

However, Aputis has other, less obvious explanations for the woman's behavior. They have to do with the boars on the horizon, which most likely signify either tractors (a source of special pride for the Soviets) or something more menacing than just technological progress. As Gvildys's father-in-law puts it, "something alien, something distant and terrible, was walking around their forests and fields, no one had seen it yet or met it anywhere, but it was right here, it stopped at every farmstead, at every home." This is the unnamed pervasive force that alienates a man from his surroundings and his family; therefore, the father-in-law senses that it is useless to try to save Gvildys's eyes because it will not solve the real problem. Gvildys declares that "No one shoots cuckoos yet" (the favorite mythological Lithuanian bird); nevertheless, the story ends with "a frightened cuckoo" perching on a birch (the favorite Lithuanian tree). Gvildys himself becomes holy with his halo of gauze wrapped around his head and "his legs crossed like a saint's." Almost blind now, he can perceive the truth that, like Oedipus, he could not see when he still possessed his sight. His wife's action has released his inner vision so that he can perceive the danger that the tractors have brought.

In "Wild Boars Run on the Horizon" the father-in-law, representative of the older generation, still retains the old values, though he has not been able to pass them on to his daughter. The father is the only one who reacts to the tragedy in a normal human fashion, kissing Gvildys's hand "like a madman, tearful and helpless, as if it were possible to expiate the inexplicable crime with kisses." In contrast, the aged couple in Aputis's story "The Flying Apple Trees," who are moving from their ancient homestead to a modern settlement, something like a Soviet-style subdivision, have already been corrupted by the system and accept its norms. They stand in direct contrast to the Rimkuses of "The Bread Eaters." Even Milašius's wife has acquired Soviet ways, drinking with the men and going along with the bribery and deception (that is why her and her husband's voices are harmonious when Milašius goes inside to see how she is doing). Under the Soviet system, state ownership was regarded as collective ownership, and theft was perceived as retrieving that which rightly belonged to one. In the story, honesty and uprightness are left to an even older generation—Milašius's mother, who flies around overhead, shaking her bony finger or growing apple trees on her chin, trying to reinforce the old values. She is unhappy with their move, a forced resettlement instituted by the Soviets. Although this relocation ostensibly improved the collective farms by draining the fields and moving the people to settlements of nondescript cement block homes with indoor amenities, it had the effect of destroying the old village way of life and was decried by most people as Sovietization. From Milašius's inner monologue it is apparent that he feels uneasy about his move.

Corruption is already quite advanced: the commission making the rounds of the farms is met with the same hospitality and ploys everywhere. Neighbors on the commission even encourage Milašius to add a few more nonexistent apple trees to his stock, but he is a moderate man and restrains himself in his wrongdoing.

In the farm person's mind, uprooting trees in bloom is akin to slaughtering a pregnant cow, a particularly vile deed. This is why Milašius has such a difficult time reconciling himself to the act—but reconcile himself he does. After the deed is done and Milašius returns to his family farmstead, he has the vision of the faked apple trees in bloom flying about furiously and says, "It's okay as long as it's only my trees that are frolicking about, but, Christ, when they get together with all the neighbors' trees, you won't be able to tell the earth from the sky, all those blossoms, why, they could bury you." All those petty crimes, light as blossoms in the execution, have succeeded in burying the economic growth of the country and have brought about the current decline in prosperity. This has been so "since the day the [Russian] soldiers . . . chased the Germans off across the pasture"—that is, since the second Russian occupation. Stealing from the state and the other realities of Soviet life have also "buried" normal values and morality. In these stories there is no mistaking the causes and the effects; this is why Aputis's work was officially banned and went unpublished throughout most of the 1970s.

Aputis and Granauskas have renewed the tradition of rural Lithuanian prose. Aputis's solution is to incorporate elements of magical realism, which may easily have come to him by way of Gogol and his "dead souls" rather than by way of the Latin American García Marquéz and his *One Hundred Years of Solitude*. Aputis uses magical realism the same way that he and Granauskas use existentialism—as a lightning rod to divert criticism away from themselves. That is not to say that existentialist thinking is not an integral part of their sensibility; it is just that it has more than one function in their texts: it comments on the human condition and brings their works closer to the universal, it gives a sense of intertextuality (e.g. the myths of Sisyphus and Oedipus in the background of "Wild Boars Run on the Horizon") and a Western cultural orientation, and it renews realistic Lithuanian prose, bringing it closer to modernism. Fiction for entertainment first and enlightenment second developed fairly recently (the Lithuanian tradition of prose fiction is now only 100 years old) from oral genres, such as the folktale and the anecdote, and relied on colloquial language. Aputis takes this feature and inserts it into the vivid inner monologue of a lower class character, flavored by idiom, a picturesque way of speaking, and even profanity. Granauskas, on the other hand, goes the route of renewing the reader's perception, making the familiar strange again by distancing the perspective, as in the first paragraph of "The Bread Eaters," where the position of the voice that is narrating and describing is physically above the characters's heads; therefore, the threshold and the path to the farmhouse appear to be a face turned up to the eaves and an arm flung across the yard.[16] For the same reasons of objectivity the voice "removes itself" from the rest of the narrative and allows the four characters to express themselves polyphonically, leaving it to the reader to evaluate the validity of their attitudes and insights. These two writers, then, can be viewed as experimenting with new ways of presenting the old village reality, bringing its means of expression up to date with its content—the sociological changes that have occurred.

Saulius Šaltenis's "The Ever-Green Maple" uses another favorite device to comment on the political relationship between the Lithuanians and the Soviets, namely, reducing it to the microstructure of family and neighbors: the landlord and the Tenant. At the same time, Šaltenis exposes the lie that is at the heart of the relationship, the Soviet myth that Lithuanians are really free. The landlord, who is a figure of speech here for the Lithuanians, supposedly owns everything, including the outhouse; it becomes evident, however, that the Tenant, a trope for the Russians, has taken over the choicest property and made himself quite comfortable by seducing the mother. The helplessness of the landlord in the face of this aggression is emphasized. Continuing to repeat the required formula that he is the owner in the face of all evidence to the contrary, the father takes refuge in saving the maple tree, even though the Tenant has poisoned it, too. The maple is in a sorry state, consisting of remnants from the desecrated cemetery, but it is all the young female narrator and her father have. Since pagan times, which in the popular consciousness are still fairly recent, Lithuanians have always empathized with trees.[17] Therefore, it is not surprising that the maple they are so desperately trying to save comes to stand for all that is sacred and Lithuanian. The Tenant cannot kill it off, even though he has poisoned its very roots.

The story deals with more than just the Soviet myth of Lithuania willingly joining the USSR and the continuing myth of Lithuanian happiness in the brotherhood of socialist nations that Russia has built; it also reveals how the Lithuanians hope to be saved by the United States, which appears in the shape of the cigar-puffing sheriff in the narrator's dream. The sheriff will enable them to retrieve that which rightfully belongs to them (the coat, the typewriter, the ency-clopedias) by taking the daughter back north. (Lithuanians see them-selves as the land of the north, thus distinct from the Russians who are the barbarian East, a perception that will recur in other stories. The view of Russians as being distinct from Lithuanians is an old one: it already saddened the nineteenth-century writer Vincas Pi-etaris, who commented on Russian homesteads as lacking trees and orchards.) The sheriff, who comes straight from a technicolor West-ern film, will also take care of the Tenant, forcing him to feel the scorn (the Russians as lice at the father's feet) that the true landlord, the owner of Lithuania, has for him.

Although "The Ever-Green Maple" was written in 1983, it seems to comment appropriately on the Vilnius Spring of 1990. It ar-ticulates the sentiments of the Lithuanians vis-à-vis the Soviets. It predicts the appeal by the restored independent government of Lithuania to the American people to recognize the validity of Lithua-nian claims to their own territory. It expresses the air of bravado that the Landsbergis government retained in the face of new takeovers and humiliations. If "The Red Forest" is a glimpse into the percep-tion that Lithuanians have of their history and destiny, "The Ever-Green Maple" envisions the injustices and hopes of the Soviet period. Both stories present a paradigmatic situation that cannot be reduced any further but can be expanded and applied to other par-allel events or phenomena. Not all the texts in the collection have this quality; most of them refer to specific sociological or political condi-tions that are extended in time instead of being symbolic structures, where time and location are immaterial because the emphasis is on presenting an abstracted situation, outlining its contours in broad, though still recognizable strokes.

Though it does include strictly local references—for example, to the collectivization of farms—"On the Chrysanthemum Bus" em-bodies more universal themes about the relationship between the liv-ing and the dead, "the great artist's" (God's) success or failure in designing humankind, and the monotony and futility of life. Invited back to his hometown to give an address, the main character feels pressured to be a "prophet" and say something profound and mean-ingful, to hand out "prescriptions for life." The story starts out quiet and reflective, but it soon takes a surrealistic turn when the narrator realizes that although he is among the living, he is riding along as a chrysanthemum among other chrysanthemums. Everyone carries along his chrysanthemum, the flower of his or her death, at all times; even in life everyone is already condemned to death. You can neither evade it yourself nor bring the dead back to life. The conversations in dialect that the narrator overhears all speak about the various guises in which misfortune and death appear, contributing to his sense of futility. He realizes that even God does not attain perfection, because He keeps starting afresh. At the end of the bus ride, however, the narrator achieves a kind of tranquillity and gets a handle on his speech by catching sight of his native soil: "how beautiful the earth is at rest, elegantly laid out furrow upon furrow. She's reclining, her knees turned to the sunlight like a woman at the beach. In places the raised furrows and the cracks in the black soil gleam with dazzling flowers of silver." He realizes that his native soil is the eternal value and that someone, no doubt the Great Artist, sprinkled the soil with these "chrysanthemums of hope" for our encouragement and benefit. A small epiphany, but a meaningful one, dependent on nature, which has been the major source of consolation for the Lithuanian people. Here it protects even against the inevitability of death.

Born in 1945 after World War II, Ramūnas Klimas's self-imposed literary task seems to be to reevaluate the myth of the guerrilla war and to examine his generation's response to it. In "What I Thought about on the Bus Ride to See My Old Classmate" he critically examines his contemporaries and divides them into two categories: "the pigeons on the grass" (the conformists and opportunists), the narrator among them, and those interested in "the flower of fiery matter" (incendiary idealists, rebels, or even dissidents), like his friend in jail. He poses a question that has bothered him since childhood: how can two boys born at the same time and identically brought up turn out so differently—on opposite poles of the political spectrum? When they are born, their fathers (significantly, one a "sharpener of knives" and the other "a former Green Thicket ranger" [so named because the freedom fighters hid in the forests]) are "convinced that each had grafted a tree. How could they have known that they picked the same trunk, only its opposite sides?" Against the background of soccer and the local team from "the rake and ax factory," Klimas raises the meaning of the game to a higher level by introducing the parallel subtext of the guerrilla war.[18] The underground and Green Thicket that had swallowed up his classmate smelled of "marshes, rotting leaves, animal urine, and clotted human blood," bringing associations of the guerrilla war. The narrator had searched for the location of the underground since childhood, but he was the son of the knife sharpener (a procrastinator who could not decide to join the rebels), receiving only the myth of the guerrilla fighters rather than the direct experience, and he has to come to terms with this fact somehow.

Klimas's narrator seems to envy his classmate, who takes a stand and risks his life for the cause. He also appears to be critical of the math teacher, who had tried to establish "functional dependence" by logical and scientific means—the "ambient temperature, the amount of precipitation," etc. (We will see how Lithuanians distrust the determinism and "logic" of Marxism in a later story, "The Suspended House.") The teacher came to realize that a "horrible antidependence," or the word that cannot be mentioned—independence—lurked underneath and could not be controlled. He remains uninvolved, and at the point when the conversation turns dangerous, while they are drinking under the honeysuckle bush at the graduation dance and the principal's informer Barčas approaches, he even takes to his heels, followed by the "future big shots," the careerists and the conformists, those who follow the rules. The vital question then was whether "human solidarity" was all-important, whether the whole country should take risks and go along with the classmate or just live in peace and relative prosperity. Most of the populace seems content to watch the game from the sidelines. They want only "the score like a grade for [their] very existence in Lithuania: the condemnation or acquittal of [their] existence." Historians have speculated that the Lithuanian resistance was so fierce and protracted because the Lithuanians had not initially (1940–41) fought the Russian occupation and needed to prove themselves and regain their self-respect. In the story, the townspeople want to withstand or even defeat the stronger, larger force, "the other town, which had a couple hundred more inhabitants." Although he disdains the "fence-sitters," Klimas saves his scorn for the "pigeons on the grass." Yielding to "gravity," to the power structure, is seen as being useful for a man's behind rather than for his soul. Nevertheless, picking "the flower of fiery matter" is portrayed as an almost masochistically sweet act; it is compared to St. Sebastian's martyrdom: when the classmate picks the flower, "his heart . . . faints with satisfaction."

Writing from the perspective of an observer rather than that of a participant, Klimas is able to interpret the sacrifice of the guerrilla fighters realistically and not romantically, as has usually been the case in émigré literature (which was the only one able to discuss it directly). Therefore, the blossom, transforming itself into a stainless-steel fork, turns on the narrator and pierces his liver, making him a sacrifice, too. And having come full circle, he is overcome by an emotion of "insane tenderness" for the young cashier selling him candy at the end of the story. He is able to love and accept the simple folk who did not directly sacrifice themselves. In this act he can perhaps assuage his own guilt at being one of the pigeons and attain self-acceptance.

Klimas continues his investigation of the time of "the pigeons on the grass," even though they are not mentioned by this name, in "Gintė and Her Man." In this tale, however, the more ambitious novella form allows him adequate space to expand the ramifications of his theme into various subordinate issues, separating the true story of the guerrilla war from legend, and examining the function of history in general—is it to record absolute truth or to be "a storehouse of unrealized possibilities" from which to draw meanings and moral compensation? In "Gintė and Her Man" Klimas has created a complicated postmodernist text, deconstructing not only history but also the myths propagated by socialist realism. For this reason, the narrative examining the immediate postwar years and their significance in the 1970s is inserted into a critique of this political propaganda trend, which masquerades as a literary one. In constructing the five versions of his story the narrator also acknowledges the limits of the allowable as far as censorship was concerned. Thus, the discussions of the problem of writing the story of Gintė and her man under various metaphors (the geometric model of the triangle, the dead child, the train in the tunnel) are not just the usual authorial comments on the difficulties of artistic creation that one finds scattered throughout much of twentieth-century fiction from André Gide on but are motivated by political reality in a totalitarian dictatorship. Examination of the different versions also shows the maturation process of the narrator, in that he starts out believing in the first version that the story of Gintė and her man can have a "happy end" and then moves to total disbelief in this possibility in the final version that the reader gets. At the very end he even undercuts the very likelihood of any true version.[19]

In what respects, then, do the first and final versions differ? Having spent eleven years of self-imposed exile in the cellar "until Lithuania returns to her heart," Gintė's man supposedly comes out of hiding and resumes normal life, receiving an internal passport, without which a Soviet person cannot get housing or work, marrying Gintė (the homemade beer for the wedding) and becoming a history teacher at Tarpumiškiai (Midwood) grade school. Whether Gintė's man was a guerrilla fighter or really just hid out, mourning his country through the tragic years, is something Klimas never feels free to clarify, but he certainly uses much of the circumstantial evidence surrounding the period of resistance: the civilians supplying the fighters with food (Gintė and her roast goose and apple pancakes); the night visits; the snowfall hiding their footprints; the "bandits' " (this is how the Russians referred to the guerrilla fighters) fondness for drink in the forests; and the imported Russian troops together with local collaborators, popularly known as wolves (they will recur under this name in Šavelis's story "In the Autumn Rain"). So only the immature and naive narrator in the 1970s can give credence to the happy ending of Gintė and her man and their silver wedding anniversary, because the fate of guerrilla fighters who accepted the two Soviet amnesties in the late 1940s was not the promised return to normal life but a twenty-five year sentence to Siberia. Gintė is right to fear and distrust the government man who claims he would have given the man in the cellar an internal passport. Gintė does reach a kind of compromise with the investigator, from the secret police no doubt, by mending his sock—she forgives him his role in these events, a reconciliation of sorts takes place, the healing process starts, and life can resume. Gone is the time when the country folk were terrorized by both the "bandits" and the wolves; Gintė's man's mother can stop acting the quail protecting her young and slicing one hunk of bacon for the partisans, another hunk for "the people's defender," trying to please both.

In the final version (the text we actually read) the narrator becomes sophisticated enough to realize that the happy ending cannot possibly be true. Having already taken away the passport, the wedding beer, and the right to teach in the second version, he also added a grim and realistic twist to the ending. If Gintė's man decided to give himself up and go to Pasvalys expecting to be amnestied, there is no way that he could have returned alive, and thus one of the alternate endings in which he is brought back dead on the sled rings true. The "good" version of this bad version is that he sat down to rest at the top of the hill, and his heart burst at the sight of a normal, peaceful Lithuania; the "bad" version implies, though for obvious reasons it cannot directly state, that he was tortured and murdered: "[he] lay on the straw curled up in an odd way. It was hard to see how a man could have died in such a pose." Not only do we have Gintė believing in this version and shouting at the government man when he asserts otherwise, but the two Wolffs (pun undoubtedly intended) who show up in the final pages of the novella laugh heartily at the naive (really the first) version of the story that the narrator, turned timid again, suggests in trying to delude them and perhaps save his own skin. At the end, Klimas seems to be saying that if the Wolffs from Wolverton don't buy this version, no one else should, either.

The novella is also about the lessons of history. Gintė's man, the history teacher, has meditated less on current history than on the fifteenth-century Lithuanian heroic figure Vytautas the Great, who was prevented from being crowned king by the theft of his crown, accomplished by "Jogaila's curs." During his eleven years in the cellar he thinks that he has come to understand Vytautas, whose empire stretched to the Black Sea but whom Gintė's man endows with a superior kind of anachronistic understanding that what really matters is one's nation and its survival. He thus uses Vytautas as a double lesson: an indirect one for Lithuania's rapacious Russian neighbors and a transparent one for his own countrymen. What Gintė's man realizes through his meditation on Vytautas is that a country needs to return to its borders, "an end to the flood" of territorial (over)expansion must come. On a map, Lithuania is vaguely heart-shaped, so in returning to its territory, it "returns to its heart." This is the only way for its "heart [to become] as hard as the nucleus of an atom," resistant to foreign influence. Lithuania learned this lesson in the time of Vytautas and had it reinforced during the guerrilla war of resistance; in early 1991 it was obvious that Russia had yet to learn it. This return to one's undiluted essence is the legacy of the resistance fighters, the Holy Grail that Tarpumiškiai divided up like a communion wafer. And that allowed the populace to return to the things that really mattered.

Gintė and her man have no children, only their pupils, to whom they obviously bequeath everything that had meaning for them. However, Gintė looks lovingly at the pregnant young woman attending their silver anniversary—it is a seed that, after a fashion, she too has helped nurture. In contrast to the danger and privation of Gintė's youth, the present period portrayed in the first version of the story is one of prosperity and peace—hence the marinated peas and the recurring fatty rolls from the Pasvalys deli that the narrator bites into at the end of the novella, and hence, too, the "rye of 1975 that was practically bursting from its ears." It is significant that the hermetic peace of Gintė's man's cellar is unsealed by the arrival of Gintė, who retained a bit of human divinity from Alaušas Lake, in which she was born, and by the birth of the calf, which also signals rebirth.

When asked what he does for a living, the narrator gives a succinctly caricatured vignette of Soviet life. He says, "I guard a warehouse full of empties [empty bottles] at night. I walk along a barbed wire fence with a gun." This presents in a nutshell the alienation from meaningless work endemic to the system, the bankrupt Soviet economy, and the paranoia of the Iron Curtain. In contrast to this vi-

sion of the absurd is "the secret law of Tarpumiškiai," which dem-
onstrates how people communicate regardless of secret police,
networks of informers, and censorship: "there were some underground canals, along which man touches man, memory touches
memory, rarely breaking through into speech, into word, the way a
tree connects with another tree—at the roots, but not at the tops."
Connected to this image of the Lithuanians' perception of themselves
as trees is another tree-based metaphor that ties in with the forest and
the guerrillas as Forest Brethren, that of the North tree and the scent
of its blossoms, which those who are tuned in can smell. Klimas
makes use of another native allusion that enriches the text. When the
narrator sets up the three-sided geometric model of the story and
claims that the rye is yellow and the apple trees are green, the native
reader instantly fills in the third color, red, that makes up independent Lithuania's tricolor flag, which until Gorbachev's reforms in
1988 was forbidden; people were sent to Siberia for any hint of the
tricolor combination. In the flag, red stands for the blood that was
shed in defending Lithuanian freedom, and the red-blood connection
appears several times in the story. When the concept of medieval
Lithuanian nationhood is discussed, the comment is made that
"Lithuania did open her eyes just in time for them to overflow with
red, for her lakes, swamps, and seas to turn red," referring to Lithuania's extended tragic history. Red is mentioned next in the context of
Gintė's man's death. He is being brought back on the sleigh, and
"the sun [is] still shining. It [is] red. The snow [is] also red," so the
geometric triangle has all the required colors in it, and through it the
author is able to enforce the truth of the final version, namely, that
Gintė's man *did* die "curled up in an odd way."

Thus, the narrator decides that the legend and sacrifice of the
guerrillas is "a vessel, brimful of positive infinity," from which his
generation can get moral compensation, derive strength, and live in
peace in the uneasy and guilt-laden years of relative prosperity that
have been bequeathed to him. "Gintė and Her Man" is not a recount-
ing of history but rather an attempt to show the problematic nature of
history in a closed society, where history was the victim of special
falsification. So there were not only the normal problems attendant to
the writing of history, there was also a lack of information and a glut
of disinformation about a very recent period that was artificially
forced to recede to an uncharacteristic remoteness for those who had
not themselves experienced it. When *glasnost* came to Lithuanian society, there were reports that young people had not actually believed
in the Siberian deportations that their relatives had experienced

(though hardly a family had been untouched). Some had thought that the tales of Siberia were a strange kind of boogeyman that parents used to terrify their children. Ramūnas Klimas tries to describe the sensation of growing up and living in that kind of society; he attempts to isolate the inherent contradictions and depicts with uncompromising subtlety the painful search of a younger generation for the truth about their past and its meaning for the present.

In an unlikely fashion the next two stories, "The Author Looks for a Way Out" and "In the Autumn Rain," show two responses to the impasse facing people living in a society based on the Soviet lie. In "The Author Looks for a Way Out" Juozas Aputis again allegorically recasts the Lithuanian condition, just as Granauskas in "The Red Forest" tries to find a tragic correlative for it and Šaltenis in "The Ever-Green Maple" articulates one in the ironic mode. Psychological and moral concerns predominate here. Soviet life is portrayed as a silage pit in which the characters cannot coexist peacefully because one side is brutalized and strong, whereas the other can still discriminate moral questions but has no power. The deep structure of the story, therefore, not only yields the opposition between evil and good but presents power versus impotence, experience versus innocence, and strength versus weakness as equally relevant in the equation. In a society that values aggression and cruelty, the working-class toughs decide to examine the wimp's manhood. He is perceived as different because he does not conform to their ways; he does not eat a hearty lunch as they do. Individualism is interpreted as a lack of guts and sexual drive; the real questions of the story, however, are reserved for the end in the moral dilemma of the student. Coming to the confrontation empty-handed, how is he to deal with brute force and the aggressive and self-confident imperative toward evil? Overpowered physically and naive philosophically, he can only "chain his eternal hatred" and accept his impotence, yet the struggle to maintain solidarity with the morally right must go on in the face of violence. Although the situation is recoded onto a microcosm as an altercation among young people, everyone can recognize the validity and relevance of the feelings that are invoked and make the connection to the political situation that persisted even in the spring of 1990, when Russian soldiers occupied the printing presses in Vilnius and searched for so-called deserters from the army. The native population still had no "way out" except to deny its feelings of shame, lock up its hatred, and bide its time while keeping its human values.

Šavelis's "In the Autumn Rain" transposes the Lithuanian experience to the realm of a love story between two horses, Bėris, the bay horse, and Whitestar, a young mare from some exotic land. As in Granauskas's "The Red Forest," the world is divided into two parts, one caught in eternal autumn, where the rain never ends (conforming to the Lithuanian climate and even to the Lithuanian name for the country, *Lietuva*, which may derive from *lietus*, the word for rain), and the other half enjoying a temperate climate and the sweetest grass. Bėris articulates the Lithuanian longing for a normal life and the tragedy of his own existence when he mentions that there was a time "when no one was tending us"—that is, when the horses were free—and he expresses envy of "people asleep in their warm houses" while he is exposed to the cold and the rain. Whitestar, the creature from the fortunate side of the world, lures Bėris to her lands, where he is shaken by her love and the prosperity that he sees. But Bėris knows that this ease and comfort are not for him, a "visitor from the gloomy and barren lands, ravaged by cold and rain." The only reason he gives for returning to them is the attraction of his native land and his sense of duty: "My fields are back there." He leaves Whitestar's many charms to go back to where he feels he belongs. Thus, in the charming fantasy inserted between two related anecdotes Šavelis manages to discuss the economic differences between the Eastern bloc and the West and also to come out against defection or emigration for purely economic reasons. Like Klimas in "Gintė and Her Man," he views emigration from Lithuania, no matter how strife-torn and poor, as surrendering to the negative pole of "minus infinity"— like the narrator of Klimas's work, Šavelis's soul is also "immigrant in nature." In spite of the discomfort of home, or even the physical danger and psychological anxiety it can produce, as in Aputis's cautionary tales, the Lithuanian consciousness does not condone leaving home behind to seek greener pastures.

Nevertheless, the injustices that the Lithuanian population has been exposed to in this century cry out for the world's attention. Before *glasnost* it was impossible to discuss the inhuman suffering and cruelty brought by Stalin's reign of terror, but since 1987 writers have scrambled to publish material dealing with these years. Because it was written somewhat before *glasnost* had become accepted, Ričardas Gavelis's "Handless" still refers to Siberia only as the Land of Miracles, but the situation of the twenty-six men and the circumstances surrounding their exile are easily recognizable and leave no doubt as to the authenticity of the location and the realism of some of the details. This is not to say that "Handless" is a true story; nonetheless, except for a few touches, like the symbolism and motivation of the main character's last name, it really could have happened. The outpouring of memoir literature describing deportations and life in the concentration camps that has taken place in the last few years certainly contains equally moving content, but it is usually couched in less eloquent and generally nonartistic form. Gavelis does articulate some of the most visible psychological problems that this experience of man's inhumanity to man aroused, but his primary goal is not, as might be expected, to record the suffering and injustice that occurred. Instead, like Klimas, he is writing from the perspective of after the fact, and this colors the kinds of questions that interest him.

First of all, he wants to stress the men's original belief in humanity's innate goodness and indubitable show of concern, illustrated by the fact that throughout their ordeal the men still want to believe that the world cares about them. As one of the characters says, "someone was bound to come looking for them—after all, they were human beings." It is beyond the scope of their imaginations that they could have been deliberately left in the snow, even though the words of the guards as they leave them with two weeks of rations are ambiguous at best. From the memoir literature and historical accounts we know that this is precisely what often happened—people were deliberately left to freeze and starve—yet such monstrosity is beyond the comprehension of the normal human mind.[20] Therefore, the only goal that the men can still focus on in spite of their hunger, cold, and delirium is, ironically, the one of sending a message to the world. Their illusion that "the whole world would drop everything and come running to [them]," if only it knew of their plight, is understandable. It was not until after World War II and the revelations of the horrors of Hitler and Stalin that modern man was forced to accept the reality of mass atrocities and genocide.[21]

Just as the raft with its human sacrifice of Vytautas Handless's hand can find no people to witness to, so Handless himself, returning to Vilnius, can find no one interested in his past or himself as the embodiment of twenty-six men. As long as Handless's partner in suffering, Aleksys, is alive, the two survivors can have their annual commemoration by surrounding themselves with the sketches of the men who perished, and then go on with their lives. For Handless, his weekly visits to his wife's grave and his communion with her soul are enough, but after Aleksys dies, Handless is left alone with his burden of memory and his survivor's guilt complex. His daughters care only about their material welfare. The neighbors do not bother to get to know him. Thus, it is not his retirement that makes Handless go in search of his past—Handless recognizes as much in looking for the reason for the obsessive desire that overtakes him—rather, it is the lack of interest of the community and its failure to acknowledge and accept the magnitude of the men's suffering. Like America's Vietnam veterans, Handless needs validation of his experience to know that it was not in vain and to come to terms with the unbearable and the unexplainable. As he says, "if the enemy takes away your hand, this at least is understandable; if your own people tear it off—it means the end of the world has come." What Handless needs above all is for the sacrifice of his comrades and himself to be at least posthumously endowed with a meaning that it did not possess at the time of occurrence.

Since society is not forthcoming with what he needs, Handless has to revisit the scene of his torment alone. Aided by fate in finding the documents of the female deputy to the Supreme Soviet, which he can easily falsify, Handless sets off to pay homage to his companions who died. He formulates his plan correctly and, having rehearsed his actions, succeeds in deceiving the zone superintendent without being detected. His clownish performance, occurring in the "dream where nightmare landscapes are more real than real ones," costs him an enormous effort that is revealed only in the doubling of personality he experiences as he goes through his predetermined motions: one Vytautas Handless is acting the part of the jovial carouser, while the real Handless is reliving the horrible events of the past and honoring the dead with a minute of silence. Handless loses his composure at only one point. Allowing the pain that he had suffered to get the better of him, he grabs his host by the shoulder and shouts at him, "give me back my hand, return my hand!"

Another component of his journey is the need "to find his past and look it in the face." Because society has chosen to ignore the ordeal that Handless and the other men have gone through, he has to relive it for himself and reconquer the stump that looks like a bull's head, as if now he were doing battle with it of his own volition and on his own terms. He can lay the stump's ghost to rest after he defeats it a second time because he has proven to himself that he can do it and has gained back his self-respect (psychologists call this desire to overcome a situation that once controlled the victim "belated mastery"). Having accomplished what he set out to do and retrieved the letters that he sent to himself because no one else was interested in them, Handless can now take his life. There is no more meaning to his existence; in fact, his survival after the experience of the camp is already an anomaly. He was just the result of the fact that "tens, hundreds could perish. But there was no power that could destroy every single one of them." Subconsciously, Handless knew (and society sent him this signal as well) that he had survived only to witness to the sacrifice of all the men. This was the meaning of his life, and because he cannot promote this goal any more, there is no purpose left in existing.

As a text, "Handless" proceeds on two simultaneous planes, mimicking the character's doubling in the scene when he returns to the Land of Miracles. The italicized narrative is set in the past and tells the story of the deportation and exile, while the text in regular type refers to the present, set mainly in Vilnius, when Handless tries to return to normal life and fails. The repeated description of the raft with the hand attached to it floating down the river and looking for people to carry its message to ties all the interspersed fragments together, lending not only a certain kind of cohesion but also a calm, flowing, even elegant beauty to the text. Borrowing its rhythm and stateliness from the river, the refrain echoes in the reader's memory after the shocking events of the story recede into the background, so perhaps one could say that the hand did find people to understand its message.

Whereas "Handless" touches on some of the circumstances of deportation and exile to Siberia, another story by Ričardas Gavelis, "A Report on Ghosts," presents a picture of the kind of person responsible for sending men like Vytautas Handless to their doom. Utilizing the first-person narrative technique especially well, Gavelis takes us directly into the rationalizations of a tortured, sadistic mind, not unlike Stalin's (or, according to Andrei Sakharov's memoirs, like that of his main henchman, Beria),[22] who ultimately was responsible for the atrocities; it is interesting to note, however, that Gavelis's interrogator (Jeronimas Šukys) is a Lithuanian, emblematic of those who were more than happy to go along with the totalitarian regime and execute its orders. Sadists and criminals exist in every society. Šukys puts his family talents and work ethic into practice. He is proud of what he considers his successful methods of interrogation, which he uses against the illiterate writer of proclamations or the supposed poisoner Dr. Ginzburgas, whom he eventually forces to confess by threatening his sons. Like the perverted totalitarian dictators of this century, especially Stalin, Šukys buttresses his "ethical" arguments with mathematical proofs and Aristotelian logic according to which "each one of us is guilty, but the ones under suspicion are doubly guilty, and those apprehended are triply guilty." He inverts the categories of good and evil, innocence and guilt, and thus suffers no pangs of conscience when he isolates the dandified teacher Kalvaitis, his early mentor in philosophy, or deports Vingelis, the mayor who saved his life from the Nazis (because he had been a communist activist during the first Soviet occupation and participated in establishing Soviet rule in Lithuania, the Nazis would have gotten rid of him very quickly). Neither gratitude nor remorse is part of his lexicon, for he has no normal human feeling, being a robot devoted to order and obedience. He easily glosses over all unpleasant facts and his own actions, such as the fact that he acquired Julė, his first woman, by sending her father and two brothers to Siberia, and Marija, the most beautiful woman in Vilnius, only by arresting her first.

Šukys is also incapable of discriminating between guilt and innocence. He misreads the fear in his victims' eyes for guilt, just as later he misinterprets the fear and horror in his neighbors' eyes for respect and submissiveness. Gavelis stresses this idea even more in the scene in which Šukys finally gazes at his own eyes in the mirror and finds them not only beautiful but also innocent: he believes he has finally found the ideally innocent man that he had been searching for all his life. He suffers delusions of invincibility and grandeur, convinced that health is related to upholding order and destroying doubt while thinking that the world owes him compensations of women and luxury for his efforts. He cannot comprehend why his younger son refuses to use the family name, or why he deserves the nicknames his neighbors give him—those of Mole and Muravjov, the hated Hangman from the 1863 rebellion—or why the aged Julė refers to him as Mr. Bureau(crat). And he is able to delude himself until the day the nostalgia overtakes him after he starts doing relative good: building the storybook house, taking care of Julė, and eventually even offering to share his apartment with the young couple, victims of the Soviet housing crisis. The arrival of the ghosts is treated fancifully; however, even in attempting to explain their presence according to the rules he has believed in all his life, Šukys reveals that he knows they are the ghosts of the people he has tortured when he says, "I'll exterminate them for the second time." Although Gavelis manages to write about a KGB man with humor and irony, we leave Šukys with an uncanny feeling that much psychological truth about the workings of that kind of mind has been slipped to us in a painless way.

"Gintė and Her Man" (1981) reexamines the myths surrounding the guerrilla fighters in the context of Lithuanian history; in "The Suspended House" (1982), Saulius Tomas Kondrotas sets himself an equally ambitious project, this time not demystification but mythification of the independent period of Lithuania. The tasks of both writers of the younger generation (Klimas was born in 1945, Kondrotas in

1953) run counter to officially sanctioned versions of history in this period before *glasnost*. "The Suspended House" does not have as intricate a narrative structure as Klimas's novella; however, it complicates its surface lucidity by simultaneously utilizing several generic conventions of prose fiction. The story allows for multiple interpretations, depending on whether it is read as a *Bildungsroman*, a love triangle, a fairy tale bordering on myth, or as an allegory of recent Lithuanian history; nevertheless, in a strange way all the interpretations tend to merge and augment each other, thus rising to the universal level (a claim not always tenable for other stories in this anthology). If "The Suspended House" is a fairy tale, it is, as suggested by the title of the collection from which it comes (*Stories of Various Times* [*Ivairių laikų istorijos*]), a story for adults that evokes a familiar world through its details and recoding of crucial events experienced by its primary audience in recent times. It contains elements of twentieth-century Lithuanian history—illusion, betrayal, loss, exile, and violence—scaled down to the microlevel of the family rather than the nation, but still recognizable as events and feelings that have been experienced, even though the plot and characters are distanced and new. For those readers who have not been involved in these emotions and occurrences the story still works as an allegory of initiation into adult life and the loss of illusion that accompanies experience, the movement from naïveté to sophistication that has been the dominant theme of Western prose fiction. This is the pattern and design of the text that would be recognized by any reader, making the myth satisfying reading.

As an account of the maturation process of a young man, Germanas, the story includes three successive mentors who are influential in his development. The meaning of his father's life lay in his taking the house left by their ancestors and turning it to face the sun (no doubt, the West), the source of civilization for the macrocosm, the young independent Lithuanian state. Although the house hung suspended for only a short time, it inspired loyalty to its ideals in all those who saw it. When the weather changes for the worse (in Soviet writing weather is often invoked as an objective correlative for political conditions even in everyday life), the father gives in to a period of stagnation for which Kondrotas finds the apt, if baroque, metaphor of the embryo, describing the disjunction and illogic of the life the Soviets brought to Lithuania and his own depressive reaction to it: "[his awakening] was as if a large and wrinkled embryo, warm and damp, were hatching from an egg, the egg of night itself, as if a soft, gentle silkworm were emerging from a cocoon, a cocoon made of black wefts, issuing from the night and the bed, contradicting the will of nature and God, which holds that silkworms don't issue from cocoons in this particular shape." While this ornate comparison may seem unnecessarily elaborate on one level, it does convey the feelings of the "silkworm"—Germanas's father—toward the new, unnatural Soviet age to which he is now exposed, which puts him into a mood resembling "that of the infants during the massacre in Bethlehem." He refuses to participate in it, leaving it almost of his own accord and choosing to die rather than succumb to its harmful effects. In fact, death seems even natural and appealing, especially after he sees the insects flying through the wall into a different state of being and realizes that transferring from one state to another is painless and perhaps even to be welcomed.

The generation gap between Germanas, an example of *Homo sovieticus*, and his father, formed by the ideals and values of independent Lithuania, is very wide. The father venerates wisdom, but he still finds room for emotion and spontaneity (and, by implication, perhaps even religion, though this is not mentioned directly) and rejects the play of cold reason typical of the dialectical materialist and the determinist. He tells Germanas, who is wrapped up in his own time, the new age, that he is nothing but an "intelligent thing," who wants nothing more than "to have no worries, have enough to eat, and be able to stay drunk"—another of the several vignettes in this anthology describing Soviet man.

Zakaras, Germanas's mentor after his father's death, appears to live in a farmyard full of manure, which can also be construed as the symbolic background of Soviet life. Although Zakaras seems unattractive at first, eventually Germanas comes to value him for his adaptation to the conditions of Soviet life, which, as we have already seen, force individuals to suffer indignity and humiliation (see, e.g., Aputis's "The Author Looks for a Way Out"). Instead of having his masculinity challenged, in "The Suspended House" Zakaras learns to swallow the rapier and survive. *How* the rapier is swallowed is important; that is, the outer form of the action must be preserved: "the expression on his face [had to] suit the occasion—it had to be dignified and mysterious and yet happy and befitting a feast." The colonized Lithuanian has to struggle to retain dignity when insulted, and as the written and unwritten Soviet laws of "the brotherhood of nations" dictated, the victim had to smile and act happy while being exploited and Russified. Presumably, this is the lesson that Germanas learns from his uncle, whom he comes to value; there comes a time, however, when Germanas forgets how to act like a slave, and this colors the rest of his life and brings about his eventual murder.

The Clever Madman, Albas Lukšas, is Germanas's third mentor and eventually his nemesis. Kondrotas uses language (and sometimes dress) primarily as a distinguishing feature of nationality. It was Germanas's father who enforced civilization by his values: "If it [hadn't been] for him, we'd be doing up our clothes the wrong way and speaking an inferior language." Thus, at the very beginning the arch-Lithuanian father's language is established as superior, and everyone else's can be measured against the standard he has set. When the gypsies are introduced, their language is also commented on: "they live among us but they are totally alien to us, our gaze has no point of reference for judging their appearance, their speech or thought." Although Albas Lukšas is not called a gypsy, he has many of the features that Zakaras had connected with the nomad tribes. When Germanas first meets Lukšas, "the idea that Lukšas was only a barbarian whose language barely resembled Lithuanian and whose clothing wasn't cut the way it should be [will not] leave him," causing a mysterious "irritating itch in his body and in his heart." If Lukšas is gypsylike, then he is a rogue and dishonest according to Zakaras's definition, and this view is further supported by Germanas's understanding of his character in the discussion of the reasons for Lukšas's drinking. Again, it provides a thumbnail sketch of the Russian mentality as viewed by the Lithuanians, a sketch that captures certain aspects of the Russian soul as seen from the colonized person's point of view, who more than anyone has spent a lot of time studying the character of the colonizer. Not only does Lukšas radiate an unpleasant energy and cause a mysterious itch, but he also wants change and power. In a description that seems to point to the Russian desire for attention and world domination, Germanas elucidates Lukšas's desire to be "renowned as a shamelessly courageous man" and shows him to need recognition, even though he periodically sits home mending the crotch of his pants. To an insider of the Soviet Union, who intimately knows that its economy is Third World while its nuclear and military ambitions are those of a superpower, it may well appear that this seemingly caricatured version of the typical Russian is the undistorted, realistic one, albeit tempered as it may be by the view from below, the perspective of the slave.

Aleksandra, being Lukšas's daughter, cannot help sharing some of his features (for this reason she is damaged from birth somehow); however, her ideas on domination and control are transferred to the realm of male-female relations. Initially, she looks somewhat like a man, and it is only when she falls in love with Germanas that her skin becomes soft and gentle. When the Hunchback tells of the female fish in the Red Sea who stay female only as long as there are aggressive males around to keep them in line, his story seems to apply to Aleksandra as well, in that she needs to be dominated; otherwise, she is the one to enslave her male partner, losing interest in him. Germanas in love is weak and under her control. Thus, she grows indifferent and her passion cools. After she has betrayed him with the Hunchback, however, Germanas reasserts himself in the same terms having to do with swallowing and vomiting that he had observed in Zakaras accepting the rapier. Nevertheless, Germanas is of a different generation than Zakaras and has not learned the art of swallowing the rapier and becoming an inner-directed man. Although he can smile at Aleksandra in bed with the Hunchback, he cannot yield to Lukšas's humiliating behavior, and in an action that is the direct opposite of Zakaras's swallowing insult and subjugation, he disgorges his disgrace by vomiting on his tormentor. This is enough to seal his doom. First he is forced into exile to some remote part of Russia; next, regardless of Aleksandra's new-found love, based on the fact that Germanas has asserted control and kept her female according to the psychology proposed by the Hunchback, he is killed by Lukšas and the Hunchback at the end of the novella. Thus, he fulfills the conditions of the story as fairy tale and as a myth that mirrors Lithuanian history. Extrapolating from details that match Lithuanian experience, Germanas may be symbolic of the left-leaning members of society who carried on a flirtation with communism only to be betrayed by the secret alliance of the Nazis and the Soviets, which the villainous Hunchback and the murderous Lukšas may represent.

In its role as the symbol of illusion, the vision of the house that Germanas's father built appears several times in the novella. Primarily, it flickers in the background of Germanas's hopes, whether they reflect on love or life, and forms one layer of his subconscious. The dream of a civilized and free Lithuania facing the West will not die, no matter what tragedies may befall ("Those who saw the house at that time could not get the picture out of their heads for years; the suspended house inspired belief in the set order of things and in the order of the world since its very creation"). In a very different form this dream underpins the hopes of the young female narrator of Šaltenis's "The Ever-Green Maple" as well, encouraging an identification with the West and a reliance on it. This is why the newly independent yet still enslaved Lithuanian state of the early 1990s felt so cruelly betrayed by the democracies of the capitalist West, of which it had always felt itself to be a part. As "The Suspended House" draws to a close, the house still floats over the river as a vision of the dream of freedom.

According to the symbolic system Kondrotas works out, Aleksandra has been dominated by Germanas, and she therefore takes over his values, even though she was originally a Lukšas (a Russian). Now she identifies with his dream and is to work for its fulfillment, thus perhaps embodying the subconscious Lithuanian aspiration to bring a light unto the Russians, to show them the path to civilization. The subjugation and conversion of Aleksandra to the cause may even be indicative of Lithuanian hopes of making up for their hidden inferiority complex by assimilating the Russians within Lithuanian borders. Although the Lithuanian complex vis-à-vis the Russians masquerades as one of superiority, at least on the intellectual and cultural front, obviously on the physical front it is an illusion. In the master-slave relationship that has predominated during the Soviet colonial period the Lithuanians have been emasculated, humiliated, and left powerless in their own land. The fantasy wish-fulfillment is transposed to the parallel male-female plane; therefore, the domination of Aleksandra, the mannish Siberian girl, through "love" and sex not only is satisfying to Germanas but makes her one of us. She is no longer the Other, the alien, the strange. Having served her indenture with Zakaras and put in her years that parallel Germanas's years of wandering, she can be trusted. Germanas, too, has grown and matured. Whereas before he did not know how to make love and Aleksandra had to mold him to her desires, after his exile Germanas has gained sexual experience and takes up photography, the Freudian substitute for sexual insight. The years of hardship were necessary to bring them both the satisfaction and sense of fruition they feel at the end. This idea that suffering is necessary to earn the compensation of happiness appears to tie in with the subliminal guilt felt for being taken in by the wiles of the stranger, Lukšas, in the first place. Instead of the alien being rejected, he is integrated in a complicated play of encompassing the opposite.

"The Point of Sticking It Out" returns to a humorous and prophetic analysis of the Lithuanian situation and, like the suspended house swinging in the mists, points to the distant hope that things will at least improve, that "once people have decided to clean up, at some point they'll decide to litter again," even if they do not totally upset the established order. Aputis has a lot of fun with his literate and literary garbage man, Tadeušas. During the course of the story he proposes three theories for reading (and concurrently for writing): as escapism (the reason why Tadeušas reads), as verification of one's existence (the reason why Fėlė, Tadeušas's mother, reads), and as a reflection of reality (the officially approved socialist realist reason). The author indulges in social criticism in the implied contrast between the two minor characters, the writer and the graduate student, inverting the maxim of "you are what you eat" into a new one, "you are what you produce in your garbage" (perhaps crudely commenting on the self-image of *Homo sovieticus*). Because the writer does not conform to the establishment and does not know how and what to write, he lives poorly; for example, his pants are patched, and he is attacked in the press. The graduate student, on the other hand, is writing his dissertation for success, including all kinds of quotations (from Marx and Lenin, no doubt) and decrees from approved texts; therefore, he can afford imported clothing for himself and his family. In this society it is not talent or hard work that is rewarded but conformism to the party line.

However, Aputis saves his heavy artillery for the Soviet myth of social progress. As the communist experiment was clearly playing havoc with the economy, making more and more products disappear from the shelves, the official version of reality still remained that life was getting better and better. Given that garbage is created only when there is food or products of some kind, the idea that the author plays with in "The Point of Sticking It Out" implies that if Tadeušas cannot find any garbage, then there must not be any food or goods available, either. Aputis merely carries the entire Soviet contradiction and falsehood to their logical conclusion. The fact that there is no garbage supports the reality (that there are no products) and contradicts the falsehood (that things are improving). The two questions that the author poses at the end of the story are the natural questions anyone would ask: why did the garbage disappear, and what could Tadeušas have done about it? Logical as these questions may seem, they are precisely the ones that cannot be answered, because one would have to talk about things like the economy, the five-year plan, and censorship, which until *glasnost* prevented the dissemination of any bad news or criticism. The reader, therefore, gets some other material for constructing a hypothesis for what really happened. The hints that are offered the reader really are "of some help" in that they point to the problem, that literature (the distorted view) has been confused with life, that is, with reality; that once people are sick of "cleaning up"—that is, pretending to be progressing—they will decide to litter or live normally again; and that what society has to do is to stick it out or endure until this happens. The 1990s have proven Aputis right on these counts throughout the East bloc. The people did decide "to litter again" and have to stick it out until they are allowed to do so freely.

The experience of twentieth-century world literature, from Eastern Europe to China, has shown that literature can and does survive and circumvent censorship, but the stories in this anthology illustrate very vividly how this is done. A pre-*glasnost* collection might have included the same stories but much of the commentary and even the arrangement of stories would have had to be less revealing to protect the authors and to avoid sabotaging the future of their writing. Even then, in those days a trick or a circumlocution of some kind quite often could be used only once; afterward, the censor got wise to it, either from private discussions of the work within the country or from foreign critical reaction and reviews, no matter how carefully they were worded.[23] Therefore, 1989 or 1990 were really the first years that a book of this nature could be published in the West in precisely this form without endangering the writers.

"*Come into My Time*" illustrates that literature has an evolution of its own even under censorship and that, perversely, state control of the media can have a beneficial effect on art—something that has been realized in scholarship in the West.[24] Nevertheless, as I have shown, it does shape the artistic output in very definite ways. Repression has an influence on the content of the literature, resulting in a decided emphasis on moral and humanistic problems, just because these values are most lacking in the surrounding society. Writers like Juozas Aputis willy-nilly become moralists because some of the normal instillers of humanistic values—the Church, the schools, and organizations for young people—are either inadequate or banned. Denied access to much of the best thought in the Western (and Eastern) world, even the self-contained individual has few resources for self-development and in any case cannot achieve integrity, dignity and self-respect because the power of repression is such that assumptions and impulses cannot be tested and internalized or rejected. The psyche is fragmented or split (not surprisingly, schizophrenia is the most common form of mental illness in Lithuania today). In this atmosphere, the writers and even the critics become the most important conduit for the kind of information that would normally be passed down by educational or social structures. They also pass down the traditions. In the case of Lithuania, these revolve around the love of nature, attachment to the land, a mythological way of thinking, pride in the nation's history, and especially, feelings of patriotism toward the homeland, which is seen as the supreme virtue. On the other hand, the literature records and comments on the disintegration of familial and social infrastructures, the failing work ethic, rising corruption and conformism, and all the other social ills that communism and urbanization have brought.

On the formal level the prose fiction became increasingly modern or postmodern and Westernized. Although the older writers still show traces of the nineteenth-century Russian classics like Gogol or Chekhov, the younger writers have obviously read and imbibed modern German writers from Kafka to the post-World War II generation (Ramūnas Klimas makes the most use of them), or the Latin American writers from García Marquéz and Borges to Manuel Puig, who have influenced Šaltenis, Kondrotas, and Gavelis. As I mentioned previously, they have adapted the international style and allegorical, archetypal, and mythical elements to their unique content and conditions, making great use of coded writing and especially of deep structures, symbols, and subtexts. Their modernity has enabled them to record and discuss the problems of their country even under strict control. Thus, the last fifty years of Lithuanian consciousness have not been lost to future generations. Translation into English makes their recent experience accessible to the world, allowing it to share their reality and their anguish and hear their cry.

NOTES

1. It is useful to compare the anthology edited by Helena Goscilo and Byron Lindsey, *Glasnost: An Anthology of Russian Literature under Gorbachev* (Ardis: Ann Arbor, 1990). The innovative elements in Goscilo's and Lindsey's anthology are direct references to informers and treatment of previously forbidden topics like mental retardation in children or Stalinist terror. These are the kinds of subjects that Lithuanian prose managed to discuss in a coded way even before *glasnost*. The change since 1987 in Lithuania is that these references are now overt. Judging by the Russian anthology, a major accomplishment in Russia is that writers are now free to present alternate realities as well. As this anthology makes clear, the Lithuanians were creating alternate realities since the early 1970s. Even more important, they continued to do so throughout the 1980s, when Russian writing was a victim of Brezhnevite stagnation. Although the thaw that succeeded Stalin's death came to an abrupt end in Russia with the removal of Khrushchev, in Lithuania it

continued, though fitfully and covertly, perhaps. Thus, openness in prose fiction was less dramatic in Lithuania; it only meant that certain topics, especially the ones dealing with Stalin or the occupations and deportations, could now be discussed directly.

2. Some reliable historical sources include the following: V. Stanley Vardys and Romuald Misiūnas, eds., *The Baltic States in Peace and War 1917–1945* (University Park: Pennsylvania University Press, 1978), 1–16; Thomas Remeikis, *Lithuanian Opposition to Soviet Rule 1940–1980* (Chicago: Institute of Lithuanian Studies Press, 1980).

3. Remeikis, *Lithuanian Opposition,* 118.

4. As late as the early 1980s Milan Kundera, in "Afterword: A Talk with the Author," an interview conducted by Philip Roth and published at the end of Kundera's novel *The Book of Laughter and Forgetting* (New York: Penguin, 1981), said, "Today the Russians keep Lithuanians on their reservation like a half-extinct tribe: they are sealed off from visitors to prevent knowledge about their existence from reaching the outside" (230).

5. One of the first writers to treat the question of coding in literature and daily life in the Baltic States was Czeslaw Milosz in "The Lesson of the Baltics," in *The Captive Mind* (New York: Vintage, 1951), 213–40. For a detailed and witty discussion of how Soviet censorship works in practice, see Tomas Venclova, "The Game of the Soviet Censor," in *The New York Review of Books* (31 March 1983): 34–35.

6. For a discussion of Soviet influence on Lithuanian culture see Rimvydas Šilbajoris, ed., *Mind against the Wall: Essays on Lithuanian Culture under Soviet Occupation* (Chicago: Institute of Lithuanian Studies Press, 1983), especially the articles by Vytautas Kavolis, Aleksandras Shtromas, and Rimvydas Šilbajoris

7. Tomas Venclova, an émigré from Lithuania, discusses Soviet Lithuanian translation policies and their literary consequences in "The Reception of World Literature in Contemporary Lithuania," in Šilbajoris, *Mind against the Wall,* 107–29, and among other things points out that many literary types in Lithuania learned Polish only to be able to follow world literature (110).

8. Roland Barthes makes this distinction in *S/Z: An Essay,* trans. Richard Miller (New York: Hill and Wang, 1974), calling it the difference between the readerly (lisible) text and the writerly (scriptible) text. The complicated texts are denoted as writerly because the reader does not just read but, in performing the required intense decoding activity, in a way also becomes a writer helping to create the text.

9. In his recent article "Lietuviškos dvasios namai" (The Home of the Lithuanian Soul), in *Pergalė* 4 (1990): 118, Liudvikas Gadeikis admits that the critics in Lithuania were not free to decipher the subtexts of writers if the writers themselves did not have the freedom or courage to make their daring points explicitly.

10. Some of their work has been translated and can be found in the following collections: Stepas Zobarskas, ed., *Selected Lithuanian Short Stories* (New York: Manyland, 1959); Stepas Zobarskas, ed., *The Lithuanian Short*

Story: Fifty Years (New York: Manyland, 1977); Antanas Vaičiulaitis, *Noon at a Country Inn* (New York: Manyland, 1965).

11. The rise of Sąjūdis, the popular front in Lithuania that declared Lithuania independent once again, showed that essentially the whole country was a "dissident" camp (even the careerists switched gears and claimed that they had joined the Communist Party and carried out its orders only to help save Lithuania). Lithuania is eighty percent Lithuanian, and seventy percent of the population supported Sąjūdis in the 24 February 1990 democratically held election. For a detailed description of events in Lithuania during this period, see Alfred Erich Senn, *Lithuania Awakening* (Berkeley: University of California Press, 1990).

12. Cesare Segre, "Narrative Structures and Literary History," *Critical Inquiry* 3, no. 2 (Winter 1976): 272–73.

13. For the structure of the story I am here indebted to Albertas Zalatorius's insightful article on "The Bread Eaters," "Novelės semantika, erdvė ir laikas" (Semantics, Space and Time in the Short Story), in *Lietuvos TSR Mokslų Akademijos darbai*, series A, vol. 4, no. 61 (1977): 167–76.

14. In the 1970s Soviet Lithuanian fiction appears to have had an unwritten requirement that characters who criticize the system, no matter how remotely, must have been drinking. I suspect that this was to protect the author from censure. The author could always blame the character's dangerous remarks on alcohol and thereby avoid responsibility for the characters' statements. "The Flying Apple Trees" by the same author illustrates this feature, but it was by no means exclusive to one author. It can also be observed in Russian fiction as well—for example, in Vasili Aksyonov, "Half-way to the Moon," Patricia Blake and Max Hayward, eds., *Half-way to the Moon: New Writing from Russia* (Garden City: Doubleday, 1963), 82–103.

15. Ilona Gražytė-Maziliauskienė first applied the idea of "dehumanization," as meaning the loss of dignity and meaning in Aputis's characters' lives, in her article "Variations on the Theme of Dehumanization in the Short Stories of Juozas Aputis," *Books Abroad* (Winter 1973): 695 701.

16. Romualdas Granauskas has shown a constant interest in renewing nature description and character perception; see my article "Language in Contemporary Lithuanian Narrative," in *Lituanus* 4 (1977): 33–44. In his *History of Polish Literature*, 2d ed. (Berkeley: University of California Press, 1969), 525, Czeslaw Milosz perceptively notes that nature description is a strong point of Lithuanian literature; therefore, it is all the more remarkable that Granauskas has successfully deautomatized the genre.

17. Lithuania was the last country in Europe to accept Christianity, which it did in 1387. Nonetheless, pagan practices, such as snake-worship and pantheism, were still viable at the beginning of the twentieth century, and even today there is still a nostalgia for an idealized version of the pagan way of life. Trees were considered to be the reincarnation of the Balt; thus, they were especially revered and identified with.

18. One of the rules that applied in writing under censorship was as follows: the more dangerous the topic, the deeper, less obvious the subtext.

19. Interestingly, the Western convention of a happy ending has so penetrated what Arthur E. Kunst calls the "international style" of contemporary prose fiction that "happy end" are the only English words to appear in the original Lithuanian of the story.

20. See one of the few translated authentic memoirs of Dalia Grinkevičiūtė, "Lithuanians by the Laptev Sea," trans. Laima Sruoginytė, *Lituanus* 4 (1990): 37–67.

21. Compare the West's disbelief and belated recognition of the genocide of the Jews by the Nazis.

22. See Andrei Sakharov's account of Lavrenty Beria, "Memoirs," in *Time* (14 May 1990): 46. Gavelis's character matches Beria on several counts, not just the tortures and executions of strangers and acquaintances: the torture of children in front of their parents to extort confessions, his acquisition of women by intimidation and arrest, and the research into the pathology of the accused.

23. For example, special attention was paid to reviews and articles in influential American journals like *World Literature Today*, edited by Ivar Ivask and published in Norman, Oklahoma. Cases where writers in Lithuania were repressed or had their access to publication limited because the true content of their writing was even hinted at are well known. This, of course, put special responsibility on the critics in the West and in effect exerted a kind of censorship on them.

24. Ivar Ivask, the editor of *World Literature Today*, once chaired a session at the annual Modern Language Association meeting titled "Censorship: Hindrance or Stimulus?" that reached the same conclusion, namely, that censorship is a stimulus to creativity.

Romualdas Granauskas

The Red Forest

A plain, stretching out in all directions, where trees dare not grow. They have concealed themselves behind the distant hills, behind the warm back of earth, winds blow in this cavity, day and night four winds at once, never are there clouds with rain, nothing but half the sun and half the moon, the other half shines for those living peacefully beyond the hills, in a forest or beside a brook. No one knows the way here: not grass, nor snow, nor birdsong. Nor could she remember how she came to be here, and she was only dimly aware of the origin of her suffering, her eyes ached terribly because of the incessant green-gold light, because of the harsh reflections from stones, smooth stones, jagged stones. Nothing but stones, nothing but stones. Seeing them she instinctively curled her toes, the memory of stubble-fields still alive between them: she was astonished that the stones did not pierce her body as she had expected, her body so heavy with tense waiting and pain. She moved her feet, they swayed gently in mid-air, touching nothing. She felt the constant blowing of the winds, drying her, tightening around her like a colorless transparent bandage. She raised her eyes, searching either for evening or morning, she hoped to organize her thoughts, to understand whether she was dead or still alive, sun and moon hung motionless, skyless, foretelling neither death nor relief. She raised her eyes still higher, but her head pressed against the wood, its hardness was warm and smooth, and it seemed that the most important signs must be hanging in the very center right above her head, and that the hardness never would allow her to perceive them. Slowly she turned her head to the left, here, too, there was nothing, nothing but stones and their glitter, making the field look larger than any of the seas or oceans, then she turned her head to the right and saw, slanting away, a row of crosses, hung with dead women. She tried to see the end of the row, she craned her neck, but the spaces between them narrowed, still further the crosses almost touched each other, until finally they fused into an unbroken wall, into a broad line, into something continuous but invisible. She sensed that she was at the very end of the row. In the immense radiance there was still just as much room for new crosses and living women, perhaps now milking their cows beyond the hills, pressing the buckets between their warm legs. Next to her hung an aged woman, she knew her to be aged, although she saw nothing but a yellowed ear, some hair, and a little patch of her left cheek. The heads of the other women were also turned to the right, they had all died facing those who had died before them.

"Mama!" she screamed suddenly.

As the scream died away, she remembered it had been early evening, her mother had been on her way to the meadow, and she had waited at the gate, a bird had perched in the maple, up high, at the very top, higher than all the leaves, an orange thread of melody stretching from its blue head, when suddenly the song ceased, the bird having been the first to see the milk pail fall soundlessly into the green grass . . . Her mother had been spinning beside her grandmother's bed, a time without complexity shining quietly beyond the window, a child playing on the floor, the child had risen and covered the motionless hand with a fur, he had sat down again among his toys and said: "Mother, grandmother's all cold . . ." Further on she saw her grandmother's grandmother, her grandmother's great-grandmother, and other women, growing less familiar and gradually vanishing, she saw bodies withered into utter weightlessness, she saw them, all fragility, hanging on small black crosses. She opened her mouth still wider to scream, as wide as she could, the lifeless light of the plain surged into the red cavity of her throat, and her large teeth glittered like fragments of stone. She kicked at the dry wood, tossing her head, her arms stretched out on the cross, hoping to free herself from that relentless row. She struggled wildly for a long time, until her strength failed her, then she hung her head, her loose hair falling in her eyes, the wind tossed her hair back and it clung to the skin of her shoulders. She hung totally naked, her eyes still open, seeing nothing but the semi-circular protuberances of her breasts, they obstructed the view of her hollowed stomach, yellow thighs, the circles of her knees, her thick calves, and large feet with flat toes. The weight of her body stretched her joints, her veins, and the lines of her waist, so that she would have looked like a slim girl to the women hanging further down, except that, with all the nursing she had done, her breasts now sagged and the nipples were withered, like a timid old ewe's.

"Children," she called softly, "my children . . ."

At the sound of her voice the wood of all the crosses, sturdily planted in stone, trembled, wounds uttered by parched mouths fell like gasping scarves to the foot of the crosses, onto the harsh glitter of jagged stones:

"My children . . ."

"My little towheads . . ."

"Joy of my youth . . ."

"My dead ones . . ."

Hundreds of names swirled among the cross-tops, tossed about in the plain, and fell, catching on stones and leaving scabs of dirty brown. Forgotten shadows filled the plain, moving soundlessly, writhing, entwining, or lying still, stretched out on jagged stones, impervious to the sharpness. A red forest sprang up from the stones, on the edge of the forest bears wrestled with men, breaking bones that had been so long in growing. She saw spears and feathered arrows whizzing by, but none of them fell at her feet, they all flew somewhere to the end of the row. Having struck, they swayed like dragonflies on reeds bending down into the water. Clutching swords in their large-knuckled fists, helmeted men wandered among the trees, alertly searching each others' bodies for places unprotected by armor. Puffs of smoke would appear, only to be dispersed by wind above the river waters, and on the banks of yellow sand countless shadows lay motionless, everything would grow still so quickly, and big river fish glistened, frightened by floating wreaths of rue and by hands of corpses that grabbed the wreaths from the water and placed them under their heads. Horses galloped down the row, their reins and empty stirrups swinging, stopping in ones, twos, and even fours by most of the crosses, awkwardly kneeling with their front legs and bowing their foaming mouths right down to the ground. Lines of bayonets surged forward and fell back like waves, everything mingled into one undifferentiated mass, and even the sharp-sighted crows that circled over the battlefield could distinguish nothing. They flew about, landing on most of the crosses. Again she turned her eyes to the right: above her grandmother's head a black bird was hunched, waiting in silence. Shadows ran across the field and stumbled unexpectedly, small scraps of paper swirled about, one of them fluttered up to her mother and landed at the foot of her cross like a snowflake. Many more were drowned in quicksand, others killed with stones, burned at the stake, hanged under elms, strangled at the very break of dawn, smothered with pillows, poisoned, tortured to death, still others died of disease, starvation, loneliness, terror, yearning or despair. Still others disappeared without a trace, and on their crosses hung just a mother's heartache. There was nothing by her cross yet.

"Mother," she moaned, "mother! You are luckier than I. All your sons are dead."

The shadows slowly disappeared, the stones, some smooth, some jagged, regained their glitter, but the red forest still stood. Again she struggled on the cross, wanting desperately to see her sons. She relaxed when she saw all three of them alive, dressed in military green, the forest was teeming with them as with ants, some flew through the air, others rushed about among the trees, still others hid among the roots, squatting, waiting, their arms clutching ammunition, their eyes, yellow with obedience, shining through the branches.

"My children . . ."

"My little towheads . . ."

"The joy of my youth . . ."

"My dead . . ."

Frightened, she turned her head to the left, but she was still the last in line. The color of the forest now began to fade, the trees began to sink back into the earth, the hills reappeared on the horizon, once more illumined by a half-sun and a half-moon. She moved her arms firmly nailed to the tree forever.

"Go. At least you can go," she commanded her thoughts.

Stumbling over stones, her thoughts waded in a little group toward the hills, crossed them, climbed down into the valley. They stopped beyond their own farmstead. The gate was open, beyond it walked a crippled goose, not doing anything to anybody. A little girl was waiting on the threshold, leafing through an old prayerbook:

"Mama, when I grow up, will they nail me to a cross, too?"

1975
Translated by Mirga Girniuvienė

Birutė Baltrušaitytė

Under the Southwestern Sky

Gypsy Running with All His Might

The wagon is running. Actually, the young, nimble mare is running while the gypsy sits in the wagon holding a whip in one hand, and with the other he clutches Izabele, who is crying bitter tears. From time to time, when the bitter tears let up, she whispers: "Oh, Aleksas, Aleksas, is it far?" Aleksas does not answer; he smacks the mare with the whip. Suddenly the girl's lips heat up, and he kisses them breathlessly, and the whip almost falls out of the wagon, and Aleksas sits up straight. Hurry, hurry, hurry.

They're not running from just anywhere. In her white bride's dress, she has escaped with Aleksas from the arranged wedding's festivities. Izabele's father, a well-to-do farmer, pressured his daughter into marrying. He started pressuring her when he spied her sitting by the haystack with Aleksas. What's most important to note here is who Aleksas is. He doesn't own the smallest plot of land. He's a bum, and furthermore, he's a gypsy. Who would ever have dreamed that a decent Lithuanian farmer's daughter would be fooling around with a good-for-nothing gypsy. So what if his eyes sparkle, and his lips, nose, and everything else are just like a Lithuanian boy's. So what if the daughter says: Aleksas is not a thief. He's a good blacksmith. He has money. We'll open a smithy and live just like everyone else. So what . . . The daughter also says: Father, you married Mother without loving her. You want me to do the same? It might be okay if times weren't so bad, but the war is just beyond the border, it will come here, too. Where will you go, my child, without a place of your own? People will make life miserable for you and that outsider. They'll turn their backs on the one who's tainted their tribe's blood.

About Aleksas the old man puts it bluntly: if he sets one foot on this farm, I'll kill him. He's a vagabond, he's not one of us, nobody would even care . . . So he kept an ax by his bed, but Aleksas still came. When he couldn't make it to the orchard, Izabele would sneak off to meet him at the riverbank. Through a black, frightening field of currant bushes under the shimmering southwestern sky, and God's eye watching from above and below, and from all around. Only the river gurgling over the rocky bed would calm her, especially when Aleksas, also black as night, would step out from the willow's shadows. Izabele, her whole body quivering, would prick up her ears trying to catch every sound. But Aleksas would be calm. He'd clench his sturdy blacksmith fists, and the two of them would stand there like that until Izabele would be off for home again, always on the lookout.

"Let's get out of here!" Aleksas said once, "We'll never win him over. Let's get out of here!"

"And if he catches us?"

"Let's get out of here, I say. Out of Prussia and into the other Lithuania. My brother lives just outside of Tauragė. There's a different law and order there."

Izabele's heart leaped out of her breast. Leave? What about Father? His hair is completely gray. He's been a widower for ten years. And it's because of her, Izabele, that he's never brought home a stepmother. She pitied him, what would become of him, all alone . . .

"But, Izabele, why is he against our . . ."

". . . love," he wanted to say, but he tripped over the word. Her father hadn't married for love, and it's not love for the dearly departed that keeps him from remarrying. It's just not the right word. Aleksas hugs Izabele even harder.

"I can't go on like this, Izabele. You decide: me or your father, me or your father, Izabele . . ."

And Izabele breaks into bitter tears. The night and the river are calm under the southwestern sky.

Then, one day, Father said, "You'll marry. You'll marry, you'll take your vows at the altar and you'll forget all this nonsense." And the groom is in a hurry, too, you see, after the wedding he's moving to the other side of the river. He's buying a brick house in Tilžė. It's supposed to be a better place to live. Father agrees, and says, "While I still can, I'll work the land, then I'll take shelter with you." But the war is marching through Europe. This is no wedding march, it's something different, but all Father can think about is the wedding. He'll sell his daughter and send her far away, anything but that gypsy bum . . .

Was Izabele ever frightened when she heard about Tilžė! The city, where she'd never even set foot, loomed over her like a dragon. No farm, no Aleksas, nothing. Alone among strangers. She knows only Marta Dalgis there, but Marta has never been much of a friend . . . Besides, Marta has Hans. To spend the rest of her life without love, her whole life, her whole life, ohhh . . .

She rushes to the river completely out of breath. Aleksas is a black statue by the willows. She recounts everything all scrambled. Without a pause, she repeats the same words over and over again. Let's run, they agree, but they know Father will be on guard so they'll have to get ready hush-hush, and they'll choose the best day to run away, nobody will even make a peep.

To make plans is one thing, to carry them out is another. Fate tripped them up—Father made them move up the wedding day, he talked the priest into it while Aleksas was away at another parish collecting some wages due him. The wedding day loomed, you won't get away, Izabele.

Fluttering linden blossoms whirl around the yard. A fiddle chirps under the lindens, an accordion accompanies it. The old man goes from one guest to another, calm and content. She's obedient, his 'Zabele, she gave up that horsethief, she came to her senses. She'll live well, dear neighbors, and how! A girl with beauty and brains, and that's good for him, the old man, too. He'd done well by his daughter.

"We'll see, we'll see," whisper the women in little groups, "Don't count your chickens before they hatch."

"Izabele gave up Aleksas too easily, if only he doesn't . . . ."

"That's a woman's love for you," one youth exclaims loudly. "She can fool around with Aleksas one day, then get into the sack with someone else the next."

"You little swine. What are you babbling about? What's better, a gypsy, or one of us?"

"We're all human beings," the youth won't yield.

"You go on. When the old man hears you, he'll pluck out your curls."

Inside the house, the groom has chased Izabele into a corner and is twirling his blond whiskers around his finger. But in his heart he's thinking, "You turned up your nose at me again and again, just wait, I'll knock the devil out of you now. You'll cry and kiss my feet."

But out loud he says, "Izabele, get ready, it's time to hitch up the horses." Izabele can't wait, when will he leave her alone? Because next to her bosom is a note, it's from Aleksas, her maid slipped it to her this morning. Just what she'd expected: her Aleksas wouldn't desert her. It says: Come to the valley. Come as you are. I'll wait for you tonight. Tonight . . . That means she must first . . . with the groom! . . . No, she'll go now. But how? The yard is full of guests, the house is in full view. Skirts in hand, she sneaks into the yard. "Where are you going, my girl?" her father appears. I'm going to the granary, I left my shoes there. The daughter is always so concerned about her shoes that her father shrugs it off, but she runs full speed through the orchard, through the granary, through the garden, off to the valley. The flounces of her wedding dress flap around her legs, and in the yard, in that other world, chirps the fiddle, accompanied by the accordion.

She's escaped! The wheels are already clattering, and the mare really is stolen, because Aleksas doesn't even own a mare. At night they stop to take a breather. Not a living soul in the forest. They get out of the wagon and snuggle up under a spruce. That's how the first night passes, but I think it will be the last because where can you go, my friends, no one cares that you're in love. Your father has called out the police from both sides of the river. But the lovers don't know this, and after their tears, a beautiful, miraculously beautiful night of love sets in. After a long cry, after days and days of worries and tears, the mind and soul are exhausted. Peace and oblivion take over, and the newlyweds sleep soundly under the cold, towering sky, and the mare sleeps nearby. But in the morning . . .

Again, it's the same story. The gypsy running with all his might. The wagon is running, and Aleksas presses Izabele's young, tired body to his side. But what's this? Plains everywhere. Was Aleksas given the wrong directions on purpose? Or perhaps they themselves . . . lost the way? They should have seen the splendid city walls of Tauragė a long time ago. But now all they see are plains, flat as the palm of your hand.

"We're lost, Izabele," he says, "We have to get our bearings as fast as we can."

"Where are all the people? They'd show us where to go." But there aren't any houses or people. Just plains. The dusty roads spin around and around and around, like a yellow circus carousel.

And this is where the trap awaits them. A few wagons are parked around the turn. They catch sight of them and urge their horses onward. Soon! . . .

"Izabele, they're from our village . . . ," he says to her, "You can still jump off the wagon and go to them, you can tell them that I took you by force . . . Let's face it, we can't both make it now . . ."

"Aleksas, keep going! Let the mare loose, let it gallop through the fields, through the meadow, across the whole world. Look, there's the Nemunas River up ahead . . ."

And she grabs the reins from him and turns the mare. Aleksas doesn't understand, why do they need the Nemunas, if she's going to . . .

"Aleksas!" shouts Izabele, standing at the reins. "That should be the Nemunas, I'm going into the Nemunas, Aleksas!"

Into the Nemunas? Dear Lord, what did she say? She couldn't possibly? . . .

"Into the Nemunas!" she shouts, turning her head, while her unraveling braids whip around her. "You can jump out and hide there in the bushes while I go . . .

"Where?"

"Into the Nemunas, Aleksas!" she shouts, while her unraveling braids whip around her, and suddenly Aleksas understands everything.

No, he doesn't turn the mare back. Now he gets up and stands next to her. The wagons are gaining on them. Many wagons. Some-one shouts, "Sto-op! You won't get away! Sto-op!"

"Onward!" the wagon rattles, and the Nemunas is dead ahead, its wide waters sparkling. The mare snorts, she wants to jump back. He feels sorry for the animal, even though he is a horse thief, that Aleksas . . .

"Take off your clothes, Izabele," says Aleksas.

Quickly she undoes her buttons, she'd like to fold the skirt neatly, but the wagon is hurtling madly. She sees his naturally brown body in the light of day. They jump out of the wagon the same way they came into the world, white arm on brown body, brown arm on white body, and the black Nemunas accepts them: it doesn't care what race or color you are.

Hands on Starched Apron

Oh, dear Lord, I'm calling you, please forgive me for being here at the market on this dusty July morning. Oh Lord, my father's gone completely mad: outside his shop he's hung up a sign in Lithuanian that reads: *Jonas Dallgis, Pretzel-Buns and Scalded Rye Bread*. Who will buy from us now, perhaps those customers from sandy Pagėgiai village. They'll swarm the store: Mr. Dallgis, the smiling mouths of the babushkas will say shyly. The other day, when they were crossing the Nemunas heading for Rambynas hill to sing hymns, Hans said, Marta, Marta, just remember you're German, and today we're going to the orchard. In Jokubinė, the orchestra will play *ein Waltz*. Father turned white as a ghost: Marta, he whispered enraged, Marta. I left, my heart pounding. I felt as though someone had placed bricks on my chest. Hans was probably teasing me because of my get-up: hair tightly braided, striped skirt, white blouse, and sash, oh God . . . Hans and Father, dear God, have pity on me . . .

"*Guten Morgen, Fräulein*," a round man lifts the ornamental cap from his bald head, "Your pretzel-buns smell lovely!" He picks up a string of pretzel-buns and shoves them into his basket. He counts his pfennigs. They stick in between his fat fingers, and Marta would almost find it funny if it weren't for the weight on her chest, if she weren't so frantic, oh Lord.

"Did you hear that they stoned some Lithuanians coming out of church yesterday?" Francas Rutelait, actually Rutelaitis, whispers in greeting. He even pulls his hat down over his face so that no one else could hear the news, or, of course, that he is speaking Lithuanian. "But you, Marta, are a church singer. Your Father shouldn't let you go to the market alone."

"Oh, go on," says Marta, watching her father and his cart appear out of thin air. He is bringing baked goods. Warm.

"Hello, Mr. Francas!" he shouts heartily. In Lithuanian. The two who had been whispering almost jump out of their seats. If Marta were Catholic, she'd call out the Blessed Virgin's name. But her father goes on as if nothing's wrong. Out loud again. For the whole market to hear. For all of Tilžė with its docks and lakes and rowboats to hear. Oh, God, everyone can hear, everyone.

"Father," says Marta, "Father," and the words don't come out because the old man is fuming mad like last time.

"You're all hunched up like serfs . . . As I always say, a Lithuanian afraid of everything is worse than an ass . . . Come on!"

The old man sits down on the cart. All around the stench of horse sweat, early apples, milk, cheese. It's quite a task to bake bread and decorate each loaf with a crucifix or a few obscure crooked letters in the night.

Out in the street, right around the corner, a march beat thunders. Youths march by, stamping their feet against the cobblestones. One can clearly read the beat: Deutsch-land, Deutsch-land, must - be our - land, our - land. This beat, mind you, will crack your head in two, and the village, and the river, and everything you thought was yours—but it isn't yours, you old man with the menacing surname: Dall-gis, scythe.

"Oh," he jumps up, "Mr. Storosta! What a miracle! You're up and about already."

The newcomer smiles, though he's very pale. He looks like he's about to fall over. Dalgis reaches out his hands, but Mr. Storosta hands him a basket and says:

"The spirit's strong. The spirit's strong, Mr. Dalgis. When a person's blessed with a sublime spirit, his body and his works ascend to heaven."

"But when he walks on earth . . . haven't you heard, Mr. Storosta?"

"No I haven't. Your daughter sang beautifully—that I heard. This morning I was walking along the Tilželė River, I heard the sweet birds in the lindens. I hope you too can hear them someday, Mr. Dalgis."

Storosta leaves with a full basket. Solid as a young spruce. Marta is blushing because Hans is making his way through the market, whistling.

"Mein Hans," feverish, not even noticing the foreign words on her lips. Words are also spirit. They can become flesh. The flesh will give birth, and to a foreign spirit if only *mein lieber* Hans desires it. God, forgive her, perhaps she doesn't know what she's doing.

Hans sees everything from afar. Marta behind the counter, her luxurious hair pulled back in a bun, slender hands atop a navy blue dress. White chest, white starched apron. Just look, Hans, she's pretty, that Lithuanian. If you want, she can become a real German. Women are like cats—they're the first to kneel to whoever is in power. She's yours, Hans. But why doesn't Hans hurry? He whistles *mein lieber* and (imagine that!) passes right by her, right under her nose. He doesn't even blink. Oh Lord. We should also add: and God, and all the saints in the church. Unimaginable things are happening here.

A fellow in a dark jacket, very similar to the local teenagers' new uniform, says with a stutter:

"Herr D-d-d, or whatever your name is. Follow me."

"But I don't know you, sir. I am a shopkeeper, as you know, my store is by Jokubinė. I sell my fresh goods here, and this is my daughter Marta . . ."

"Ha!" says the man. And adds, this time more seriously, "Ha! Ha!"

"What do you want, sir?" Father cries out, a bit nervous now.

"Who are you?" retorts the other.

"Jonas . . . Johnn Dall . . ." Father stumbles. The intruder's eyes betray no shame. He's raising his arm. Suddenly he strikes the old man across his clean-shaven cheek with a long rubbery object. "You're a Lithuanian!" he shouts. "*Ein litauisches . . . Schwein*" others will come to say after many more such incidents.

"*Ja, ja*," the crowd of townsfolk that has gathered around them is getting agitated. True, not everyone is shouting, some mouths are too stuffed with goodies from the market. But everyone's eyes are gleaming. The old man glances at his booth and takes a pretzel-bun. It's so warm, he strokes it like naughty child. I don't understand why he does this, but I know he notices that Marta is ashen. She blends in with the cobblestones in the marketplace. Soon the townfolk will walk across her, all of Germany over there—and beyond—will rise up and walk over her soft stomach, over her chest and neck. A pleasant walk, no cobblestones to break the tips of your shiny shoes.

There's no point in waiting for help, Jonas Dalgis, at least not until I've written about you, but by then it will be too late anyway. Mr. Storosta is almost home. The villagers from the nearby towns are watering their horses by the Nemunas. Look for yourself. There's only one word that's worthwhile—yourself.

"I am Jonas Dalgis," he says in Lithuanian. "I fed you, we all fed and nourished you . . ."

I still don't understand why he is talking like this, because everything is meaningless. There is meaning only in holy blood, shed early in the morning. Look, everyone . . . Mr. Dalgis hasn't finished his sentence, and for some reason he's down on the ground. Horse droppings right by his head. That doesn't matter, but something is falling: words perhaps, or curses, perhaps the first hard apples of the season. Most likely it's stones. In 1939 the clever villagers wouldn't be throwing newly bought apples. Just lie there, old man, stay, until they drag you past the gates, roll you into the wagon, and Marta? Marta will sit, frozen, white hands atop her navy blue dress or on her white apron. Starched.

By This Window

Lord, help me. It's so quiet when you're frightened. Over there, past the brick walls, beyond the Gothic *Kirche* tower, flows the black Nemunas. A steamer still sounds its horn at the dock, the cows moo on the other side of the river. But can you hear the cows from over there? . . . From the station, the harsh whistle of trains. And silence again. Rather than turning on the light, I'll just part the curtains ever so gently . . . Better not, better sit in the corner at the white cloth-covered table. The clock is ticking, and Father . . . Where is Father now? Marta doesn't know. Oh! Nobody told her, and she didn't ask. Beyond the window, the street is black like a long narrow coffin, its pointy end disappearing into the distance by the station. Lindens on both sides. Instead of candles, huge, bright lanterns from the city of Tilžė. Sitting here all evening, her long thin fingers gripping her white hands. Ouch! As she sits down, she stumbles upon some-thing—a small, soft object falls noiselessly at her feet. She touches it with her hand. Brrr! It's slippery and cold like a fish. Father's Bible. As if repelled by it, she quickly puts it away at the other end of the table. Oh! Footsteps! God! It couldn't be Father, could it?

"Clink!" A sound from the side window, not the one that looks out into the street . . . Who can it be? . . . Marta stands up: she fixes her apron, quickly smooths out the wrinkles, and pats her chest. Her heart is bursting out of it. She stands, tense, I must hold my breath, that's the only way. To become a table, a Bible, a colorless fish . . . Oh! someone's tapping on the window again, more and more boldly and insistently. Perhaps Marta can't find the right words, but she finds the right pose perfectly—starched, frozen Marta. Go to the window. It's only a few steps, her legs are not a girl's—they're made of stone. Marta, someone outside the window says. Hey, Marta . . . Oh, it can't be, no, no, it couldn't possibly be, oh Lord God, all thoughts drain from her head like the sands in an hourglass, but the window won't stop quivering like Marta's bright red heart, when it and her soul and body walk toward the window. Once there, Marta jumps back.

Yes, it's Hans at the window. A hardy young man. Horse whip still in hand. There must be a bright moon outside, otherwise, how would she recognize him in that dark, gloomy courtyard. On his face there's just one command—hurry and open up, Marta, Hans is here!

So the doors are opened. First come Hans's feet (the horse whip next to them), then his hands, followed by his trunk and head. Blond, neatly combed and parted hair. Clean, shiny teeth. Hans smells sweet. Why not, he uses first-rate soap. *Ja, liebe Marta,* and the horse whip goes swish, swish.

Mein Gott, Hans, Marta mumbles. Miss Dalgis's German vocab-ulary is limited to a few archaic phrases. Hans grins and looks around, where should he put the whip? He says he'd like some *Kaffee,* and afterward . . . *Ach so,* Marta rushes to the kitchen. She gropes for the copper coffee pot handle, looks for the matches. A string of pretzel-buns is still on the kitchen table. The ones that nobody bought . . . Perhaps she should give him some pretzel-buns or some bagels . . . but then she remembers what happened that morning, and Marta shivers. She grabs the buns with two fingers and shoves them into the cupboard, far away, deep into the darkness. Her little white fingers are trembling. O God, please don't let the *Kaffee* boil over! "Marta!" Hans's baritone is heard, "bring it here." I'm bringing it, Marta is hurrying, but she can't find the sugar bowl or the tray. The kitchen utensils are fearful and dark, it seems that every one of them is retreating back into its own corner, where the moonlight's claws can't get at them. Marta rushes into the sitting room. And you, utensils, do whatever you like: hang there until dawn, hiding from the moon—the way people do. Because objects that are made by people become their reflection and shadow: you love, you fear, and you suffer, just as they do. And Marta . . .

And Hans? No, he doesn't want any *Kaffee*. All he sees is Marta. What a beautiful girl: gorgeously pinched-in waist, her hands are smooth and elegant, her stomach, flat, her breasts are firm, not droopy like other girls'. If only she weren't a Dalgis . . . And then, without taking his eyes off Marta, who stands bewitched, Hans comes closer and closer, and Marta backs away, farther and farther, although she knows very well that the wall is right behind her, and she won't be able to walk through it. You'll have to stop and shut your eyes, like all women do. When it's awful, they shut them . . . Hans's hand, slippery and cold (oh, that Bible again!), clutches her shoulder. Marta's eyes are closed. Hans's other hand grabs her other shoulder. Ha! ha! ha! she hears, you're a pretty broad. *Ja*, I'm telling you, Marta . . . What's he saying? Marta doesn't get it. Her body stiffens, as if turning into a cold fish. Inside, her heart gasps. And Hans's hands slip off her shoulders. Marta's breasts are firm, not droopy. A hand can rest there. Both hands. Later they'll squeeze her breasts painfully, and Marta will stifle a scream . . . She'll gasp. Outside the window—not this one—is a long, dismal street leading past the storefronts to the station. Long and straight, it shoots into the distance like a coffin. A strange, flying coffin. Oh! Hans's hands are like steel. They have no mercy. Mercilessly they tear off Marta's clothes: the dress with the white bodice, and the apron, of course, the crocheted petticoat. Ha, ha, ha, Marta hears. Her legs spread in the air, she flies along the ceiling, who knows where she'll end up. *Ich*. . . Marta . . . *mein*. . . again it's Hans's voice, becoming a drawn-out whisper, without harmony or musicality. Marta's head bangs against something hard. Dear Lord, it's Father's bed! Marta would like to jump up, but Hans's strong body is made of steel. And you, little woman, are made of lace. You sink deeper and deeper and can't see the moonlight anymore. For a long, long time, until Hans leaves, cracking his whip. Of course, he'll stop at the door, put his arm on Marta's shoulder, sweaty and bare, and say: tomorrow. Wait for me tomorrow, Marta, every night, Marta. But only at this window—not at the other one.

Marta raises her head. Until now she's been staring at the ground. Her luxurious hair reaches the ovals of her knees. Her eyes stare at Hans's whip with dull obedience, and then at his—this is strange—unshaven cheeks. That's why Marta's cheeks burned and are still burning. But, *mein Hans*, she says tenderly, just this morning you didn't even . . . she stops herself just in time from saying "recognize me." This is Hans, Hans! She remembers the two of them paddling around the lake, and Hans dreaming out loud about the new red-tiled house they would live in. Your father, according to your customs, will certainly give you a *Krait*, or dowry, as you say it. Father didn't even want to hear about it. And he complained to Storosta: did you hear, my daughter is all googly-eyed over some German. And what will their children—my grandchildren—be?! Mr. Storosta, he said, look, you married a German, tell me, forgive this old man his bluntness. Were you two happy? And if it weren't Marta Raisukytė . . . But, what a coincidence, they're both Martas! . . . Mr. Dalgis, Storosta says angrily, people of all nations must abide by love's commandments. They must, repeats Dalgis, but do they, Mr. Storosta? and Storosta straightens up, a woven tie under his white shirt collar. The tie, you see, was woven by Marta. Dalgis's stare stops Storosta in his tracks—not even the blameless could escape this gaze. Storosta and Dalgis take a long walk along the Nemunas river and discuss the matter. Yes, Father wants a Lithuanian for Marta, from the other side of the river, from Pagėgiai, but Marta loves Hans, only Hans, and no one else, because a woman's heart pays no heed to racial or national laws. And tonight she hadn't resisted him. She flies to Hans like a swiftly kicked ball, she hugs him tightly, she presses her weary body against him, and whispers over and over, *mein Hans, mein lieber lieber*, don't leave me, please, remember how we talked about those red-tiled roofs . . . Do you remember, Hans? . . . Can't he hear, who knows what it is, but Marta's loving lips must repeat it over and over again, and Hans remains standing in the same place. Then he reaches for the door. When Marta realizes that Hans is leaving, and she will have to be alone until morning with two sins on her conscience, she becomes very frightened. And for the first time all day, she is afraid of her father, of Jonas Dalgis's cold Bible, the arm chair with the wicker back, his clothes hanging in the closet, the sign at the shop's entrance. No, no, says Hans, flashing his clean, white teeth, I tore it down, don't worry. What? the blood drains from her face. And suddenly her whole body shaking, she starts out softly, but says louder and louder:

"Hans, tell me, where is my father now? Where's my father, Hans?"

But Hans shuts the door from outside. The moon peeks in, illuminating Marta's white body, as if covering her with frost and spraying her with silver polish. Again silence fills her ears into which Hans's words force themselves. Tomorrow, wait for me tomorrow, Marta, every night, Marta. Not by the other window (it looks out onto the street), but by this one, by thissss one . . .

. . . And His Very Own Home . . .

That night he dreamed about his dead wife. Apparently she'd come back, and it was that same room again, where it wasn't just the two of them, but also their three puffy-cheeked kids. What joy to return again to that cramped cottage! But why weren't the neighbors saying anything about seeing them with Petrikė again? At first they listen, astounded, then not a word. Perhaps that's why Petrikė disappeared. A strange girl brings Petrikė her clogs. Here, she says, put them on. And he cries, sobbing from time to time—is it because she's disappeared again, or is it because of those old, worn-out clogs, bought way back when, at the famous Tilžė market? He cries and cries so pitifully that his elder daughter, Elė, nudges his arm, calling in a frightened voice: Father, oh Father, wake up . . .

By morning everything is different. By morning Jurgis has even forgotten the dream. Silently he leads the cow out to the forest to graze, checking back every few steps: some no-good German might pop up, so help me Lord. Dry twigs crackle under foot. The lingonberries are ripening on the hillocks. He runs his hand across a branch and gets a whole handful of berries. He puts his head back and pours them into his mouth. His teeth sting from the tartness, but it's all right dear lingonberry, better your red nectar than the blood that flows all too readily in Pagėgiai forest. Jurgis listens, but this time there's no shooting to be heard anywhere. All is calm except for the rumble of cars from Jurbarkas. Then someone from near the station calls. It's old man Einikis out walking. He certainly has been cursing his job with the railroad lately! Yesterday when he stopped by, he sat there all hunched up, picking splinters from his cap. I was born by the tracks, he said, and that's where I grew up. That's my people's profession, but to live to see times like these, I never imagined . . . The convoys rattle on toward Königsberg, what they're carrying only God himself knows, the other day they brought people. And where do they put them? Jurgis asked then. Are you stupid? Don't you know there's a camp on the other side of the tracks? The Germans are packing them all in there. There are all kinds there: French, Russians, and young Poles. It's all on my back, who do you think meets these trains and who do you think sees them off? I do. Einikis punches himself in the chest with his fist—a fist, no, it's not much of a fist, it's a dried-up, withered little fist. What can you do with a fist like that—you can't do any harm to yourself, much less the Germans. But we used to live side-by-side with the Germans, continued Einikis, we were neighbors, with no problems, we got along. The German masters, oh! they sure kept things in order— brick farm buildings everywhere, cleanliness, the women always freshly bathed. They had culture, not like our naked wretches . . .

"Shove that culture where the sun don't shine," Jurgis can't help saying.

". . . not like our miserable wretches," Einikis rambles on as if he hadn't heard. I used to envy them that, I would have envied it to my grave if it hadn't been for the *Krieg*. What a nation, such order, but what's going on in the camp now, Jurgis, you wouldn't believe it . . . Old man Einikis presses his chest against the white edge of the table, then suddenly he rubs his eyes with his fist, gets up, pulls his uniform cap over his head, and without adding another word or taking one back, he reaches for the door.

That was Einikis yesterday . . . And now Jurgis, perched on the rise near the lingonberry field, watches the cow grazing greedily in the tiny meadow, the grass—sparse and dry because of the summer heat. Jurgis awakes from his daydream and scans the area again. As long as some German doesn't drag himself here. If they take his cow away, what then? He has three kids to feed, and no pigs, no chickens, nothing at all. And on her deathbed, Petrikė had said over and over again: Jurgis, take care of our little cow . . . And three kids to feed, his responsibility, the oldest one a young woman already, I must protect her from the soldiers, you never know . . . But women show up all the time, even women from Mikytai dart straight toward the young Germans. The other day, with his own eyes he saw a couple sneak off to the pine grove. Rumor has it that they pay with canned goods . . . They're disgusting! The tramps! If that happened to him, he'd club his very own daughter with an ax. But as soon as he imagines his blonde-haired Elė's head on the chopping block, he shivers with dread and spits into the grass: God, protect me in the evil hour that makes me say such things. Then his thoughts begin to jumble, unconsciously his hand picks the autumn-tinted cranberry leaves over and over again. His fingers rest on the ground. He puts one black, muddy finger to his nose and smells it: nothing, just the smell of earth. That's all. Above, it is silent and calm, not too far away a wandering rooster crows (how the devil did he end up in the forest?). And the cow looks at Jurgis with calm, drowsy eyes. Get up, my human master, let's go, look, I've licked up all the grass here with my sharp tongue. I've plucked it all out with my teeth. It's time we were on our way.

It's time, Jurgis agrees. They go together. And when the path narrows, he lets the cow go first and he follows, and so they proceed. Jurgis would prefer for the path never to end, it feels good to walk, it's a peaceful evening, no shooting anywhere, not a single German in sight, and home is close by. You may be going for the last time, Jurgis . . .

"Daaad," yells little Anė at the gate. Her white head cocked to the side, she grabs his coattails, she is close to the ground, hardly touching his knees, she's such a . . . I'll have problems with her, he is thinking, but he says: Anė, do you want some milk? She shrieks with joy and follows him, hopping along on one leg like a grasshopper, still pulling on his coattails and stretching them down almost to the lawn.

That evening they all sit down around the unpainted white wooden table. It's Elė's chore to scrub it, and it's a chore she doesn't forget, because it reminds her of her mother, who would bring a block of soap and a bucket of warm water on Saturdays and scrub the table for a long time until it was white and smelled sweet. Now Jurgis cuts the bread into thick, uneven slices and heaps them right onto the table. The wooden-handled knife is right there. He pours milk for everyone into tin cups. They eat the bread, washing it down with milk, as the room gets darker and darker.

We'll have made it through another day, thinks Jurgis, as he brushes the crumbs from the table into his hand. God be praised. Out loud he says: "Girls, go fix your beds, it's time to call it a day. I'll make sure everything's all right outside."

When he returns, the cottage is silent, little bare bottoms and legs flicker in the light from the wood-burning stove. One of the girls laughs softly, and Elė, wearing a stern face, is quieting them all.

Shhh, says Jurgis in his bass voice. Quiet, no fooling around, I want this house as quiet as a church . . . He'd like to pat their little behinds, but they'd go wild again, and he'd have to calm them down with anger. Oh, there had been times, but Petrikė was always gentle. And she'd advise Jurgis: gently, gently, gently, Jurgis, take it easy . . .

Jurgis sits down at the table. It's time for bed, it's getting dark, but why are people still out, they're so quiet, so quiet . . . He opens his mouth in amazement because someone is rattling the front door. He goes to open it. Again, just like yesterday, it's Einikis. What a tough old guy, he keeps coming over . . . Most likely it's because of these nighttime talks with Einikis that Jurgis can't fall asleep at night, and that he dreams such dreams.

But this time, Einikis looks around the cottage like a stranger, and with his finger he motions Jurgis to follow him away from the stove where the children are.

Einikis presses his uniform cap to his lips. He never used to do that—he just used to pick off lint. Now: Jurgis, he says, listen, Jurgis. And when the latter doesn't catch on, he whispers a confused explanation: Jesusmary, one of them's escaped, he's run away . . . Overhearing him you'd think that Jesus and Mary had escaped their torturers, but it's no joke to use Jesus' name in vain on such a dark night. For some reason Einikis is behaving oddly: his muddy cap at his lips, he's rambling—run away—run-run-nn . . . Who? Jurgis can't help asking. Talk like a human being, did you lose your head over there by the tracks?

Finally he understands that a prisoner has escaped from the camp—he ran down the tracks, straight to Einikis's, and using all the languages he knew begged him to hide him and not turn him in. Where could he, Einikis, hide him, he lives in hell itself, right next to the station, but Jurgis—he's out here by the forest. Just for tonight. Better yet, they should take him to Mikytai to Jurgis's sister—she could take him somewhere even further from evil's eyes. You can't just let him die, Jesusmary . . .

Hmmm . . . but how . . . you know . . . I'm alone here with the girls . . . The Germans will figure it out, they'll come here, they'll smash our brains in, and then . . .

Either Einikis doesn't hear or he doesn't want to hear. He goes on: listen, my friend, you've got to help us . . .

But do you know him, he might be some Anglican or . . .

What's it to you—Anglican or Russian. We're all creatures of the same God . . .

So, you'd say a German is of the same . . .

Oh! What's all this chatter, my friend? You've got to decide, because he's out there waiting in the bushes. They'll notice soon, they'll start looking for him, and the bushes are probably the first place they'll . . .

Now you've done it, Einikis, you've put all the guilt on me, and you keep chattering away, you keep pleading, says Jurgis, as if in reproach, as if trying to convince himself. He looks around the cottage helplessly—in the corner is a painting of Christ, his heart pierced. Jesus Christ, what should I do. There's the children and the cow, and that man waiting in the bushes. What's it to Christ? He just points to his pierced heart, but you, my friend, you have your own troubles. Touch his heart with your finger, maybe he'll answer, as long as you're not standing by the door or by Einikis.

Shhh! Einikis is practically shouting. They both prick up their ears. Over there, somewhere beyond the shiny railroad tracks, it sounds like gunfire. They're on his trail! They're looking for him! The thought flashes through his mind like white lightning. There's no more deliberating, my friend. It's yes or no. Einikis bolts out the door first, but Jurgis remains struck dumb until through the half-open door he notices a shadow strangely huddled up in the moonlight. The shadow keeps falling to the ground as it crawls toward Einikis. Fear paralyzes Jurgis's arms and legs, he wants to move but he cannot, and the shadow is coming closer and closer, and from Pagėgiai station the dog's barking is getting louder and louder. They're looking for him! And something under his rib cage snaps as if they were out to get him, Jurgis, the owner of this cottage. Oh God, his three little girls are asleep here, and out there they're hunting down a human being . . . If only a human being could forget, just for a moment, the desire to live, to live the way you've lived until now, if you could just hide this desire in your pocket like a shiny coin, while . . . that's why Jurgis is gulping air as if he were standing before the hangman's noose. Jurgis wearily crosses the threshold. The shadow is right there, it's lifting its head, how can you avoid it? It's not a human being, but a ghost, barely skin and bones, makes your hair stand on end. Einikis hisses: Jurgis, I'm telling you, don't be a jerk, hurry . . .

And Jurgis hurries, but it's too late. He's dragging the shadow by its ragged sleeve, but where can he go? The basement? The barn? But time has a ready answer, it's faster than the slow thoughts of a human being under the moon's dwindling glow. Oh, you Lithuanians, walking along behind your cow or looking into the jaws of death, grinning, grinning, grinning . . .

Lord, while he was thinking, flashlights flooded the yard. And it's amen to the shadow—Russian or Pole—and to the old railroad man, and yes, to Jurgis, dumbstruck on the threshold.

He'll cry, oh how Jurgis will cry now (if there's time), cursing himself, and even Elė, awakened by the human and canine barks, she'll come to the door, barefoot. But Father isn't asleep, if he is, he'll wake up (perhaps he'll wake up wiser), and Petrikė, poor Petrikė, she'll lie on Pagėgiai hill, not knowing how or why Jurgis is leaving his children, his cow, and his very own home . . .

The Butcher

whom everyone in our town knew. The shop stood near the marketplace, a square paved with heavy stones. Surrounding the square were pubs, small taverns, and a little restaurant in which a copy of Matejka's painting "The Battle of Grünwald" hung on the back wall. Drunken men waving their arms, their cheeks flushed, graying hair falling in tufts over their foreheads and ears—the scene echoed the painting. And the butcher shop was next door. Near the marketplace.

Sundays, wearing a dark blue jacket and black, well-polished shoes, he'd hang a heavy lock on his door, close the shutters, and set off for market. Treading on cobblestones overgrown with wheat and wild daisies, past the long rows of tables laden with wares, eyes fixed straight ahead, he'd walk clutching something tightly under his arm. When he could make out the tiny black figures of the villagers, their wagons, and their horses covered with blankets of elaborate design arriving at the other end of the square, he'd carefully pull the rumpled hat from under his arm, blow on it a few times, slap it into shape, and put it on his head. And then with big, heavy steps, he'd make his way toward the wagons.

Look, look, Rupšas is coming, Rupšas is coming, the women selling honey, cheese, butter, berries, linen and woolen threads, and fine cloth would say. They'd say it with subdued respect, or perhaps it was envy—without a doubt, his was the best butcher shop outside Lauksargiai.

Rupšas is coming, Rupšas is coming, the girls gathered at the corner by the confectioner's would automatically turn their heads. Then they'd whisper to one another until their mothers would appear out of nowhere and tell them to shake the straw from their skirts and wipe their mouths. Time for church. The shrill bell of the Protestant church was already ringing. Soon the Catholic bell would begin its melody on the banks of the Jūra river. But when the girls still couldn't keep from whispering, their mothers, overhearing his name, most likely, would scold: shhh, you little fools, he's not interested in the likes of you. He'll get himself a German, a lady, if he wants. Choose from among your own kind.

Rupšas is coming, Rupšas is coming, the farmers would stir. They'd spit into their palms and rub them in anticipation of the bargaining. We won't sell cheaply, men. Then they'd wait, puffing on pipes filled with homegrown tobacco.

That's the kind of attention they paid to Jeronimas Rupšas as he crossed the market square on sunny summer Sundays, overcast autumn mornings, and even frosty winter afternoons. The children, diving like sparrows under the horses' haunches or circling the pretzel-bun vendor, would holler:

> Rupšas, Rupšas, rat-a-tat-tat,
> With your fancy German hat,
> Rupšas, Rupšas, down you'll fall,
> No place left for you to crawl.

And when he looked back, they'd take off in an uproar, falling over each other through a hole in the fence. Through the hole and across the street was the Protestant churchyard. Once in a while when they jumped through the hole, they'd bump their heads on some dignified stomach. And while the stomach would try to brush off the microscopic dust that the Lithuanian children carried, they'd be off again, zipping through the market square.

Business was good for Rupšas, even though he was young, not even forty yet. Look, everyone: white apron, white shirt, sleeves rolled up, of course, and his hands moving swiftly, fingers clenching and unclenching as if to some beat—one, two, one, two. The clean pieces of meat: red beef, the freshest veal, smoked ham, fattened geese and ducks flying from the freshly scrubbed butcher's block to the scales. You'll lick your fingers, ladies. Please, thank you, okay, what pleasant customers, please come again. And so it went from morning until evening, not counting market days. And sometimes there wasn't any need to go to market. Coming to town early, the villagers would stop their horses by Rupšas's store and knock at the shutters with their whips. Sometimes the butcher would go to Lauksargiai, well-known for its cattle trade for as long as anyone could remember. And he would return with a cartload.

How did he manage by himself? His parents had died many years ago, and hadn't hired servants. He was alone. He could have married. Any number of townspeople would have been proud to act as matchmakers. But he would have no part of it. He had a butcher shop; good profits, he drank seldom—only if the occasion warranted it. A man in his prime: blond hair, blue eyes, fair face. And his lips weren't fat like the other butchers', whose very appearance gave away their trade. Not Jeronimas. When he'd go out, dressed in his light-colored suit, you'd have said he was quite a guy, you might even have mistaken him for a teacher . . .

Rupšas received many special orders. A wedding for one, a funeral for another, a christening for a third—they all needed meat. And thank God, he could satisfy everyone, and he himself was satisfied—until . . .

They always decribe a person's life as until . . . And a town, too, until . . . And this town had always been on the border: Lithuania on one side, East Prussia on the other. Poor people from the surrounding villages would travel to Lauksargiai to find work as hired hands. When the war broke out, the first thing the Germans did was take over the town. They made their presence felt in the countryside, not to mention the town. And everyone knew Rupšas— businessman, famous butcher, so . . .

That evening after sunset, while the last stray beams of sunlight still clung to the clouds' edge, while the wind slowly swept the deserted market square, after Jeronimas Rupšas had counted out the day's money and had poured it into his chest, a man entered the store without knocking. Jeronimas slowly raised his head. By the counter, where the large wooden-handled knife still lay, stood a broad-shouldered stranger. He didn't say anything, even though it's rude, and even strange, perhaps, but it takes all kinds. The businessman's duty is to please everyone; that's why Rupšas first greeted him in the several languages he knew and asked him what sir might like, perhaps he might still have some . . . The man took the wooden-handled knife into his hands, flipped it over a few times, tried out the blade's sharp edge, scratched off a coagulated drop of blood with his nail, and then looked the shopkeeper straight in the eye.

Nobody knows what those eyes were like, but Rupšas was taken aback, and the stranger, noticing this, smiled, exposing two rows of even metal teeth.

"Peace, honored sir, peace," he said. "I have some business to discuss with you."

A kerosene lamp burned next to the counter. Unconsciously, Jeronimas dimmed it. He spent a long time wiping his hands on a white rag, then he came closer:

"I'm listening, sir. Do you need some meat?"

"Hmmm."

"I can get you some."

"Are you from out of town?"

"Hmmm," he muttered, "I said I could get you some meat, we can split the profit." And he banged his fist on the counter. The light dwindled and started to flicker.

"What kind of meat?" Jeronimas then asked. "I buy only the finest quality."

"Don't worry about the quality. It will be special meat."

"What?" Jeronimas' mouth dropped open so low that it was disgusting for the stranger to look at. Then he came to his senses. This must be a joke, what a joker this man is. And I didn't even catch on. So he laughed: Ha, ha, ha. Where will you get first-quality meat these days?

"I'm not joking," the stranger retorted sternly. His piercing eyes fixed on Jeronimas. "I have a product to sell, you're a buyer, there's nothing else to discuss."

"But, sir," Rupšas stammered, "what can I say?"

"You're not accustomed to buying from strangers, you mean? Then listen, my dear man. Soon there will be no more pigs, no more bulls or horses in these parts, and what will happen to business? Business must continue. So I am offering you the finest product. There will be more and more of it. It will last for a long time, I tell you."

"There won't be any more pigs, or bulls, or horses? What are you talking about?"

"I'm telling you. I know," the stranger answered. "Your people will work for us, but who will feed them? You will, Herr Butcher! So, do we have a deal or don't we?"

And he grabbed Jeronimas by the arm and led him into the corner of the store. The chairs, eager to be of service, slid themselves into place. The men sat down, the stranger spoke, Jeronimas answered, loudly at first, then more and more softly. Outside the wind swept the littered streets and whipped the drooping willow branches into the black waters of the Jūra River.

So how's business now, Jeronimas? You say it's horrible to take a product you don't know into your own hands, especially when you know your clients so well, and they are wondering where Herr Shopkeeper gets such good meat in such bad times. The market square is emptying out because every bloody day of the week the young men are being hunted down and taken to the railroad station. Convoys of train wagons take them far away. It's true, Jeronimas receives shipments in white linen bags and business is flourishing. Don't worry, ladies, my products are clean.

Many shops have closed already, but Rupšas is still in business. The strangest rumors abound, they reach Rupšas's ears as well.

Tonight Rupšas picks up his lamp with trembling hands and examines his padlocks for a long time. Then he sighs, picks up his money chest and begins to toss in his money as he counts it.

"I can't go on, I can't go on, Jeronimas," someone whispers.

"Who is that?" he stirs.

"I can't go on, I can't, Jeronimas!"

"What? Who's saying that?" he grabs the lamp and turns to the opposite corner. It's empty.

"Quit this work, Jeronimas," it pleads.

"Ohh!" he jumps up suddenly, runs around the room, and presses his wet forehead to the window. The shutter's still there. Everything's locked up, but . . .

"Jeronimas, do you hear me, Jeronimas . . ."

Now he's running through the room frantically, the lamp casting a gloomy light on the table. The lamp is a keepsake from his father, but Jeronimas, unable to understand anything, grabs it with both his hands and . . . he wants to smash it to the ground, but he controls himself. A gust of wind. It's quiet and dark.

Strange things are going on under the southwestern sky. Jeronimas neglects his business and takes to drinking. He slips into the restaurant and sits slumped over his plate, a bottle tightly grasped in his hands. Sometimes a few other men join him. The restaurant is overflowing with noise. Blind Zigmas is singing love songs. Black-haired Mockus whispers to his neighbor about the shootings in Pagėgiai. Zigmas keeps singing, and the restaurant owner sits smoking a pipe and, intentionally or perhaps not, pays no attention at all to the men.

"Men, you scoundrels," Tadas Dautartas suddenly jumps up. "Why are we all sitting here with our asses next to the butcher? He kisses up to the Germans."

They all turn toward Rupšas. A murmur fills the room. The word has been spoken. Yes, of course, of course, he sells meat by the cartload, from where, tell me, my friend, where do you think these diseases are coming from, if not from over there? . . . The murmur grows, the men get up, Jeronimas remains sitting alone. In Matejka's painting the men bluster forward. Aha . . . Blind Zigmas senses this, and accompanied by the accordion he roars a new song at the top of his lungs. As horror encircles everyone in the restaurant, Jeronimas continues to just sit there. Tadas continues:

"Let's throw the dog out by the scruff of its neck!"

Then Rupšas is out the door, running for his life, though there's nowhere to go. At home there are only walls, shutters, the old, beat-up butcher block. He needs a human being now, he desperately needs a human being, otherwise he won't have a life at all. The butcher decides to get married. Nothing else will do!

Rupšas looks around for a long time: he needs a healthy young lass, one with all her teeth. Through her he will revive and forget everything. And you wouldn't believe it, but he found her in some other parish, in a big family, the kind he wanted, she was innocent and didn't believe the rumors that preceded him.

No big wedding. The young couple quietly moved into the butcher's lonely house. Occasionally a little smoke would rise from the chimney, or one of them would go outside to shake out the bedding. Otherwise the shutters were closed, the inhabitants nowhere to be seen.

Several months after the wedding, a heavy hand knocked on the shutters. There was no answer for a long time. It knocked harder. Even the closest neighbors hid their heads under their pillows. Finally Rupšas slipped out: unshaven, disheveled, it seemed he hadn't even bathed.

"So, man, in bed with the dame all day long!" the visitor shouted. "Come on, invite your guests in."

"Where?"

"Inside. Show us the wife, set the table. Don't you remember your old pals?"

"I don't want to," he managed to say. He shoved his hands into his pockets and stood there.

"Now, now," the other said and knocked him on the head so hard that Rupšas bounced up like a spring. "Move it, or we'll fry you like a goose without grease."

In the doorway stood a woman in a long linen shirt, Rupšas's wife. Her big stomach was already showing. One of the men slapped it with his stick and laughed, the other said to Rupšas:

"We'll try her out, too. These are lean times. People are restless."

"I won't give you my wife, she cost me too dearly," Rupšas answered sharply.

"Now, now," said the other. And to the woman he said: "Do you know what kind of business your husband was in? You don't? Well, you'll find out."

Rupšas rushed toward the men, who pushed him away laughing, what a worm, slithering on the ground. And the men kept bringing in pieces of meat and throwing them on the ground, saying: "Man, woman, child, man, woman, child." Rupšas's wife was screaming and slapping the visitor's faces with her little hands, until one of the men kicked her in the stomach. She doubled over and fell to the ground, the other man immediately slammed her in the head with his revolver. Then he picked the woman up by her hair and threw her onto the other pile. Sell it, Rupšas.

Rupšas rushes in with a flaming firebrand. Red, thick fire spreads over everything; the men fumble at the door, it's locked, so they break it down, outside they secure it with a boulder and get into their wagon. They ride casually through the streets of the town. That's what you get, butcher, for not keeping your part of the bargain.

The next morning the townspeople stood by the burned rubble of the butcher's house.

"The butcher's burned," they whispered.

"Praise be to God," the women whisper softly.

The boys whisked to and fro between the onlookers's legs and shouted: "Rupšas burned! Rupšas burned! Hurray!

To cover the hurrahs, blind Zigmas came and belted out a song.

1981
Translated by Jūra Avižienis

Romualdas Granauskas

The Bread Eaters

It's not yet clear where on the horizon the sun will rise, its red hues are still nowhere to be seen; the only thing is the black trees have moved closer to the door of the farmhouse and something, something vaguely large, lies in the doorway, its white face turned up to the eaves and one crooked arm flung across the yard, touching the well. This is the oblong stone threshold and the gravel path; all the other paths are still lying motionless on the grass, they need someone's feet to rouse them from their early morning torpor. Or they need the red light of the sky, awaited by the faces of four people still asleep in the warm darkness behind the wooden walls, two faces at one end of the cottage, two at the other; eight closed eyes, but one pair will open before the others, and the stone threshold will hear awakened thoughts, wanting to go out, silently creeping inside, along the walls, beside the hall door.

Old Rimkus's eyes were the first to open. He listened a while for drops falling from the trees; did it rain last night, no, it didn't rain, although it might as well rain: now rain isn't bad for the rye he sows every year on his land (a plot the size of a good calf hide). They carried sheaves, the two of them, sometimes two apiece, and carried them all into the garden, then they threw them down, then threshed them, then hauled them to the mill by bicycle. By evening there'll be bread baking in the only bread oven left in the whole village, the young housewives don't even know how to bake anymore, their children will grow up without having tasted homemade bread. He heard the dried-out cottage wall creak just once, very softly: creak. Mornings and evenings the house sinks slowly into the earth: creak, creak . . . While he was thinking about the wood in the wall, he thought to ask himself if he had kindling in the woodshed. They light the oven only once a year, but there should still be some large pieces of dry branches from before, there should still be some, he finishes his thought, and the window seems much whiter, he can make out his wife's head next to his own: a black braid tied with a little rag, such a sad braid, got to get up, can't stay in bed so long, and he still has to go to the riverside for clay to patch the oven with, he won't be able to manage a full pail anymore, clay is heavy, heavier than water, black soil, or gravel. He puts on his pants and goes outside barefoot, he stands on the oblong stone facing the ruddy light of the sky, which has just absorbed the quiet thud of the door.

The son-in-law hears it, wakes up, and wrinkles his face from the pain in his head, but he refuses to open his eyes so he won't have to see anything. His mouth is dry, Narkus is really an idiot: last night he told everyone that the vodka he brought won't give you a hangover. And what's more he hears his father-in-law, padding on his way to the barn. In his head he can see the bare feet and hunched back; you'd think he could stay in bed this early in the morning. He's still fooling around with the rye. Marytė says: they sow a little bit each year, there hasn't been a year yet when they didn't. He cuts it down himself, the old woman ties it, they don't let anyone near them: no, no, we'll manage ourselves. They only make people laugh, hell, his head feels like wood, when he opens his eyes he sees his pants thrown across the table, he must have come home a pretty sight, the store doesn't open till nine, Marytė won't give him a ruble, she'll be mad as a witch, maybe he still has a few kopecks of his own, if she hasn't grabbed them. He gets up and, still staggering, goes to relieve himself in the pail, the hell with drinking: it's brown—like a horse's. He goes back, sits on the bed, rubs the soles of his feet together and tucks them under the blanket. There's a painful spinning in his head, and something, he can't quite figure what, keeps rolling before his eyes: colored spots or black and white branches. As he falls back to sleep, he hears: something is coming from the direction of the barn, shuffle, shuffle . . .

Someone is coming through the big, empty dream; the old woman always has these dreams: something like the potato fields at harvest, something like mowed meadows, only there's no one anywhere, many have died, and at the very edge of her dream lie their grass-covered mounds. Father, mother, the children, the neighbors, can't even remember them all, fall after fall the grass dies and in winter—no mounds, just a white plain, the old woman wades to its edge, poking her cane before her: maybe she'll find one? But it's only a dream, it's not even winter, just a week ago they were cutting rye, each carrying in two sheaves, and if it's this hard now . . . no, it's not winter now, you'll see the mounds dotted with wildflowers, that's why the footsteps on the grass are so soft and go shuffle, shuffle . . . It feels so good to go barefoot early in the morning, barefoot through the grass, in your own yard, but why is he up and about when the sun has barely risen? She remembers: we're going to bake bread, the neighbors will come over, he's up and I'm still lying here, shame on me. It's already red outside the window, I'll milk the cow, he can take her out to pasture, then I'll start getting the bread ready, my God, did I just now wake up or have I been lying awake for a long time?

She's lying on her left side with her face to the wall, and the wall is red, so the sun is rising, maybe it's already up, then she feels her husband's hand on her thigh, last night he came home drunk as a skunk and fell asleep, mother is rinsing a pail with water, got to get up, father will be taking his cow out to pasture, he can take our cow, too, the front door is already open, the pail strikes the door frame so clearly, and the clanking of the handle echoes throughout the yard. She goes out sleepily, halfway down the road she sets the pail in the grass, goes behind the barn herself, and when she comes back, mother's white face is in the barn door and the pail's green edge is spattered with milk, they set out toward each other, mother's glance travels over her breast and stomach, down to her feet still warm from the night. You can relax, she thinks, suddenly angry. Not yet, unless it should happen accidentally, we'll build our own place first—then we'll be ready. But not now, the two of you can have your shack to yourselves.

"Where's father?"

"He went down to the river for clay."

"He can take our cow out to graze, too."

Their skirts touch as they pass each other on the road; father is coming back, bent over by the weight of the pail, a trowel sticks out of it, and its handle is red. His hands and his pants are covered with clay, father is quite close now; she says: father, I'm just about to milk her, will you take her out? I'll take her, says father, but hurry. I'll just bring the pail home and then I'll be taking my cow out, he's breathing heavily, he sets the pail on the ground and walks around to the other side of it. Now she sees that it's not even a pailful, barely a half, and she hurries to the barn, swats the cow across its back: leg! she shouts, leg! She kneels by the udder and for a moment does nothing because somehow she feels very sad.

The old woman, down at her end, is enjoying straining the milk into an old-fashioned milk can with a glass window at the bottom:

she'll lower it into the well, and by evening it will be cold as ice, the bread will be straight from the oven. She fills a pitcher with milk, saving some for breakfast. She lifts the sheepskin jacket from the kneading-trough, the dough has already begun to crack, she pinches off some and eats it, then smooths over the spot. After lowering the milk into the well, she looks for the baker's peel on the porch but she can't find it, her son-in-law hung his quilted jacket over it, now it'll stink to high heaven of gasoline; she carries it outside, washes it at the well, rinses it several times, and keeps smelling it; no, it doesn't smell, it only seemed to. She stands the peel up on its handle, takes it in both of her hands, and looks to see if the old man is coming back from the pasture, over her head a white board is sparkling, that means the sun has already climbed higher than the roof, she leans her forehead against the damp wood and stands that way for a long time. Then she carries the peel back, slaps the clay side of the bread oven with her hand: scat, scat, you beast! Sometimes it crawls inside and lies there, and the old man will come home and light the fire from the front of the oven, it's already been trapped in there once.

As she's lighting the fire, she glances toward the bed, a foot with a yellow big toe is sticking out, father is already opening the porch door on their end of the house, instead of his own. Son-in-law, he says, stepping inside, are you still sleeping? Of course he is, she hurries to answer, it's Sunday, isn't it enough that he bounces behind the wheel all week? Son-in-law, the father repeats, are you going to sleep through lunch?

"What?" he asks.

"Can you move those sacks on the porch? They're yours."

"And where am I supposed to put them?"

"Take them up to the loft. Pour the flour into the big bin. I need to get at the bread oven."

"Why?"

"Because I do."

"They're going to bake bread today, didn't I tell you?" again she hurries to explain, he's leaning on his elbows, his large head looms black. The father stands and waits, his soft voice has just stopped echoing. "Father," she wants to say, "you go, he'll get up and bring in the sacks in a while. When I need flour, I'll bring it down in a pail, it's not heavy."

"The things you come up with," says the son-in-law.

All the while the father is standing there, he looks at the pants thrown across the table, she grabs them and hurls them on the bed, so will you bring 'em in, he asks again.

"The things you come up with," says the son-in-law. "All kinds of nonsense."

He takes his pants, swings his feet onto the dirt floor, then the father leaves. He finds a smoke in his pants pocket, holds it in his lips, and sits there without lighting it.

"You should go right away," she says. "You look like a horse nodding its head."

"It's my last cigarette. I'll have to go buy some more."

"You're gonna go fill your tank with beer already?"

"Tank up, tank up. You sure gave me a lot to fill my tank with, didn't you? The day before yesterday I brought home eighty rubles, and did you at least buy a bottle? I would've had some now."

He goes out the door to the porch, now he'll take the sacks up, no, he goes behind the barn, the father is standing in the yard, they say something to each other but she can't hear the words.

When I was young, the old man thinks and goes into the barn carrying a rope, stretches it out as straight as a stick on the dirt floor, piles the kindling across it, and slowly continues his thought: "When I was young, the oven needed four armfuls, later it was six, and now it'll need eight. And maybe even twelve," he realizes sadly. It'd be good if it only took eight, and he stacks three more logs on top. He ties the rope, lifts it onto his back, and a sharp pain stabs his back but the pain passes immediately, and bent over but happy he goes out to the porch: "Back and forth another seven times and then I'll light the fire. Then I'll be ready to light the fire."

"Come and eat!" the old woman says.

"After I light the fire," he answers.

As the flames begin to rise he bends down to see if the top of the oven has caved in. Not yet. He opens the door to the house, but his wife is nowhere to be seen, he can feel her spirit everywhere. "Are you ready yet?" he says to the spirit. "Do you need anything else?" "I don't need anything," the spirit answers, "only some maple leaves."

"You're not going to pick them yourself, are you?"

"And neither will you. Your head will start spinning and you'll come tumbling down. Don't even start climbing. I'll ask Maryté."

"Go ahead and ask her. I already asked our son-in-law to do something."

They're old people, they don't eat bacon anymore: they slice some cheese and pour themselves some milk from the pitcher. Then he looks out the window:

"So whom shall I invite?"

"Why, you know."

Slowly he sets off down the road through the blue potato blossoms, white butterflies circling around his head all the while, up to the very end of the field. He looks back at his house, his son-in-law is following not far behind. Let him catch up, if he wants to, what will we talk about walking side by side, young people's lives are so strange now, it'll be hard for them when they die unless our grandchildren learn from their parents and begin to love everything in life. The whole village can be seen from the road: eight homesteads scattered between the forest and the river, but the forest only seems big, there aren't even any mushrooms in it, in winter another village lights up beyond the forest, and Rimkus sees his son-in-law disappearing under the branches.

She cleared the plates from the table, there were only three, and as she did so she thought: how few plates they still needed to eat. Mother's face was strange when they met this morning with pails in their hands: one empty and one full. He's already gone to to the store for cigarettes and bread, maybe he won't come home too drunk, now a lot of people drink, not just him. She went to the window and saw her father walking on the other side of the potato field, why aren't they walking together, she wonders, do other people see mother and me that way too? Then the mother can relax, now she's ready to bake bread, she keeps going out to the porch, getting things ready around the oven, she comes back: she needs something. She says: pick some maple leaves. Your father's set up the ladder, climb up and pick some, I can't, my head spins round.

"Why? You're not ready to bake yet," she turns around but doesn't pull her hands out of the warm water where she's washing the dishes. "Later."

"Later then."

The old woman returns, remembering her daughter's back, which she saw when she opened the door, but then there were other words that had to be said, she couldn't bear to think about what she was seeing: narrow shoulders under a cotton dress. "The children are growing old," she walks around the house in mourning, the green of the yard gleams outside the window. Even without looking, she knows what's happening: the goose is walking around the well, the swallows are darting along its sweep, a pretty white cloud is hanging above the maple tree. But sometimes a sudden premonition pierces her heart, and turning around she sees a large raven perched on the gate post, looking straight at the windows with an evil eye. Flailing her arms, she rushes to the window, and the bird flies onto the barn roof, caw! caw! she hears; terrified, she throws open the porch door, hurries into the yard, and yells at the bird, scaring it back into the forest.

Now he's already made his way through the woods, he breaks off a branch, strips it of leaves—it becomes a whip; nearing the store, he slices the tops of the tall grass, but doesn't quite chop them off, they just bend their heads downward, they'll never straighten up again, he thinks, not after it rains, not ever. There might not be any people at the store yet, but he wants there to be some, he imagines Vanda's face and her blond hair, the smell of freshly washed floors, it always smelled that way in her room, everything happened so recently. After all, he never said he'd marry her. Even so, it would be better not to meet her face to face in the empty store: those first words they'd have to say. Two young horses, their heads down, are standing in front of the store, in the yard, behind them a long wagon stacked with milk cans, a whip sticking straight up, just waiting to whip someone. He runs into Mineikis in the doorway, he already has a pack of cigarettes in his hand, over Mineikis's shoulder Vanda's face flashes by like a memory. Mornin', mornin' they both say. He follows Mineikis back to the yard, there's a beat-up wooden bench by a scraggly lilac bush, the edge of one of its white boards ripped up by beer bottle caps.

"I was looking for you yesterday. The guys said—he's out drinking."

"Oh, we were under the oak tree," the oak was visible from where they were standing, there used to be a large farm there, now there were only rocks and wormwood.

"Then you must be feeling great?" Mineikis gets up. "I'll go get some beer."

He stays there, his palms pressed to the chewed-up edges of the bench. Could get a splinter easy here. Sure, Mineikis asks you to bring him something, and he won't buy you squat, never mind beer, but when someone springs for him, he slurps it right up. Now he's building himself a new brick house, you can see the white chimney, he hasn't taken down the bottle and the cheese yet. The jerk—he does it so everybody can see there's been a roof-raising.

"They're out of beer," Mineikis says, "I got some wine. It's sour, so it'll do the trick."

Together they walk toward the oak, Mineikis stops, turns, and shouts: "Whoa! . . . You bastards," at the horses, so they'd remember not to stray while the two men are off drinking, but the animals only raise their heads apologetically: we know, we know, what are you shouting for?

Under the oak tree they strike a deal: tomorrow after work I'll bring you some gravel.

"And when are you going to build a house of your own? Are you going to live with your in-laws forever? Take out a loan and pitch in."

"I don't want to stay with the in-laws, that's no way to live, with the old fogies. I would have started already but I can't decide on where. Maybe I'll figure out a way to build in Skuodas, or right outside of Skuodas."

"You should have married Vanda . . ." Mineikis laughs.

"What do you mean—Vanda?"

"You wouldn't even have to build one. She's got more money than she knows what to do with. You think she doesn't? You'd buy one already built."

"Don't start in on me about Vanda again. Go get another bottle, and when I bring you the gravel, you won't have to pay. I'll bring it tomorrow. My head still doesn't feel right."

Mineikis sets off, while he sits thinking anew about how the floor in Vanda's little room used to smell. How many times a week does she scrub it? You just turn the steering wheel in the opposite direction . . . It's a crossroads, he thinks, a real crossroads. That village is like a quagmire. Getting stuck there is easy, but getting out . . . If you're not married yet, you've only got one leg in the mire; when you get married, it's already both legs, and if you have kids, you can see your head going under, too. He stretches out on the grass, while beyond the woods, in the direction of home, a pretty white cloud hangs in the air.

She also sees the cloud. It's time to start dinner, but on Sundays they always put it off until afternoon. The dew evaporated long ago, she'll pick those maple leaves for mother, then, while the meat is cooking, she'll go to the pasture and back to move the cow, but maybe father will have moved her on his way back from the village? Father's a good man, but since he started getting older, he's become kind of sad. She climbs up the ladder to the crotch of the maple tree, sees its clusters of white seeds, as children they used to stick them to their noses and pretend to be birds, their arms spread, they'd glide over the village, over the woods, over the rye field. I'm up in the clouds! but I'm already above the clouds! I'm even higher! Higher than the sun! The moon! Everything! They couldn't think of anything higher, so they would float down to earth slowly, back down to the meadow, without the slightest idea of how painful it would be to remember all this later. A little while back she had started thinking about childhood—ever since she got married—and she felt fear: how hard life will be when I'm old. I'll be sad every day just like mother and father are now. She carried the leaves in to mother, put them down on the table, and sat in the chair near the window. Mother studied her face. She's come back different somehow, the mother is thinking, what happened to her? Well, she says, here they are, is that enough? Of course, it'll be enough, why wouldn't it be, there's not going to be much bread—four little loaves. The daughter looks out into the yard, she sits there so silently, and her mother waits for her to say something else, but she says nothing, what's the matter with you, she asks, unable to restrain herself, it's as if you were going to pack up and leave tomorrow.

"But I will leave sometime."

"I'll be the first to leave."

"I'm not talking about that kind of leaving. In the spring we're going to start building a house."

"But you won't be far away. Just beyond the woods."

"We might build in Skuodas."

The old woman is afraid and doesn't know what to say. Then she begs:

"At least don't tell father now. You were born and raised here . . ."

"That's what he wants."

They pick up the dough kneader and carry it to the porch, putting it down on the dirt floor next to the oven, the heat is already coming out of the wide-open outside door. The chickens come close and stop, they don't dare go inside. Suddenly they beat a retreat, the shadow of the father's head is on the stone threshold. He looks at the two of them, bent over the kneader. Did you move my cow, she asks and hurries toward her own door, it's already time to peel the potatoes, she sits by the fire, lifts the basket onto her lap, and begins to sing, but very softly. Her parents are talking on the porch, soon they'll put the bread in the oven and go look at the clock, and then the whole house will become very quiet, but when the clock chimes—can you keep from crying? I seem to have everything, I'm only twenty-seven, and we'll be building our own house soon, and yet sometimes it's so hard to keep going. He's probably lying drunk somewhere, loaded, and he doesn't understand anything. It's easier for men. They always have it easier, at least the ones who don't have good hearts like father.

"One-thirty," says Rimkus, sitting on his bed, the old woman sitting on hers, above their heads hangs the wall clock. Only now do you realize that you're tired, you really didn't do any hard work: you brought home half a pail of clay, and firewood, you lit the oven, then you loped off to the village. Let's take a nap. As long as we don't oversleep, she says, worried, no, we won't oversleep, in an hour I'll go see how our bread is doing. It's so silent now that everything seems to be submerged in deep, murky water, and Rimkus feels himself sinking deeper into it along with the things in the room, with the midday light beyond the window, with the swinging of the pendulum on the opposite wall; everything that was on his mind today sinks with him, and there's a soft, painless bottom that you can rest on, where you can stay a while, and when you come up, you'll start life anew. When I was walking through the potatoes, he thinks, still sinking, and he wants to remember what he thought about then, he seems to remember something but not very clearly. It's midday, a great and holy time, and a painless helplessness envelops all the thoughts of his daughter's aging face, the village farms, the cat, which for some reason he hasn't seen since morning. When I was walking through the potato field, he suddenly remembers, there were butterflies circling my head.

The old woman drifted off before he did. Now her back hurts, and images float before her eyes, she's standing at the open gate and looking in the direction of the woods, but even she doesn't know who it is she expects to come home, only her heart is heavy because the road is so empty, she shuts the gate and goes back inside. But inside . . . the door is wide open, there's garbage everywhere, everyone's gone off somewhere and they've left her alone. Maybe Marytė's down at her end of the house, she thinks, dozing, or maybe her son-in-law. She opens the door but it's even emptier there . . . They've gone, she realizes. A green and white scarf is lying in the middle of the floor, the one she bought when her daughter was still in school. A skinny-legged little girl standing behind the gate with a schoolbag, calling at the windows in a squeaky voice: "Chase the goose away, chase the goose away, can't you hear me!" And now she's gone to Skuodas, she'll bear his children there and grow old, her heart aches so at the sight of her child's old age, if only they could all live together under the same roof, a maple grows behind the barn, the yard is so green, there's a pretty white cloud hanging over the chimney. "Father, father!" she walks through the empty rooms crying, she wants to tell him something. He's lying with his ruddy face turned up to the ceiling, the old woman is watching his eyelids twitch: "Father, father!" she says, out loud now, "It's time to check the bread, my back hurts so much that I can't do it."

"What time did you tell them to come?" she asks, sitting down.

"I said toward evening."

The old woman gets up and goes toward the kitchen door, bent over, dragging her gnarled, bare feet along the floor, and he thinks about what he started and that he'll never be able to finish. And why did those potatoes upset me today, as if I'd never seen potatoes before? He's already gotten up, too, he's carrying the whetstone and bread knife to the threshold, he looks down the road, where the neighbors will be coming, look, they're already on their way, but they're still so far away you can barely see them: maybe it's the old Narkuses, maybe the Rimgailas. Then he carries the knife to the table and smiles for the first time that day.

"Look out the window, mother, our friends are on their way!"

There is still plenty of time before they get to the gate. The bread is on the tray, the whole house is filled with its scent, and the peel is put away in the corner until next summer, the Rimkuses are proudly standing by their bread. Now he goes to fetch the milk from the well and looks down the road again. The old Narkuses. And past the ditch three more: the Rimgailas and Mrs. Medutis. The old woman spreads a linen runner on the table, brings the bread in as if it were a child—in the crook of her arm. But the guests are taking their time, poking their canes just a little ahead of themselves, stopping now and then, looking around at the crops, or maybe just catching their breath, and then creeping forward again, straight to the gate, they know this gate, they've gone through it hundreds of times, a few of its posts have rotted since the first time they opened it for a visit. The five of them gather in the yard, the women in their black Sunday dresses, but even so it seems that they've come in white, dressed all in white. There are eight places at the table: three along each side, one at each end of the table, in all they're seven, this year no one will be sitting in Medutis's place, but a glass of milk is poured for him and a slice of bread placed next to it. When you hold bread in your hand you never know if it's going to be your last, that's how life works.

He was still staring at the white cloud when Mineikis came back with two other neighbors, each carrying two bottles, one in each hand: what good is four bottles for four men? They sat down, leaned back against the oak, talking about all kinds of things, the kind you won't remember the next day, but everyone's feeling good anyway. When the wine is finished, Mineikis gets up and glances at the store: "Well, I'm going. So it's a deal?" "I'm going too," he gets up, but the other two stop him. They stick five rubles in his hand and say, "Go on, go get some vodka, you can get it."

"Why me?"

"If you can't get any, no one can."

That pleases him, he wants to see Vanda again, more now than before, so he goes off, carrying the five rubles, looking up he sees a cloud in the shape of his wife's face, the hair is the same and everything. "All right," he thinks, "but what can I do?" He opens the door but there's no one in the store. Blond hair behind the counter, no face, no hands, but then the rest of her stands up, she doesn't say anything.

"Hi, Vanda. All alone?"

"Not anymore. You've come in."

Her hair is even brighter from this angle, damn it, damn it all, how you can screw up your own life like this, and you can't even tell anyone about it. She stubbornly looks past his shoulder at the door, as if he'd come in without shutting it.

"Do me a favor and give me a bottle of the clear stuff."

He opens his fist, and there are the five sweaty rubles, even he can see they're sweaty. "But that's just because it's so hot outside," he thinks and looks at her face again.

"I wouldn't give them any, so now they're sending you?"

"What are you talking about?"

"Those two drunks. Your friends. I can see—it's the same bill, the corner's ripped."

"What? You think I don't have five rubles of my own? I could get fifty, if I needed to!"

"Sure, you could . . ." she smiles at the window bitterly. "Such a rich man. You're gonna build yourself a house."

"Are you going to stop me?"

"Oh Lord! You can build a palace if you want for all I care."

"Let's not fight . . . Give me a loaf of bread and some cigarettes," he takes his own ruble out of his pocket, ashamed and angry. "And a bottle of booze."

"Can't you see there's none on the shelf?"

"And how about what's in back?"

"If it's not on the shelf, it's not for you. You'd better leave."

"Well fine," he almost says "bitch." "Now I know."

He takes the bread and leaves, slamming the door, and just past the threshold he stops; maybe he'll catch her crying? No, not a sound. He heads for the oak, muttering all the way, "You lousy bitch, you lousy bitch! . . ." The other two are still sitting there, he throws the money on the grass, there isn't any, he says, if there was, she would've given me some. One of them sighs and stands up, "Those poor slobs, the hell with them. They don't even have anything to make vodka with anymore. I'll go get us some rotgut. We've got to have something to drink anyway." Got to have something to drink, he thinks, clenching his teeth, got to have something to drink, otherwise I'll go crazy. His eyes follow the one who's leaving: the seat of his pants is baggy, the backs of his knees are wrinkled, should he catch up and kick him or should he punch the other one in the mouth? Keep smashing the bastards' faces. And feel the old guilt become smaller and disappear as the new one grows. Later they drink four more bottles, he takes his bread and heads home, seeing large red circles before his eyes. He stumbes along, all the while singing a song, the kind of song you can't get out of your head, not singing out loud, or under his breath, but only in his head so there'd be no room for anything else there: "On the woodchips stands a goo-ooat, goooo-ooat, on the woodchips stands a goo-oat, whoo-ose goat, nobody knoo-ows noo-othin." And as soon as he finishes, he starts in again: "On the woodchips . . ." And here's the road. Red circles are above the potato field.

"Help yourselves, neighbors," says Rimkus.

"Please do," says the old woman. "I don't know how it turned out."

They each take a slice and bring it to their mouths, deeply inhaling the all-embracing smell of bread. The sour-sweet taste makes saliva collect in their mouths, and they wash it down with milk. Bread is their sons, earth, horses neighing, the clang of iron at the smithy, frosty wagons of logs from the woods, the desire to live a long and righteous life; milk is their daughters, their barns, a clean linen towel by the well, a white face waiting behind the warped windowpane, the longing to die a beautiful and peaceful death. "Let us live long, neighbors," they want to say, "we can no longer do anyone any harm." Mrs. Rimkus raises her eyes to the window, dear Jesus!— what is it? She rubs her eyes and looks again. No, a huge raven is not perched on the fencepost, she only imagined it. A green tree, the potato field, her son-in-law, coming down the road with his own bread. Marytė runs out, takes the loaf away from him, and brings him into the house, scolding.

1975

Translated by Rita Dapkus, Gregory M. Grazevich, and Violeta Kelertas

Juozas Aputis

Wild Boars Run on the Horizon

Oh, rue so green,
Let me go home,
Oh, rue so green.

He even felt strange to himself that evening. But maybe it was
everything around him that was strange, for Gvildys had never felt
the things around him so keenly before. Swaying a little, he climbed
up the hill on which a white tower, made of crisscrossed logs, had
been built last year. But there was no need for the tower really—you
could see for miles from the hill itself. The sun was already setting
anyway, it waited for no one, with merciless speed it thrust the forests into darkness, and the peat bog where Gvildys had left his tractor, and only then would it swallow Šatrija hill looming in the
distance and the fields of clover in bloom. Gazing in that direction,
beyond the horizon, Gvildys felt a sorrow that seldom comes in life,
a sorrow that makes you feel you're the world's clock, not the windup kind but the kind on which everything depends: you radiate
lights and colors, you give animals and people water from the rivers,
you build nests for the birds and guard their naked young from
hawks, you manage the most complicated affairs, and if you did not
exist, everything, both living things and objects, would fall to their
knees. And Lord, oh Lord, you realize that the time will come when
you will no longer exist. Then the great pain and longing comes because you understand that you are a god who knows that he will
have to die.
　　Gvildys sat down on a large moss-covered rock, his head was
reeling, he had no desire to go home. The man in him still wanted to

be a god, to return to childhood. Childhood hounds us in every hour of sorrow and longing, we run to it as if to a source, there's never a lack of water, for only in childhood are we truly gods, and only in childhood can we find the water that will quench our thirst. Then one day it dawns on us that we have just been rolling a rock up a hill and that we will never make it to the top. But we really don't want to let it roll back down.

He looked around. You could see very far, the sun lit up the fields and on the horizon, into infinity, tractors crawled over the hills, they looked like the boars that, back then, after the war, Gvildys remembered, used to come from the forest and climb up on the mounds of potatoes. His head was spinning from the bottle he had drunk, it was hard to make anything out. He got up and set off down the hill. He had to go home, you can't stay on the hill forever, you have to come down and go home. He opened the door quietly and went through the hallway carefully so as not to give himself away, he tried to shake off his sorrow and be cheerful. Two little children ran in from the kitchen, clung to his hand, and pulled him along. Gvildys didn't say hello, he only placed his hand heavily on his wife's shoulder. A vague foreboding pierced his hot and giddy head. His wife was still silent, she kept banging the dishes around and scolding the children, she gave the chair a shove, her inexplicable anger kept growing and growing. Suddenly she grabbed a broom from the corner and slowly came toward her husband. Her eyes were horrible, Gvildys had never seen them like this before, he tried to laugh but he didn't get a chance, sharp twigs were poking at his face, and he felt a terrible pain in his eyes as he heard his wife shrieking with a stranger's voice. Covering his face with his hands, he could barely see her. His wife stood there like a madwoman, her arms hanging down, her hair disheveled. She was shaking and kept repeating:

"That's for your drinking, that's for your bottle, you don't care about your home, nothing here makes any difference to you . . ."

She probably didn't hear what she was saying, she hadn't the slightest idea why she had acted this way. And she never will. She was a woman, she was raising her children, she had looked out the small cottage window more than once when the children were screaming or were being aggravating, she had stared out the window many times, strange sounds lured her from her home, where almost nothing mattered: not the forest, not the fields, not the animals and—a terrible thing to say—not even the children. She would remember her mother, who had also been young and raised her children young and who used to tell her daughter about a similar feeling, but what was it her mother had found to cling to in her hour of despair, what was it?

Holding his face in his hands, he sat down at the table. A fierce pain was stabbing at his eyes, the children stood huddled together in the corner, dirty and frightened, their mother too stood frozen to the spot. Gvildys got up, groped around, and found a towel hanging on the wall, tied it around his face, twisted the towel over his left eye, he could still see a little with the right one, then hunched over, he staggered out of the house and, coming across his bicycle in the shed, got on it and rode off.

It was hard to ride, the sun had already set and it had grown completely dark, but Gvildys knew all the paths, so he pedaled quickly through the field of clover.

At the clinic they told him that he had definitely lost one eye, they weren't sure about the other, if the nerve had been damaged, anything could happen. Could he, they suggested, go to Šiauliai or Kaunas right away, there were more doctors there. He should hurry, tomorrow might be too late. If he had no money with him, the doctor could lend him some for now, his wife could pay him back tomorrow or the day after.

Gvildys was standing in the clinic, looking through his swollen right eye at the small lightbulb in the ceiling, he decided not to hurry, he'd make it tomorrow, things could wait. At the clinic they bandaged his face better but his left eye was gone for good, only a terrible fire was left burning where it had been, and his right eye was so swollen that he could barely see anything with it, either.

Without saying goodbye, Gvildys walked his bicycle over to the beer bar, where they could get the stronger stuff as well. It was crowded inside, everyone noticed Gvildys, they hurried over to ask questions, some tried to make fun of him, others commiserated, after all, it wasn't often such incidents occurred in their village. Gvildys didn't answer their questions. Perhaps if he hadn't climbed the hill this evening, if it hadn't been for the painful longing, maybe he would have sought comfort from his neighbors and told them all about it, but now it wasn't that simple. Gvildys found an empty, banged-up table in a corner and sat down. If he had ever had occasion to see it, surely it would have occurred to him how sadly he resembled the self-portrait of the painter without his ear.

The people didn't let up, they were constantly coming up to him asking questions, but Gvildys didn't open his mouth. When a young girl in a dirty smock came up to him, he quietly asked her for a bottle and some bread and then continued to gaze out over people's heads through his white bandage.

He drank a glass and rested his chin in one hand. He looked awful, already there was talk in one corner of the room that it might not be a bad idea to call the police: Gvildys had gone out of his mind, can't you see? But someone else swore and laughed at this coward.

Gvildys had downed his second glass, his wife's father, his father-in-law, came up to the table, old and wizened like a stick, he was shabby and gray-haired, his hands were gnarled. The old man sat down with his back to the people, and just this made Gvildys feel a little better. He asked the girl for a second glass and poured his father-in-law a drink.

An hour or so had passed, the drunks had dispersed, not many people were left in the bar, but the two of them were still sitting there and drinking in silence.

"So tell me how it happened. What did she do it for?" the old man finally spoke up, scratching his grizzled jaw.

Gvildys downed another glassful.

"I don't know, father. That's just it, I don't know. Yesterday I brought home half a month's wages, I made out pretty good, I hid some for a bottle and drank it today for lunch, I didn't drink much, just enough to cheer me up, you can go out of your mind it's so sad, what, can't I have a drink once in a while, don't I make a decent living, don't we get enough to eat in my house, father?" He felt his tongue beginning to get twisted, and the spot where his left eye had been started to burn even more.

"But my daughter was so . . . like an angel she was."

"That's just it, father. I don't think we ever even had a real fight before. I just came in the door . . . and all at once she pounced on me, you can see what she did."

It seemed that only after hearing his son-in-law's sorrowful words did the old man realize what had really happened. He dug his nails into his cheek, drank a glassful, and felt a few large tears rolling down his face onto the table. He looked at his son-in-law with tearful eyes, and then the thought came to him that something alien, something distant and terrible, was walking around their forests and fields, no one had seen it yet or met it anywhere, but it was right here, it stopped at every farmstead, at every home, it sat in the tractor or on the plough attachment, but people couldn't see it yet, no one was aware of it yet.

"Something's wrong here, son-in-law."

"We've had quite a bit to drink, father."

"There's not much I understand anymore, son-in-law."

"I don't think it's because of the alcohol, father . . . Just like that, she lunges at me like I was some stranger, some murderer. She pokes my eyes out, and all you can do is moan and drink like some bum, and that's all. There's no way to get even, no one to fight, you're blinded in your own house and that's that."

As Gvildys got steadily drunker, he retained less and less of the controlled manhood that can carry you to your destined end through the biggest misfortunes and sorrows in life without spilling your gut. He felt his fingers and his whole body begin to quiver, and his right eye, which hadn't been poked out altogether but whose future was uncertain, kept blinking. He realized he was like the good kitten that a child who can barely hold back his own tears is carrying to the river while slowly searching for a rock. The kitten is sad, it knows what's coming, yet it can't bring itself to claw at the sobbing child . . .

"What's going on, father, can you tell me? Huh? You're just an old man! You can't do anything, you just sit there, that's all. And what's to become of me now, huh? Did you hear what they said at the clinic? They said the other one can go, too. Do you know what that means?" Gvildys slammed his fist into the table, and his father-in-law, not knowing what else to do, grabbed his hand and began to kiss it like a madman, tearful and helpless, as if it were possible to expiate the inexplicable crime with kisses.

"She never hurt an animal or a bird, but this . . . ," the father-in-law started.

"It's easier to hurt a human being, father . . ."

"The rye is in bloom everywhere," the old man was talking to himself as if he hadn't heard his son-in-law, "the air is filled with pollen, and you start to feel warm and good inside, you start to feel whole. Without meaning to the cuckoo still calls out in midsummer, and everyone sees you and you see right through them. How can you hurt anyone, when all of creation looks up to you as if you're the most intelligent and the best?"

"Ah! But after all, the rye and the cuckoos haven't disappeared. There are plenty of them, no one shoots cuckoos yet, father. But, dear Jesus, that's small comfort, small comfort to me; nothing helps, not money, not bread . . . I can scarcely hear the cuckoo, it's as if its voice is drowning in a barrel of tar . . . Last night, when I climbed the hill, the tractors were crawling over the hills like wild boars, just crawling over the potato heaps . . ."

"It was a comfort to me . . .", the old man sighed. "What can an old geezer like me tell you, how can I help? I sit here slobbering like a calf and I can't say anything that's sincere. I have centuries weighing me down . . . My daughter Onutė poked your eyes out and now her old drunken father is slobbering at the table . . ."

"What the hell is there to say . . . ?"

"You think I don't know that the first thing I should have done is to make you get out of here and take you to the city right away? And that's what I planned to do when I first found out, I ran around looking for you like a wild man, but later, the closer I got, the sillier it seemed. Why, taking you to the hospital doesn't solve anything anyway. Maybe the alcohol's making me talk in circles, but if your wife poked out one eye and the doctors fix up the other one, that won't solve anything, will it?"

"So you want both my eyes bandaged up?"

"Don't you understand that you can't undo what's happened?"

"Ah, why complicate things, father! I feel bound and gagged as it is . . . Maybe only time heals all wounds. I remember as a kid I couldn't possibly imagine how I'd live when my mother and father died. And look, fifteen years have gone by, and I don't think about my folks for months at a time . . ."

"That's the way it is. But death is something else again. As soon as you learn to think, you already know you're going to die. And you know that others will die, and you know that that's the way it has to be . . ."

"Maybe that's the way it was meant to be, my wife was supposed to poke my eyes out, only I didn't know it, no one did, just like death: that's just the way it has to be . . ."

They each downed another glass, and the bottle was empty, there were only a couple of people left, though some were still walking around and waiting outside the windows; they both got up, the old man and the son-in-law. The old man carefully held his son-in-law by the arm so he wouldn't trip over the chairs. Outside Gvildys found his bicycle against the wall, he leaned against it and felt it as if he were checking to see if it was still real, then he hung his head.

"Well, I'm going to go, father."

"Where are you going to go? It's dark, let's go to my house, you'll make it home tomorrow or you can go to town straight from here."

"What do I need a place to stay for, father, don't I have my own home?" Unsteadily, Gvildys pushed the bike forward and got on.

People made way for him, everyone had had more than their share to drink, but they still retained some common sense, they understood that it was no ordinary person getting on the bicycle, but someone not quite like them, someone quite different. And the old man, tripping as he tried to chase after the bicycle, was also not like them.

Gvildys was already out of the village, he was pedaling through the meadow, in the dark night his head shone white like a flag and his swollen eye followed the road unerringly. As he pedaled away from the village and past his house, thoughts of what his wife was doing, what the children were up to, flashed through his head. He wondered why she didn't come running after him, why she didn't fall to her knees like a sinner at Jesus' feet, and why she didn't begin to weep. After all, the old man had blubbered up a storm. He felt sorry for his wife, his home and his children, there was something almost sacred about his pity, while a painful yearning constantly drove Gvildys further and further away; one would have thought that he was trying to ride back to childhood, where all of us were gods.

Early the next morning the old man hurried to his son-in-law's house on horseback, he found his daughter, Gvildys's wife, sitting outside in the potato bed, dry-eyed and sad. The old man became very frightened, rode his horse into the village, then turned down the path that his son-in-law had taken yesterday; people also sensed what was wrong and dashed after the old man, some on bicycles or horses, some on foot; the tractors stopped on the hills like wild boars, their drivers set out across the fields, at that moment the old man jumped down from his horse and ran headlong like a dog on a fresh trail.

They found the bicycle seven kilometers from the village, tears were already streaming down the old man's face as he followed his son-in-law's footsteps stepping on the tufts of grass. Suddenly everyone stopped dead in their tracks: in a nice little clearing in the grass, his legs crossed like a saint's, surrounded by a halo of white gauze, sat Petras Gvildys, the old man's son-in-law, calmly eating. He had remembered that yesterday his wife Onutė had packed him a lunch, but he had been drinking by the tractor and completely forgotten about it.

Petras Gvildys sat there calmly, he seemed to see neither the people who had run up nor the old man who had turned pale in astonishment. With his one eye, Petras Gvildys was staring through the white gauze at a birch tree growing at the clearing's edge. On it a frightened cuckoo perched.

1970

Translated by Rita Dapkus, Gregory M. Grazevich, and Violeta Kelertas

Juozas Aputis

The Flying Apple Trees

. . . they bloom and bloom
in the subconscious, under water and earth.
                              Liūnė Sutema

Hell, aren't they ever going to come? That's the way it goes with
commissions—they promise to come, tell you expect to them at such
and such an hour of the morning—we'll be there, take care of everything, if they'd at least have the goodness to show up by noon! Naturally, what else could you expect, someone's pumped them full of
whiskey, that's all. Sure, there are plenty of excuses for drinking
nowadays, but when haven't there been? Ever since the day the soldiers crept out of the woods, shooting sporadically, and chased the
Germans off across the pasture, only yesterday they'd been playing
football in the manor flowerbeds—and this is the way it's been for
twenty years, no—it's a good deal more than that, whoever makes
the rounds of the farms doesn't do it with a dry whistle: there are
mortgages, requisitions to the state, next they're distributing acre-
ages, surveying them again, then the next thing you know a body
gets the urge to keep a cow or two.

The bastards, they're still not here. Once more he'll go into the
barn and see how much hay's left over from the winter, the early
spring sun feels warm on his back, soon he'll put the cows out to pasture, save on feed. You're so dependent on old mother nature, just
last fall you were complaining about the biting cold, the unseason-
able snow, and here it's an early spring, all to the good, quite un-
foreseen and unplanned. That goes for the move, too. Sure, the
rumors had been flying, everybody'd been saying that they were

going to tunnel underground, cram the good black earth full of clay pipes, and look—it's already here.

The barn would make for some good boards, they'll come in handy at the new house, that's for sure. It's only now they're promising the moon, but once you make the move it'll be kiss their ass: you won't get this and there'll be a shortage of that. Rip the ceiling from the clay barn and you'll have some good boards, too, it'd be nice to slap some on at least one inside wall of the new house, cement's so rough to brush up against.

And the apple trees this year! . . . They were late, the bastards, fixing the papers—today's not the only day they haven't turned up, all in all they were supposed to be finished by the beginning of April, so what's going to happen now that the trees are already full of buds, will they come to uproot them just like that, just when they've come back to life back again?

Just now, staring at the apple trees, Milašius caught himself feeling perhaps just a little discouraged. There were the young oaks and birches, too—getting quite tall on the south side—and the mountain ash. They say you can find a place for your every hardship and every joy on the mountain ash's berry. And nothing ever spoke to Milašius in quite the same way about the end of summer and coming of fall as those berries. So, now, having put everything away and expecting important guests, it was a bit sad, maybe, damn it, not that sad, what has to be done has to be done. He was gazing at the smoke-colored ash and seeing only autumn in it when just then Milašius's mother appeared before his eyes, everyone had known her as mother-dear until the day she died, but here she was, frowning and angry, she flew by like a blackbird, sweeping the ash treetops with her skirts, scattering berries right and left, one even seemed to pop Milašius on the nose, and there mother was, shaking her bony finger at him.

"Well, what are you going to tell me, why are you shaking your finger at me like that?" Milašius was about to say, but decided to keep his mouth shut one more time. He'd be damned—it was just the way it had been when she was alive—here he'd almost started an argument with her again. Mother-dear would always complain, he could never do anything to please her, she'd always say, "It's not like the good old days."

Mother flew about the orchard, took a final turn over the alder grove, and whizzed into the barn through the chink used by the owls, frightening the pigeons away.

And Milašius caught himself giving in to it again, to something that never helps but only plunges you even more deeply into the morass, and taking his switch, he lashed himself briskly across his rubber boots as he peered in the direction of the blue woods; nearby, Santvaris's bog rippled under attack by screaming lapwings, their voices echoing, their wings whirring, they swept downward with a hissing sound as if to extinguish their flaming wings in the water.

The cuckoos had returned early this year, too, but none had reached his trees, they hadn't had their fill of the birches, where the trees grew more densely and the birds felt more free. The starlings, they had been laboring since early morning—taking turns, some recovering twigs from the field and wood, others in the meantime singing on the roof and in the poplar. What cheer—one of them put so much feeling into his work, he began to shake and ruffle his wings and back and did heaven knows what with one of his legs, sending some old chips flying from the roof.

By now the bulldozer, put to work on setting his, Milašius's, affairs in order, could be heard roaring, soon Milašius caught sight of it as well, it came rumbling along straight from the former manor and with a terrific racket came to a stop right at Milašius's pond. It was not much of a pond anymore, just a sort of pit. Once it had been a place for children to splash around in—the pond was left over from the time they'd been scooping out clay to throw together the barn. It seemed that the driver knew how to maneuver quite deftly because he parked his machine on the very edge of the pit, running the caterpillar treads a bit over the edge, and now the machine stood, eager for an order to attack. The driver turned out to be someone he knew, a neighbor kid, not a bad kid really, too lazy to study, he'd even had a fight with the teacher—told her those classes of hers weren't worth one bulldozer tread, he'd make more money on construction any day—now he jumped out onto last summer's dry grass.

"You'll catch your death of cold," said Milašius, while the driver laughed; as yet no illness had ever penetrated his clothes.

"So where are the big shots?" Milašius spoke out anxiously. "They promised they'd be here a long time ago."

"I saw a flock of men, they should be here, if they didn't get waylaid somewhere. Anyway, I'm the most important one and I'm here, old man," the driver spat on the ground.

Milašius suddenly remembered that in all this business of gaping at the trees and birds he'd quite forgotten—how was the wife doing inside? He hurried into the house, their two voices could be heard, but they weren't angry, everything seemed to be all right, and by the time Milašius came out the door, from the direction of the wood he could see four, or was it five, men with briefcases come wav-

ing, their raincoats flying. Somehow, Milašius started to feel a bit uncomfortable then, luckily the driver chose that moment to ask:

"How many apple trees is it you have?"

"Fifteen good ones. One's withered away—the rabbits got it."

"That one doesn't count . . ." The driver scratched the back of
his head. "You could have more, you know, other people are selling
more . . ."

"I've got what I've got."

"Don't we all."

Just then the winged contingent arrived at the orchard.
Milašius went to meet them, the driver brought up the rear.

One of the new arrivals was in charge, the rest were just witnesses, this leader wore boots of rather good quality, and his raincoat
was imported, Yugoslavian. He said hello and mentioned the purpose of their visit. By the way, comrade Milašius was probably aware
of the reason for their coming. Well yes, yes.

"So then, how many apple trees do you have in all?" asked the
same man in the Yugoslavian coat. "On our way, I'd guess we
counted about fifteen, only one looked like it was dead. The state
can't pay for that one."

Milašius kept nodding his head, scarcely daring to raise his eyes
to the man in charge; therefore, he turned toward the other four men,
all of whom he had seen before, they were all from neighboring villages, having been chosen for this commission only at the meeting.
The one standing closest to Milašius, the one he knew best, began to
wink at him imperceptibly and seemed to be trying to step on his toe.
It wasn't the first time that something like this had happened, so now
Milašius raised his eyes more boldly to the chief and stated what was
on his mind:

"What's the hurry? . . . Maybe we could . . . To tell the truth,
chairman, it isn't every day I sell trees, the occasion should be
marked somehow . . ."

"Marked, you say?" the person addressed as chairman asked
rather grimly, and at that moment the driver slapped Milašius on the
back saying, "If I've understood you correctly, then thank you, comrade Milašius, thank you. But we do have to get to work, we still have
a huge job ahead of us."

"Chairman, we all have plenty of work, you think I'm not
swamped?"

This equation struck the chairman as amusing. Milašius did not
notice it, of course, but the chairman smiled and cast his eyes over
the four men, who, even though they didn't raise their hands, clearly

indicated their preference, and then the chairman gave in, while the driver was already heading to turn off the bulldozer, which was still shaking like a frog on the bank of the pond.

When he stepped onto the porch, the cat jumped out over the threshold and Milašius started, his scowling, angry mother again appeared before him, flew off with two small birches, and nailed them not to the house but to the barn door.

Milašius's wife was a good housekeeper, and her husband's shirts were possibly the very whitest in the village. For her guests she set out the best of what she had in the house, after his second shot the driver got up to thank her, Milašius wanted to force another drink on him, but the driver refused.

"Thanks, old man, thanks, I'd have another one, but, you see, I'm not alone, the machinery's outside waiting, so I can't have any more." And he wouldn't have a third drink, machinery had certainly put discipline into him.

The chairman, thank God, was not so full of himself, he caught on quickly and made himself at home, he carried on a polite conversation, now and then he cast a glance out the window, his eyes were smallish, the youth was making a racket with the bulldozer over there, the birches and oaks and the poor mountain ash fell to the ground almost without protest, they weren't hundreds of years old, nor had they managed to take root deeply yet or grow stout, but with the help of his machinery the kid took care of them as well.

From time to time swallows skimmed by the window, by now Milašius had downed his share, maybe even more than the others—he kept toasting them and setting an example, he sat at one end of the table as a host should, and it was the chairman himself who brought his wife out of the kitchen:

"Where's our lovely hostess, we haven't seen her yet. She's seeing to our needs and neglecting herself."

"Teklė, dear, come, they want you here."

Milašius's wife came in beaming, happy that she hadn't been forgotten and remembering also to poke her husband in the ribs—maybe now was the right time? She had to drink two whole glasses—first for one leg, then for the other, to ensure that life in their new home would stand on its feet firmly. The chairman said as much, proposing yet another toast to her diligent hands, but she shook her head—everything was already spinning around in her head as it was.

The bulldozer chose this moment to rattle violently, Milašius had the feeling that it had hooked the tresses of the fir tree his father had planted some fifty years ago; at that moment a crow cawed over the yard. Milašius, stunned, again feared that mother-dear might slip inside, and so he told his wife to shut the porch door. The chairman pulled out a thick blue notebook, he spent a long time looking up and down the lists for Milašius's name, finally he found it and stared at the number written in pencil.

"Hmm . . . How many apple trees of Milašius's was it we counted?" he asked his witnesses, smiling and looking at Milašius, who felt uneasy. The wife in the meantime stood in the kitchen doorway. "It seems to me it was fifteen and the sixteenth was dead."

"Are you sure that was the number, chairman?" interrupted one of the witnesses. "No, it couldn't have been fifteen. It seems to me it had to be at least twenty."

"Isn't that too many?" There was hesitation in the chairman's voice. "What do you think, comrade Milašius?"

"Whatever you make of it, chairman, that's . . ."

"We only plough them under anyway, chairman. Why don't we put down twenty. Well, there's sixteen for sure, and the dead one, we could have missed it. And even if we add five, in a stand of trees like that—that's no great number."

For a while the chairman fidgeted with the eraser in his fingers, thinking, and then slowly he rubbed out the number written in pencil, pulled out his pen, made a few scratches with the tip of his pen, and this time he wrote the number 20 in ink, initialing it himself and letting his witnesses and comrade Milašius sign as well.

"Thank you, chairman, thank you," said Milašius, while the chairman and the witnesses downed one more shot and got up, reaching for their raincoats. Milašius held up the Yugoslavian one and helped the chairman on with it, while the latter cheerfully extended his hand to Milašius's wife.

But they ended up staying rather a long time, the kid had already knocked down the last live apple tree, old and bent, and could be seen driving his bulldozer over the fields to another farm. Following the chairman's lead, the men also headed in that direction, straight as the crow flies, since the ground had dried over, the rains came only intermittently that year.

By this time not a tree was left upright, they all lay on their sides, and from a distance it was even hard to make out which end was the tree's feet and which the head—the muddy branches lay black, and the roots were encrusted with dirt, water oozed slowly into the newly gouged pits.

Toward dusk a truck pulled up, it was driven by a different driver, though the kid from earlier in the day was along. He jumped out of the cab and made straight for the house, now that he didn't have his machinery along he could have a drink.

Having loaded up his belongings, not all of them but only some, Milašius downed a few more shots, locked up the house, and climbed into the truck with his wife, but by now it had grown dark, and making the turn from Milašius's yard into the road, the driver cut it a little short perhaps, and Milašius fell out into last year's grass, he didn't hurt himself at all but jumped up immediately and waved to his wife to go on, it wasn't far, he'd go on foot.

His head reeling, he returned to the farmstead, all the trees, large and small, were resting on their sides, when suddenly five apple trees detached themselves, flapped their branches, rose up into the air and, buzzing strangely—like bees—began to circle over Milašius's head. Milašius tried to plug his ears, but it didn't work, he could still hear them because the trees were flying wildly at furious speed, and when the watery moon appeared, the trees began to shake off their blossoms, and the tiny blue dots, spinning in the air, fell into the hollowed-out earth, covering both the pits filled with water and the black roots of the apple trees. Milašius watched the flying apple trees scattering blossoms, he was still sober enough to think: "It's okay as long as it's just my trees that are frolicking about, but, Christ, when they get together with all the neighbors' trees, you won't be able to tell the earth from the sky, all those blossoms, why, they could bury you." At this thought he began to walk backward, then he set off running down the road. By the strawpile, where they kept the potatoes and beets, he had to stop because he heard somebody calling him. Coming closer, he bent down. Under the thin cellophane, he saw his wasted mother-dear lying there as if she was under glass. With her withered finger she pointed at her chin; there, instead of her long whisker, now grew a small white apple tree.

1970
Translated by Violeta Kelertas

Saulius Šaltenis

The Ever-Green Maple

I wish I'd been born in Corsica because then I'd have long long hair down to my waist. But we don't even own a mirror . . . In the movies everything looks beautiful, even the puddles look different from the way they really are.

We have it pretty good now, the worst was the winter dad drank his coat away. My dad never gets depressed, though, and on the whole he's really amazing. It's okay, my little girl, is all he said, it's okay, pretty soon we won't even need jackets . . . The subtropics, where it's always green, are returning to Lithuania. And my dad knows French! He always wears a hat and tie, he doesn't drink in gateways like other men do . . . and even if he does drink, at least he spreads his handkerchief out first and cuts his tomato up in neat little sections . . . He always has to keep the others in line, too, by saying: don't tell me the Lithuanian language is so impoverished that you can't use anything but swearwords when you talk? My father doesn't drink like other men—he doesn't drink because it tastes good, after all, medicine doesn't taste good either—he drinks to cleanse his festering soul . . . My dad has a soul. But we're not poor. We're the landlords, dad says, and this is our house, our woodshed, our garden, our outhouse. The dying maple is ours, too. But the Tenant hates our maple. He paid his rent at first, of course, but then he stopped—then he took our mother for himself, and then the big room and even the little hallway, the garden, the woodshed, he even wanted to cut down the maple tree, so it wouldn't choke the potatoes . . . He would have taken me, too, but I grabbed my clay piggybank one winter and ran over to dad's side of the house because you can't just rely on the coming of the subtropics . . . Dad's not working at the paper anymore, now he's a night watchman. We're not the least bit afraid of the Tenant; just the opposite, we laugh in his face: ha ha, says my dad, I'm the landlord, I don't mind renting out three rooms and the kitchen for a while, or the whole house and even the outhouse with your own personal lock, I can even rent you my wife, if you want her that much, but this maple tree of mine—never! . . . And he grabbed the ax from the Tenant's hands and threw it over the roof. Then the Tenant knocked my dad down and pinned him to the ground with his knees under the maple tree. Our Tenant keeps his college badge pinned to his chest day and night, it's kind of a rhomboid shape, but my dad doesn't give two cents about that, either: ha ha, he laughs, with all your fancy education, you've still got a plow handle sticking out of your pocket!

We're doing okay now, just great, you might say. We've almost completely forgotten the winter when my dad sold his body to science. After he dies, the students can learn from my dad. My dear, my only child, said father, how bad could it be, if we still have our souls? I'm alive, aren't I? I'm like the maple, as long as they don't cut me down I'll flourish.

We have some money, we'll buy a new school uniform and a winter coat, we've already put up some curtains, and no commission on children's welfare can move me over to the Tenant's side anymore . . . I'm guarding the maple, but what good does it do if it's turning all yellow and dying right in the middle of summer. There's a clothesline running from the maple tree to the fence: those diapers belong to the baby the Tenant and mama had. I taste the dirt under the maple, but never tell my dad that the dirt burns my tongue. When we're away, the Tenant pours sulphuric acid on the maple . . . Don't die, maple tree, hang on if you can! Today I'm going to see an American movie in technicolor because everyone has to have some kind of weakness . . . like my dad does . . . The movies are my biggest shortcoming, but it's good for me to have shortcomings, too. The movies eat up a lot of our money, and afterwards I always have dreams . . . I dream, at least I always try to dream of Corsica and long golden hair . . . I don't want to dream of war because in wars they have no pity, not even on long golden hair . . . I'm seeing another technicolor movie today, but I won't give dad a ruble, it's still a week till payday. And of course he'll be waiting patiently for me outside the movie theater because I've forbidden him to meet his friends, they never shave and they don't wear ties.

I left the theater with tears in my eyes, still in love with that wonderful, kind sheriff.

"Was it about Corsica?" asked dad.

"No," I said, "but you would have liked the sheriff, too."

"Oh," said dad, "and what was his name?"

I couldn't really remember his first name or his last name, maybe he was a sheriff with no name, but I made one up anyway:

"His last name was Jefferson . . ."

Dad was staring at the shop window where bottles of cognac we couldn't afford were lined up.

"Wasn't he the one who invented the steam engine?"

"No," I said, "that was somebody else . . . That was Polzunov . . ."

And I saw dad lean toward the window, and fine beads of perspiration broke out on his forehead.

"Dad," I said, " maybe you should take that ruble."

"No, no," he was pulling at my elbow, "we'll wait a while yet, we'll wait!"

And he walked slowly off toward home, not directly but along Marija Melnikaite Street, and all of a sudden we could see from a distance how bare our maple tree really was, it looked like it had turned gray overnight.

"They got it," said my father and blew his nose in his handkerchief a few times. "They poured some lye on it."

"No," I said, "it was sulphuric acid."

"What's the difference," said dad, "if it's lye or sulphuric acid! . . ."

We didn't get home till evening, dad stretched out in the field behind the cemetery by the brook and covered his face with his hat. I spent some time wading in the river, then we went home to fix supper. It was dark by the time dad got home, he had a drink and climbed into the maple tree, dragging the tin wreaths on a rope up after himself. They had been desecrated and were rattling around beyond the cemetery fence.

"Well," said my dad, "now we're going to flourish again! . . ."

During the night a wind came up, and illuminated by the moonlight, the maple tree revived, and the leaves of fantastic palmtrees, oaks, and other plants I didn't know, which were attached to the branches by wire, some of them still green, others completely rusted, started to rustle, clattering and scraping metal against metal.

On the other side of the wall and then beyond the fence, not on our side but on the other, we heard doors slamming and voices and mother crying and the sound of blows, as if someone were hitting the wall with a mallet:

"You damned old drunk, you!"

I was standing by the window in a long nightgown, father had his jacket on. Radiant and happy in some strange way, we were both looking at our maple tree.

"Yes, I am a damn old drunk," yelled father, "yes, yes, I agree, I drank it all away, even my body, I managed that, too . . . But I'm not a Tenant! . . . We still have something! We still have some kind of soul! . . . Even if it is ragged and delirious . . . Tenants! . . . Lord, look at the lice that swarm beneath my soul!"

Then dad began to cry and started to rub up and down on his chest.

We lay down in our beds. Our maple tree kept clanging and moaning in the night . . . And if you shut your eyes very, very tight, and if you wish it very, very much, then the bright southern sun blazes forth and your hair grows long and golden . . . Of course, everything will change when I get my identity card, dad, I'll take you south with me, to the Crimea or to the Caucasus . . . We'll pick grapes and get suntanned and make a pile of money, we'll get the coat back, and the typewriter, and the encyclopedias, and even our own bodies . . . And then he'll simply appear, my one and only, good, kind sheriff, the one I fell in love with after that movie . . . Now he's taking us back up north in a convertible sportscar through the canyons of the Caucasus and the prairies, and without noticing it I fall asleep . . . I fall asleep on his shoulder, but he just keeps smiling with his cigar between his teeth . . . The rotted fences flash by, we come to a stop in the shade of the maple tree, and I wake up . . . My suntanned father is calmly drinking coconut milk, our priceless sheriff hops out of the car, the cigar still smoking between his teeth . . . He throws his two pistols in the air, his two terrible Colts, and they land back in their leather holsters by themselves. Then he folds his arms across his chest and stares through narrowed eyes, from under his inimitable hat, at the quivering sweat-covered stinking little creature, spits between its legs, and forces one word through his clenched teeth:

"Listen up, Tenant . . ."

1983
Translated by Violeta Kelertas

Eugenijus Ignatavičius

On the Chrysanthemum Bus

He awoke as the clock struck seven, its mystical copper tones resounded and dissipated into infinity, while sorrow forced its way into his soul, for in this house no one hears these chimes any more, no other heart beats in any corner. For an instant it even seemed strange that no bed was squeaking behind the thin wall, no one was yawning deliciously, deeply drawing in the morning air. The corridor is silent, having swallowed forever the careful shuffle of footsteps toward the kitchen. The parquet floor does not creak, water is not gushing from the tap; there's no sound. If he were to hear these comforting, ordinary morning sounds now, he wouldn't even be surprised—all is as it should be, yes, this tune was played every day at dawn. No one else could appreciate the knells of passing time as he could . . .

Don't think about it. You just woke up, and that's a miracle in itself. Just be glad you've come back from there. A few minutes ago you were still soaring along the treetops over the highway telephone poles and then, with a firm shrug of the shoulders, you escaped the earth's gravity, and you were swallowed up into the azure of the sky. Now no one can prove that you're not here. Of course, you're still here: the light switch clicks under your hand, the lamp light flashes on, the letter you threw on the chair glimmers before your eyes: ". . . we're expecting you . . . because of your prophetic words . . . we miss you very much, we want to see you and hear you . . ."

Prophetic? My head is like a lead pot, devoid of thought, and they want prophecies. There are none; the sky swallowed them up into its void tonight . . . You can even see the fatal point in the vault of the sky. He glances out the window, as though wanting to point out the exact spot. It's a pity, the sky is still pouting from yesterday: gray and sooty, a dank night sky. The city is invisible, its huge, bulky body with all its towers and chimneys is still dozing, wrapped in the black cloak of night, meticulously fastened with glittering snaps. Here and there on the rain-sprinkled asphalt clumps of light dart about like a worn-out zipper; car engines honk tonelessly. In time the sky will open its eyes. People are already getting up, lights flash on, other people scurry, carrying sleeping babies on their shoulders; briefcases and bags in hand they scramble to their jobs, meetings, coffeebreaks, to speak tired words, to express last night's and last year's ideas. They fly even faster to warm the chairs that have cooled overnight, to take their places behind shop counters and the most complicated machines and mechanisms, they hasten to barber shops, hospitals, stores, cemeteries . . . Already an ambulance shrieks past, casting blue flames to its sides and frightening the city with its heart-piercing wail. Morning claims its first victim. The hospital gates instantly swing open, sleepy orderlies spill into the yard and lay the moaning victim, wrapped in rags, on a stretcher.

Just try to stop someone on the sidewalk, offer him or her a cigarette or strike up a conversation, raise your arm to flag down a ride; forget it, they're in more of a hurry than you are because no one has time to utter a single word. Hey, you'd better fly, too. Get up, wash, and take off. Grab a few manuscripts from the drawer; if no thought or soul-soothing phrase turns up in your "lead pot," you can read out loud what you thought about them when you weren't in such a hurry, and you'll force them to pause in their well-trampled circle at least for the moment.

Where are they all hurrying to? And for what? If you'd straighten out all their meandering paths and roads, you'd get the swift, even motion of someone planing a board.

Get a move on, brother, do something. Come on, they're waiting for you. See, they miss you and love you . . . So what are you waiting for? They're already waking up with thoughts of how to get their work done earlier and come home on time so they can scrub off the tar their hands have absorbed, the paint and the dirt, rest their aching shoulders and backs and their heads full of the motorized din. Later they'll get dressed up, they'll put on bright, fashionable shirts, knot the most fashionable ties, comb their hair that's all in clumps from their salty sweat. You have to try, too, sir. You can't show up like the village idiot in musty trousers and no hat. But the most important things are a tie and good spirits. What's in style now? God only knows. Take an extra tie and put it in your briefcase, the whole shebang, in your briefcase. If only your eyes weren't so sad and there were fewer wrinkles on your forehead so they wouldn't give away the anxiety that oppresses you, especially in the morning or when you wake in the night acutely aware of the process of existence, uncontrollable and relentless, like an icy hill that can creep up and break through the brick walls of your solitude, shatter your windowpanes and burst into the emptiness of your rooms, an emptiness that's sometimes hard to fill when you're alone. Give them no hint that at moments like that you're ready to pick up the phone and place a call to the forgotten cottage at the edge of the forest under whose roof a lonely old woman draws in the last whiffs of rationed oxygen; you'd like to kneel before her, place your head on her shriveled knees, and say: I made a mistake, dear friends, I was wrong, my entire life is a chain of irreparable mistakes. What should I do? Let me warm up in your yard for a little while at least, stretch out under the maples, press my face against their loyal trunks, may they at least shade my troubled brow, bless me with the rustling of their innocent leaves and forgive me. Perhaps then, caressed by their shadows, you will be able to sleep the sleep of the innocent, as you once could . . .

Go. Go and fulfill their request; say that you were successful in life: say it's easy to work and rest and rejoice. Whatever will be, let it be. Soon day will break. Soon the curtain of ashes will fall, the morning glow will start gleaming, and over the roar of the obscure city the azure of a starless sky will appear. One more morning will break, when all the roadside trees will fly into your arms afresh. Cars, hungry for trips, will swallow the asphalt ribbon greedily. And maybe you will succeed; the native clay, alive and breathing, will help, you'll touch it with your feet, and its invisible powers will penetrate your vinyl soles. Vistas of days gone by will open again, and as you force your way into the abode of shadows, you will recover them.

It's decided. The prophet is off. He doesn't know what to tell you, but he's on his way. He has a quick bite of breakfast, gulps down a cup of coffee, shines his shoes, and knots his tie (he might very well have forgotten). He dons a hat; what's a prophet without a hat?

Outside the windows a taxi is honking. The prophet sails down the stairs head over heels. A dank, drowsy city skates past his sorrowful, troubled eyes. At the station a comfortable bus awaits him, its metallic mouth wide open. It will soon swallow up our prophet. Soon, soon he'll bounce in; have patience, dear hearts, in the meantime keep yourselves busy. Clear the fall harvest from the fields, plow the land, bind the apple trees, now's the time. And finally, just for once, drain the waters that have flooded the fields of rye.

He's off! The last of the city lights slide past the windows. Autumn blinks its yellowed lashes from the groves stirring in the twilight. The grayish sky slowly turns blue. From time to time the faces yawn. The sound of crackling cellophane can be heard, and a truly funereal smell spreads through the bus. "What's this?" thinks the prophet, astonished. Flowers burst into flame on people's knees: nothing but chrysanthemums!

The bus seems stuffed with gentle, small-flowered, ruffled chrysanthemums. Drowsy faces are stuck among the white drifts of blossoms. From time to time their eyes gleam through the thick, bushy branches. The prophet sees only bouquets embraced by young and soft, stiff and veined hands.

Dawn greets the flower-covered travelers. In the morning light their bodies begin to resemble clay vases or pots, overgrown with blossoming flowers. Not people, but living, moving flower bushes seem to have boarded the vehicle and are now showing their tickets to the conductor in all earnest and traveling on. Only now does he notice a forest of the same type of white-blossomed chrysanthemums lying pale on his knees as well. He's lying in a bier of blossoms—is he awake or is he dreaming? He's awake, for he can clearly smell the bitter, sorrowful odor of the blossoms, evoking corpses, cemeteries, and tears.

He presses his cheek against the damp, cold glass and glances out at the roadside: God, the same kind of flowers are shimmering through the windows of the cars flying in the opposite direction, even the cars passing them contain smiling chrysanthemums. That means they're traveling everywhere. He notices that even the shiny, rain-covered ribbon of asphalt is cloaked in a thin, gentle layer of petals. What's going on here? What's happened to Lithuania? A catastrophe! The great mourning. There's a funereal gravity and silence on the bus. No one swears, no one engages in idle chatter; the drivers, they're not cracking jokes either, they aren't discussing yesterday's adventures, they're not even smoking; instead, they're stopping respectfully at each station, gracefully opening the doors of the vehicle and sucking in several "bushes" standing by the roadside. Their eyes flash and sink into the overgrown blossoms. That means he too is not on his way to meet people coming home from the fields, but . . . people who are already under the clay, shielded by the sunset not only from him but also from all the rest who remain. So how does one bring them back? It's like in the fairy tale: walk anywhere you please, pace by the gates of yon ruddy courtyard, not guarded by man or beast, but after you've turned over your thousandth stone, you still won't find the hidden key. So what can you do, how can you get in?

And if you could open the red-hot curtain just a crack and glance out of the corner of your eye to see how they're doing out there? You know for certain that they're already there, barred from our sight, there, on the other side of the hill, beyond the dim horizon, the forest, on the other side of the ocean's bubbling glow, maybe even on the other side of the evening star, growing quiet, growing smaller, melting with every cloud and drop of rain, vanishing into our embedded footprints, newly imprinted in the road. They're there, you cannot restrain them, you cannot bring them back with their words, their days and their nights, all wound up into one huge ball like a dahlia blossom, transformed in the evenings into a purple colophon.

Brother, there was no point in going out on a day like today: how will you look carrying flowers of mourning onto the stage, the platform of hope and enlightenment? You're not going to throw such serious flowers out the window along the way. You can't hide them under your jacket, either. And anyway, why invite a person to a rendez-vous on a day like this and demand gaiety, jokes, and wisdom from him? It's all the same to you, it seems, to hell with it all, it's nice on this earth and that's enough. You've risen very high, dear friend, you can sail tranquilly through the chrysanthemum bushes and hand out prescriptions for life all around. But what makes you so sure that they don't understand more than you do?

Don't let that slip. Not under any circumstances. They'll boo you off stage. They don't want to hear that the child in you is still alive, that he buries his head in his pillow and is capable of sobbing because he'll never hear his grandfather's baritone in the parish choir again; he'll never descend the cement church steps from the choir loft, where the organ booms, like Moses from the mountain. And it's not just your grandfather, you'll never see your mother as she rises from the presbyterium, her face as pale as the Host, her hand clutching the manifestation of God that has just settled in her heart. You'll never again find a button on your jacket, newly sewn by her hand. Not a single button. Rail against injustice and God if you want to, pray or sow your oats, pave every single road and highway with chrysanthemum blossoms, but your mother still won't come walking down any of them with her thin cane. Your city's awakening without her, it's coming to life, full of births and deaths, hate and love, vice and virtue, a lazy city, a laboring city. All things in equal measure!

What an amazing scale this world is balanced on; how accurately everything is apportioned and meted out without your assistance and without your prophecies.

So why are they calling on you? What do they expect? Why don't they leave you alone? Let's live, each of us locked up in his own shell! But no! Come, we want to see you, comfort us, cheer us up, prophesy a little! Has feeding the pigs and fattening the cattle become too dull for you? Are you fed up with plowing the fields, boozing it up, and falling into bed every evening to enjoy your wife's soft body?

They probably want you to cheer them up, say something funny or witty, perhaps even sing! See, they still think you're an actor, like when you visited their homes as Santa Claus and passed out toys to the children. Or like the time in the pasture, when you struck up a heart-rending "Why did you desert me, world?"

Why, they sang their hearts out, too, that same day, dragging the plowshares into one of the fields, they sang and drank while they plowed and plowed while they drank, and they sang in frustration at having to leave the horses in the common pasture and trudge home on foot. Later, come evening, they'd gather in someone's house, smoke homemade cheroot, curse, and redistribute the world among themselves anew, they'd reestablish the old "colonies," discuss how to remap the boundaries, how to take their animals off the collective farms. The ones they had to surrender themselves, no problem, but what about the ones that were born in the collective pen?

Those men won't come to the meeting. You can count on that: they won't ask inappropriate questions, for time has straightened their ever-disheveled crests and the stubble of their prickly moustaches. Their solid arms, helpless before the judgment of time, are folded on their proud chests like broken branches and have sunk into the damp clay of their parishes. What these men "propped up on their elbows were merely skeletons." Their passions and desires have cooled like a long-unkindled bread oven. They've gone. Gone without having seen the farms divided up, and the deeds to their lands, stamped with the ancestral white knight, have smoldered away in the same ovens as the logs from their cabins, dragged from the demolished private farms. They certainly won't show up for the meeting. And they won't be upset over the boundaries, they won't bloody each other's noses or cut each other's throats over a plow that has crossed the property line and strayed into someone else's field. Even two worms, passing each other in their decomposing coffins, will not meet. Time pays no heed to hopes and desires, the incoming wave seizes them and carries them off. It's over. Fate! What an amazing thing is fate, redeeming every mistake and every injustice—like the Nemunas river, appearing through the bus window as one approaches Vilkija hill: it seduced the tribe of this land, bewitched it and left it to live and yearn on its banks for thousands of years. Now, calm and passive, containing within itself the reflections and destinies of all those who ride by, it flows off to the west.

How loyal and apathetic is the calm of the waters, like a transparent autumn void with the sun ever mocking beyond the window, so like a morbid chrysanthemum blossom. The blue-tinged, smoky vault of the sky only intermittently flecked with clear little clouds—delicate mesh on the cold body of a beautiful woman.

How slow and quiet is the advance of time, the imperceptible change of color: someone cares whether the world grows green or not. The great artist, it seems, did not like the scene he created, or he got bored—again he cleans off the canvas, soon he'll blot off the last remnants of paint, the wind will scrape off the most subtle strokes of the brush that still sparkle on the vanishing picture of summer. Is it because he's noticed a mistake that he's tearing off the last leaves from the trees, burning the blossom of every flower, weeding out the tiniest blades of grass with such fury and haste? In a week or two he'll polish the terrain, cloak it gently with a white sheet of snow like a tablecloth on Christmas Eve, during the long winter nights he'll patiently think how to create everything anew, with more justice and beauty. If only man could do the same—erase the previous day from memory and the next morning start everything over, without mistakes.

But maybe that's how it is. Don't you try to avoid yesterday's absurdities and errors? Until you make new ones. But maybe there is hope—newborns are like white canvas, paper that hasn't been written on yet. Isn't it the children who magnify their parents' sins? That means there's no way out—weakness, sin, and goodness in a closed circle and no exit? You've got to come up with something. If you want to create something new, you have to be able to visualize the model of the scene that is to be. And, dear prophet, who's going to confide its secret to you? . . .

So what advice are you going to give them? Soon the road will come to an end, and in an hour or so you'll find yourself face to face with them. Open-mouthed, they'll hang on every word of yours, take everything to heart . . . You'll tell them that next spring the same types of grass and leaves will grow, only the fir trees will sprout higher, and there'll be nothing new. Why, there might be children there—they'll realize that they'll grow up to be like their parents and grandparents, just like theirs, their teeth will ache at night, their foreheads will wrinkle, the most luxuriant of curls will retreat down the back of their necks, and sorrow will make its home in their eyes. But maybe they can . . . just a little, a little differently . . . avoid some curve or wrinkle and be a shade happier? Perhaps . . . This is eternal progress? This is it? Is this what it means?

The prophet gets depressed at this idea. His forehead breaks out in a cold sweat, and just in case, to make sure that no one pays too much attention to him, he puts his hat in his briefcase, furtively undoes his tie and stuffs it in his jacket pocket. There's no point in standing out too much. Arriving at the bus station, he fails to notice how in the twinkling of an eye he transfers to a different, somewhat smaller bus, where he can't even budge in the crush of chrysanthemum people, and it's suffocating. He's happy to find a secluded corner where he can perch on one foot and keep the chrysanthemums from crumpling. He can't bring himself to meet the eyes twinkling through the bushes—they might recognize him. Fortunately, they don't notice, they don't even suspect that it's he, he himself, whom they raised from childhood and from whom they have every right to demand an accounting. He shrinks back and listens to what the bushes are whispering to each other, quietly and secretively, in the all too familiar dialect.

". . . you mean Antanas? Collapsed in church. His heart . . . ," mutters a bouquet of tiny blossoms to seven yellow chrysanthemums of a newly developed hybrid variety.

". . . how about l'il Motiejus, went out with a band playing . . . he had it so good with his daughter in Kaunas, hot water and heated floor, indoor toilet, died anyway," interrupt some miserable and scruffy blossoms.

". . . poor Domicelis," whispers a weary bouquet with shriveled leaves to a split-leaf variety. ". . . He conked out in a ditch, only a kid . . . whaddaya s'pose . . . some big shots give a speech . . . some kinda dope they says . . . He's a big athalete . . . ODed . . . Spent ten days in 'tensive care in Moscow . . . Wouldn't even let his ma see him, rules is rules there, y' know . . . Brought his body home for just a hour . . ."

Two rows back, a few more bushes had settled in the corner and were hissing at each other. The disheveled chrysanthemum heads, as huge as rabbits, nodded to the more dignified royal blossoms.

"Hey, see the shed in the middle of the field? Right near there, that's where they got that li'l Pulmonas . . . poor kid got hisself pounded. Just out of the army. The director started it hisself, then the mechanics took over and whupped him good. He starts crawlin' home through the furrows still alive. Tractor drivers think he's drunk. By evening they look—and he's bought it. So what if his paw's an alcoholic, he's still a human bein', ain't he!"

". . . and old lady Pliauskienis? Šikalius's daughter-in-law, they plowed her furrow."

". . . wrapped a rosary round her hands and hung herself under an alder . . . it wuz a small branch, but it held up good enough. What's the big deal . . . got knocked up . . . but her foolish pride . . ."

Shaking and rattling, the minibus hits the gravel road, pitted by cars and trucks, the conversations break into small fragments. While the vehicle makes its way over the potholes, the chrysanthemum bushes bounce around in their seats like rubber balls and prop up the rusty ceiling with the tops of their heads. Their meek, sneering faces, long since reconciled to their fates, poke out from under the bushes from time to time, and the prophet turns away to avoid their curious glances. Let his arrival remain a mystery. You never know. Maybe he won't be able to utter a single word, or catch his breath, or . . . better not start anything . . . You can't stuff their heads full of fairy tales. But maybe he'll come up with something yet. Let's say the speech begins with the feudal days, when master Kriučkovskis loved cats better than people. And Mister Silvestravičius gave his grandson, who was plagued by worms, over to die in the hands of strangers, raised him up to the creamery ceiling and nailed him there. No one's going to find that amazing.

It's a good thing our prophet can go unrecognized and can listen to the bushes whispering, he may latch on to some little idea yet, and after that it'll be a breeze.

". . . the poor bastard on the end, he sez on his death bed . . . ," the silvery chrysanthemum leaves lean toward the purple bush again. The prophet pricks up his ears. But whatever he said—whether he asked for a shot of vodka or uttered something extraordinary—it was impossible to hear. As the vehicle paddled its way over the flooded road, the motor started to backfire and sneeze. The bus began to pause at every village, where a candle or two would be flickering in the cemetery, and one chrysanthemum bush would detach itself from the main body of blossoms and make its way toward the crosses. The other bushes stayed in their vinyl-covered seats, as if they had been nailed to them, and meditated silently. They avoided the slightest movement in their seats, as if they didn't want to disturb the shadows of those who were already everywhere and yet nowhere sitting next to them. Why, it wasn't so long ago that they really were sitting on this very same worn upholstery, trading mocking and covetous glances, sharing words. Maybe they haven't gone anywhere, perhaps they're still in the blood of those who are sitting there, they tread the same paths with their feet, their thoughts and occasional words force themselves into the things the others are saying. Their final moments and looks of despair at not having found salvation on earth linger in the memories of the living. The bushes had thinned out a little, and on some of the faces you could begin to read anxiety and helplessness at the well of eternity continually in turmoil. The great artist doesn't seem to be too satisfied with our images either. He can't obtain perfection, no matter what he does. That's why he puts us in the same row with the dogwood bush and the dandelion . . . But maybe the clay lacks fertilizer?

People get confused and start to say "excuse me." They offer the labor of their hands, they pick the most beautiful blossoms and hold armfuls of them on their laps, like a significant letter or a declaration of their love. They'll go to the gray mound, light a candle in the wind, and maybe that way they'll be able to warm the thickening wall of ice a little and melt it. And the roots of the chrysanthemums, stuck in the damp clay, should penetrate even deeper, pierce the shield of oblivion, and witness those who mourn the dead, remember their names and their work, the words they've spoken, so that they not only diligently resume the broken thread of the others' desires but try to be faithful to the precept they bequeathed—to be honest. Only it doesn't always work out that way because they're human, too, and must submit to their own fate.

The edges of a very familiar forest and the slopes of a former estate flash by the mud-covered windows. The tips of red rooftops poke out. The bus dives into the yellowed pits even more quickly and bravely, splashing a slushy liquid to the sides, the motor wheezes, howls, and explodes as it labors, as if mischievous children were sticking tiny grenades inside it. The noise deafens the prophet, and he stops caring. Any minute now the azure church steeple will emerge beyond the turn, the belfry built by serfs will appear, impressive haystacks—the sanctuaries of the new times, and then the schoolhouse will appear, from the platform he'll be able to see the stairs and windows through the auditorium window. That same school smiles in front of him, the school that seemed like a shrine many years ago, and the high schoolers, gathering around the cedars, had seemed like the chosen people. The stairs, which will appear through the window of the facade, were the ones that he had climbed to the second floor and from which he had looked out at the shingled roofs of the cottages for the first time. Later in his life there were to be many more staircases, quite a bit higher, but none as memorable. And what was it he saw looking down at the ground, what did he learn? What will he tell them, when he has to leave the safety of the chrysanthemum bush and come out into the open? The living gardens will throng to the cemetery; he too will leave his flowers of sorrow for the spent generation and will have to confront the living. The hat and tie won't help, nor will a cheery disposition.

The prophet becomes uneasy, anxiety makes his knees throb, his chest ache, and his temples twitch. Maybe it's not too late to turn back. No one has recognized him. Timidly, he peeks out the windows, as if hoping to avoid the confrontation and run away. But at the crucial moment the low autumn sun comes out and generously strews its beams over the huge, black, plowed field. He calms down: how beautiful the earth is at rest, elegantly laid out furrow upon furrow. She's reclining, her knees turned to the sunlight like a woman at the beach. In places the raised furrows and the cracks in the black soil gleam with dazzling flowers of silver. Perhaps the sun sent them for the unfortunate Pulmonas, or are they blooming for us all? Strange, the black rows reflecting the chrysanthemums of hope so brightly. What does it mean? Who dared to plant the fields with flowers?

Perhaps he could start his speech with these words? The prophet cheers up, and, enveloped in blissful peace, he climbs out of the bus and plants his feet firmly on his native soil.

1988
Translated by Rita Dapkus, Gregory M. Grazevich, and Violeta Kelertas

Ramūnas Klimas

What I Thought about on the Bus Ride to See My Old Classmate

On the bus ride to see my old classmate, the dampness and odors of the gloomy underground melancholy or the Green Thickets would intermittently drift by, or more precisely, it was the underground melancholy and the Green Thickets. Later a trite thought kept humming in my head: *He who uses only his eyes is not the one who sees. He is just a lost, half-blind wanderer, walking away from the flower of fiery matter, continuously away, all his life—away . . . A Gertrude Stein pigeon on the grass, reflected in Koeppen's mirror . . .* I doubt that I myself thought this way. Someone else was thinking for me (about me?), forcing a sickness upon me. Perhaps it was my classmate, who was drawing closer at a speed of fifty slow kilometers per hour.

The bus was early. A meek Indian summer sun appeared, cloaking the hills and lakes with the quiescence of a weary animal. People for the most part took short trips; the bus would suck them in from the roadsides along with sacks and baskets and, after two or three stops, spit them out in some sleepy village. We would stand there for a while longer, the driver would shut off the motor, thus severing the thoughts about my classmate (or maybe his thoughts about me?), and with a sense of relief I'd give myself over to abstract meditation: *Souls converge only at the height of tragedy or farce . . .* A poor excuse for an idea would break loose and slide along the glistening pavement ahead, disappearing behind the nearest hill. The driver would spit out the window and forge on, not realizing that for me the distances between the stops were an attempt to vanish without a trace into the gloomy underground melancholy that had one border, but probably not another, making its measurement impossible in any known spatial dimensions. The driver had blue eyes, a frank, sincere face and light, curly hair like a lamb's. He was a typical *pigeon on the grass.*

He who uses only his eyes is not the one who sees. I now knew that the underground, which had swallowed up and kept my classmate forever, smells of late autumn forests and thickets—of marshes, rotting leaves, animal urine, and clotted human blood.

Since childhood I had searched for its location, as if for the location of paradise. I longed to experience the point from which he suddenly emerges into the light and stretches—anxious, energetic, determined.

Quod licet Jovi, non licet bovi, I thought during the bus ride to see my old classmate. *Non licet bovi,* a bull is only allowed so much: to rush with its horns a small white cloud, born of the dew of Eden's olive trees. Too massive a structure of nature to penetrate an alien dream and feel the lick of fiery matter.

I was completely in his control for a long time. And I was happy. I was in seventh heaven, embracing his duffle bag with the jersey bearing our town emblem's colors and other soccer gear, figuring out his algebra, although he knew his algebra a hundred times better than I. These, no doubt, were just marks of a superficial dependency. On the bus ride to see my old classmate, I saw myself as a sooty, hard-working vessel, hurling an astronaut out into limitless space to capture a badge of honor. He walked with bulging pockets, while I spent my time mending the vessel's flanks, banged in by meteors. I could not do otherwise. Nor, it seemed, could he.

We were twins.

Not brothers but twins. The fence between our yards was merely symbolic. Our mothers went into labor at the same time, and our fathers hailed the only taxi in the town square simultaneously, ruining the driver's day by not losing their heads and sharing the cab fare. On the way to the hospital the driver grumbled that nothing under heaven is a sure thing anymore, you count the stomachs of the broads in town, you cultivate them like watermelons, but now two stomachs only get you one fare.

I can easily picture them letting the cabbie go by the hospital and returning by the only town road. Two men, bound only by a deck of cards and a jug of homemade beer. A skillful sharpener of knives and a former Green Thicket ranger, who had purchased a house in the neighborhood a month or two ago. They returned proud as gardeners, convinced that each had grafted a tree. How could they have known that they picked the same trunk, but opposite sides?

On the bus ride to see my old classmate, I thought how handsome he had been in the ridged and grooved stadium arena.

While still in eighth grade, I believe, he tasted the laurels of victory as the local soccer team favorite. Heated up by the activities on the field and in the stands, where a glass traveled from hand to hand, the townspeople predicted an intoxicating future for him: "I tell you, I'll be damned if we don't see him on TV some day."

The rake and ax factory team is not televised. But the critics nodded in assent, washing down mouthfuls of sunflower seeds with cheap wine. Wine distorted their sense of distance, and they saw their idol on a green, smooth field in a thousand-seat stadium, attired in the most brilliantly colored uniform, not in this dusty wasteland, almost bald of grass.

I'll note what could be seen from the stadium's only grandstands: the town, overgrown with linden trees on all sides, gardens at the foot of the bluff, and, rising above all, the steep Gothic nose of St. Peter and Paul cathedral . . . The town was laid out on a hill, and at its foot, in the valley of the Nevėžis, the rake and ax factory team chased after the ball and the competitors. The competitors were not allowed to leave smiling; this sacred rule had been laid down to meet the crowd's demands, and eleven of its enforcers worked their tails off in the town valley. The eleventh was my classmate. The left wing.

On the bus ride to see my old classmate, it occurred to me that it wasn't right to say that eleven enforcers worked their tails off. There were only ten. Even when he came out onto the field, the left wing couldn't break out of the gloomy underground melancholy, out of the damp Green Thickets in which he was begot; between whistles he often skulked along the edge of the game, indifferent to the ball. The officials didn't run after him much either, the crowd said, because they more or less knew my classmate. The crowd also knew what was most important—his sluggishness was filled with the potential of a dozing snake. But the crowd did not now know what was most important—when the snake would strike.

It did not know the system.

A kind of childishness covered the town valley. Those forty-year-old fathers of nearly grown children (balding, pot-bellied, eyes swollen from sitting too much in the local hot dog joint), when they huddled together in their arena of punishment and, like St. Sebastians, pulled arrows out of their opponents' bodies, were infantile. Disapproving of scrimmages, they poured generous libations to Dionysus and simply huddled together, pulling arrows, and as a result the hour was really dedicated to keeping the ball from being kicked into the current of the Nevėžis.

On the ride to see my old classmate, I thought that maybe the valley believed it could bathe in the score as if in a spring, while like a granite cliff it withstood the other town, which had a couple hundred more inhabitants. Maybe the valley needed the score like a grade for its very existence in Lithuania: the condemnation or acquittal of that existence.

Empirically, it seemed as if the opponents could endure everything: the elegant and unusually rational technique of my classmate, his ability to concentrate every force of Newton's last law into one spot on the ball; they seemed to have as much time as they wanted to prepare—to dig their trenches, build reinforcements, put up a barbed wire fence—they had also seen the dozing snake's potential more than once. But they did not know what was most important—the system. They did not know when my classmate would emerge into the light—anxious, energetic, determined, burning everything in the vicinity with that gloomy, wolflike, Green Thicket melancholy. That is why, with naive fury, they assaulted the small white cloud, born of the dew of Eden's olive trees—*quod licet Jovi, non licet bovi.* They hunted the small white cloud as if it were a spirit, those *pigeons on the grass,* while the balding and pot-bellied Dionysians from the rake and ax factory team would tear out the remaining arrows, stretch, and raise such a storm of dust in the valley of the Nevėžis that, after the dust settled, only a sad token of the opponents' ambitions would survive. The crowd would whistle, the crowd would howl, the crowd would pass the wine glasses faster, the crowd would be swallowed into the depths of childishness, where it could wash away all of Cain's blemishes and return with a fine grade for the town's existence on the hill, for the gardens at its foot and the linden trees in the evening sun.

There was only one thing the crowd didn't care for—having stung once again, my classmate went back to flitting along the edge of the game.

On the bus ride to see my old classmate, I remembered our math teacher's attempts to establish functional dependence. After some observation, he concluded that my classmate's outbursts did not depend on the ambient temperature, the amount of precipitation, the size of the crowd, the crop yield, or sunspots . . . Later he discovered a horrible, from his point of view, antidependence—the outbursts did not depend on the score. *Quod licet Jovi, non licet bovi*—and the math teacher stopped going to soccer games.

He had done all that he could. The next step would have been for him to attack the small white cloud, born of the dew of Eden's olive trees. Or to convert to a different system of measurement, a system created, of course, completely from scratch. This backwoods teacher was slight and myopic, he kept a flock of chickens and prepared an outline for every lesson. Of *the pigeons on the grass* breed. Afterward it seemed to me he even began to fear my classmate and started giving him good grades for almost no reason.

Here again it is more than appropriate to state: *He who uses only his eyes* . . . The math teacher had discovered the antidependence but hadn't taken the next logical step over to the side of truth, so he remained in the tepid dusk of falsehood, where the shadows that fall on the prosecutor's white toga are pretty and the prosecutor's finger, held up toward heaven, looks gallant as it incriminates my classmate during the rare moments of inspiration, during the rare toasts in honor of the town heraldic crest. Tossing your head back, you might not see that the chickens he's raised himself are tearing up his toga with their beaks, and sometimes even answering the call of nature on them. But more about that—later. After I come to the part about the tables, which were lined up for our graduation in the basement gym.

The girls dragged in flowers to kill the smell of armpits, which had eaten its way into the walls and floor. The principal spoke a little about azure spaces, then she sat down and bit into her cigarette in agitation. A literature teacher depicted these spaces in a poem of her own creation. My classmate sat under a basketball hoop intertwined with birch branches, and his face shone with unconcealed contempt. On his face for the first time I could discern open emotion, which had broken away from the gloomy underground melancholy. A shudder went through me. They announced the dance. Some people dashed into the auditorium, and a good-sized bunch, grabbing the math teacher along the way, took to the honeysuckle in the schoolyard, where a fairly large stock of intoxicants had been stashed. The math teacher put on airs, mumbled something about official reprimands, but once he had a glass in his hand said: "What else can we mere mortals do, when soccer stars won't pass up a drink."

"You saw me play?"

"I used to. But now I only hear. I hear the whole town singing in the hot dog joint after the game."

"Do you like those songs?"

"I vote for almighty human solidarity."

"Just solidarity?"

"That's too little for you?"

"Is it enough for you?"

The question was to hang in the air permanently. Someone shouted that the principal's messenger Barčas was coming, and the math teacher was the first to evaporate at the news. He slid along the fence, away from the official reprimands, and a section of future big shots slid after him—three Ph.D. candidates, a couple of journalists, one famous surgeon, and all sorts of small-timers, too. Again contempt shone in my classmate's eyes. We sat down on a stack of old planks and lit a cigarette.

"Solidarity," he repeated. "But, to tell you the truth, maybe nothing means more than miserable solidarity."

"What are you talking about?"

"About the fact that Sir Newton was an idiot. Gravity exists for a man's behind, and not for man's soul."

"I don't think he denied that."

"That's why our math teacher denies it. He invented a form of gravity of the soul—namely, solidarity."

The school guard Barčas strolled into the honeysuckle thicket.

"Pardon my interruption," he said. "Would you happen to have any empties?"

"Go ahead and take them," my classmate said.

Then he asked: "Barčas, do you like your job?"

"Job?" the guard straightened up, holding the bottlenecks between his fingers. "Job? And what, in your opinion, is there for me to do? If it wasn't for my leg, maybe I'd be a chauffeur."

"You heard him," said my classmate. "Barčas's dream is to own a chauffeur's jacket."

"And what should it be, soccer?" said Barčas, shrugging his shoulders sadly.

My classmate carefully climbed down from the woodpile and went up to the invalid.

"Boredom, Barčas, soccer is sheer boredom," he said.

Barčas threw his head back as if he'd been spit at. My classmate crept even closer to him.

"Yes, old man, boredom. It can put you to sleep."

Barčas stepped backward and whispered: "You greenhorn. You pig."

And my classmate laughed in his face.

Suddenly he struck. Barčas let the bottles slide out of his fingers and doubled over, squeezing his stomach with his hands. I don't remember jumping down from the planks, grabbing my classmate by the wrist and pulling him toward me. I collected myself only when his eyes seared me and pierced the whole of me through and through with the cold, sharp, Green Thicket melancholy of a growing wolf cub. Its tongue lolling, it panted with unexpected joy (I thought) at the idea that it was finally allowed to explode. It struck me that the enemy's goalie used to see it; he would lose his coordination over it and forget the very colors of his town emblem. That was by far worse than the kick in the groin that made me double over a second later.

Barčas was lifting me up by the armpits, and I couldn't tear my eyes away from my classmate, who, with his hands crammed into his pockets, took off across the schoolyard, becoming smaller and smaller, until he disappeared altogether into the graduation evening twilight.

During the bus ride to see my old classmate, I thought about the chickens that had torn the prosecutor's toga with their beaks. The prosecutor's finger raised toward heaven was a gesture of naive gallantry, with which the math teacher expressed his incriminations during the lukewarm twilight of falsehood on the rare toasts in honor of the town's emblem. What toasts? For what town? What kind of foothills and grandstands, what kind of St. Sebastians from the rake and ax factory team? My classmate merely struggled closer to the flower of fiery matter, blooming in the gloomy underground melancholy and Green Thickets, until in the end he picked it, stole it, held it in the palms of his hands for a few seconds, and fainted in satisfaction, at which time the flower there scalded his heart with an inhuman coldness.

Later the flower died out.

But that didn't happen in the honeysuckles, although back there he was especially close to the flower, already reaching for it, laughing in Barčas's face.

He crossed the schoolyard and disappeared, leaving an irritability to hang in the air for an hour or so, like Satan's: Eh . . . he spoiled the song . . . the fool!

At the station, when I stepped off the bus, I thought about what I would say to him. In what respect do I differ from the math teacher, who, frightened by antidependence, slid the length of the fence, taking a whole university department of future big shots with him? How am I any better, even if I've stepped out of the tepid dusk to the edge of truth. *Quod licet Jovi, non licet bovi*, no one is allowed to manage things in a stranger's dream exactly like in one's own, I thought, drawing closer to the tall stone walls with the iron gate shut tight and the wide open wooden door next to it. I went through the door into the cramped premises, where not a single person was present at the moment, and knocked on the little barred window. The bust of a uniformed man appeared. I told the guard whom I had come to see.

"You're his brother?" asked the officer.

"No," I answered.

"And you're not a relative?"

"He was a classmate of mine."

"In that case, there's no way I can help you. Only people who are close are allowed to visit."

"But I am close to him. Can't you understand, or do you just not want to understand?"

"Show me in writing. Where's a document?"

"Here," I said, rapping on the left side of my chest with my fist.

The officer spat out the dry crumb of tobacco stuck to his lip and said, "That there's a poor document. But I'll do what I . . . Bring him a package."

"A what?" I asked.

"A package. The store's right around the corner. You can bring bacon and butter. Fried bacon is always popular, but you're not from around here, you wouldn't have anywhere to fix it. How about candy? But something plain, not chocolate."

"What do you mean, don't they feed them well here?"

"We feed everyone here according to his or her merits," the guard growled, and I head a pigeon on the grass intonation.

In the store, packing the groceries into my briefcase, I thought about how this could have happened. I had heard the story about the restaurant and the fork, although my imagination created a mise-en-scène with such facility that, whether I wanted to or not, I began to believe that it hadn't been the student but me sitting in front of my old classmate.

I dug into my first scholarship lunch cutlet. My old classmate sat in front of me. He sat alone. He didn't even look at me. He tarried, immersed in the gloomy underground melancholy. Tarried? The student didn't know, the math teacher didn't know either, but I knew already that he never tarried there without work, that his soul is forever diving to the very depths of the underground; flung back to the gate, it howls in fury and dives again into the depths, where the flower of fiery matter blooms. He sits in the restaurant and feels its cold breath, and the breath turns to frost, and my old classmate stretches his hand toward the stem of the flower carefully, carefully, still forever doubting his luck, he picks the blossom, holds it as if embracing a tiny bird with his palms, and his heart, scalded by the frost, faints with satisfaction.

And to all the others dining in the restaurant of life—to me, to the father of several children at the adjacent table, to the couple sucking on a cocktail, to the orchestra's musicians playing blues from

Satchmo's repertoire, to the math teacher frightened by antidependence, to the guard whose instructions are the only things keeping him from admitting that he who is close on paper is not the only one who is close, and to the St. Sebastians from the rake and ax factory team, striving to get a good grade for the town's existence on the hill—to all, *quod licet Jovi, non licet bovi*, to all the *bovi*, to all *the pigeons on the grass*, it was not a blossom, nor a tiny bird, but a stainless steel fork, whose shaft my classmate still grasped at that instant, although its teeth had already torn through my clothes, my skin, and had pierced my liver. I still stand with the fork in my liver, while he falls half-dead, weakened, like the old fascist in Koeppen's novel who disgraced and raped the Jewish girl.

"Is that all?" the sweet young cashier asked me.

"And some candy."

"What kind?"

"Assorted. A little of each."

"They're just different wrappers. Other than that it's the same old junk."

She scooped up a handful from each box, threw the bag on the scale, and said, "If you're getting these for a child, you'd be better off with chocolate."

"This child doesn't like chocolate."

I studied her small face, the protruding collarbone, the scarcely discernible mounds of her breasts under the smock. After all, you're also *a pigeon on the grass* longing for a good grade for your existence in Lithuania, I thought, overcome by an insane tenderness.

1981
Translated by Rita Dapkus

Ramūnas Klimas

Gintė and Her Man

That summer I saw that rye had overgrown Gintė's path. Until then I thought that it had been snowed over forever in 1950. That summer the rye was billowing there, and only someone who knew that the path was there twenty-five years before could feel it.

In 1975 they remembered me and invited me to Tarpumiškiai, to the silver wedding anniversary of Gintė and of her man, who had mourned Lithuania in the cellar for eleven years. Maybe they sensed something, maybe that's why they remembered me. I had been patching their story together for several years. I had already written four versions, but eventually the fruitless, smoke-filled nights would creep up on me, and I would gnash my teeth at the thought of putting the Tarpumiškiai story on paper—of putting it in a cage.

I went to congratulate them.

Gintė's man was puttering around in the garden, hammering some old, unfinished boards on a sawhorse. He had aged somewhat and was as thin and tall, as straight as if he were a single bone. He could stay upright even when he bent down to pick up a nail.

I asked if there would be a lot of guests.

"There will be room enough for everyone," he answered with quiet conviction in a voice that seemed not to have changed.

But we ran out of boards, so we took off the woodshed doors. Gintė came out into the garden and covered our work with white tablecloths. She covered the woodshed doors as well. She, too, was no longer young, but, like him, she was straight and upright, and I saw how they suited each other. A beautiful thing it is to grow old together. I listened to their wordless language, which to me was like music to a deaf person, like a billet-doux to a blind man.

Through the kitchen window Gintė handed me an extension cord with a two-hundred-watt bulb. I climbed into an apple tree and hung the lightbulb above the table. More women appeared in the garden: on the table they were setting out platters of fatty meat rolls from the delicatessen in Pasvalys. Gintė's man took a platter right out of someone's hands, carried it back to the kitchen, and then came out of the woodshed with a pitcher.

We both sat down at the kitchen table.

I sat opposite the window. This place was the apex of a triangle. The triangle is the geometric model of this story. Its surface area was now overgrown with rye. The whole area billowed with a parched yellowness, and it seemed that the grains would spill from their ears if a stronger gust of wind came up.

Only someone who knew that Gintė's path was there twenty-five years ago could feel it. The path was one side of the triangle, and the triangle's second apex—a green island of apple trees—now appeared in the very center of the yellow billowing. No farm buildings could be seen amidst the apple trees, which grew as if merely by habit.

"We tore them down after mother's first anniversary, " he said, looking me in the eye.

"Did she live there until she died?"

"That's the way she wanted it. A mile in the village is no more than a block in the city."

And the cellar?

Are the apple trees still bearing fruit? Have they grown wild?

The road still rose up a hill with a white post at the top—the third apex of the triangle. The post once said that it was an infinity of miles to Pasvalys. The shops and the bar in Pasvalys, the streets strewn with horse-apples, and the market square were submerged in fog.

Large and prosperous, the classical town of Pasvalys was as unreal as the promised land.

Now only twenty of those miles remained.

We discussed the warm summer, Africa and Thomas Mann, the fish in the Mūša River that the little tanning factory was killing off, soccer, land reclamation, my kids. Here too he was upright, both talking and sitting at the table. An early old age had already started weaving cobwebs around him. But they were still thin and transparent, and he didn't even seem to notice them. He had reached that age when time seems to hesitate for a year or two and then vanishes in the thickets of the fullness of life to prepare quietly for the lunge of the beast.

What disease could be eating at this man?

Leukemia? Hardening of the arteries? Just some chronic infirmity?

Just old age?

Gradually the blood surged to my head.

I didn't come to Tarpumiškiai just to pickle myself in beer. I came to breathe some life into the fifth version of my story, and here we sit smoking Bulgarian tobacco. Sooner or later the kids will learn to stand on their own two feet and all the blacks will have liberated themselves, sooner or later *A Death in Venice* will be translated and the willows will grow back along the river banks, maybe we'll have more trouble with the head of the factory, he'll be paying fines for a long time and he'll still be giving the Mūša's fish tanning brine to drink. We'll have more than our share of trouble with that jerk. But why is he coming up in our conversation today? Why tonight?

Ginté's man was straight when it came to details, but I had come here to get straight to the heart of the matter.

I had come for an explanation.

It seemed that his brain, too, was inundated with angry blood, for he stood up and went to put on a tie.

I remained in the kitchen alone.

The edge of the big sun had already crept behind the hill with the milepost. The orange pavement rose straight to the sun. Everything was close, everything smelled of the constancy of time. I looked at the green island of apple trees in the rye. The mature yellow of the rye made it seem like the grains were already scattering from their ears. The triangle of the story suddenly came back to life, and I ran out into an early morning in the winter of 1950 and waded off through the snow to the garden fence. My mother and Ginté came wading behind me. Ginté's man had come out of the cellar that morning. In the farmyard, on the second side of the triangle, two black figures appeared. For a moment they merged, then separated, and one little figure turned toward Pasvalys. The other followed it with her eyes. This was his mother. She waited until her son reached the road. We waited until he climbed the hill with the milepost and stopped to look around.

He disappeared behind the hill as if beyond the horizon. We all went into the kitchen. Ginté sat down at the table and set her hands, rough and chapped from work, before her. She could see the hill through the window. On it, toward evening, her man, who mourned Lithuania in the cellar for eleven years, might appear. Or he might not appear.

He appeared, but was he the way I need him now?

How many miles is it to Pasvalys? Twenty or an infinity?

And finally, what have I set out to write? A true story or a legend?

God knows I really did want to be objective, like Publius Cornelius Tacitus describing Nero's antics. I wanted to be documentary, to be like a bookkeeper's ledger.

In the first version (could it have been in 1970?) I stated everything the way it was. It turned out to be a dozen pages or so "with a happy end"—with a stamp in an internal passport, homemade beer for a wedding, and the right to teach. And so it was—passport, beer, and a class full of pupils devouring all the colors of history with their eyes, beginning with the gold of Pericles' Hellas and ending with the blood-red of Rome in flames.

That night I felt as though I had given birth to a child. But it lived only until morning. Perhaps not even that long—when I woke it was no longer breathing. I decided not to give up. I threw the child's mummy over my shoulder and crept off along the path to documentation. I came back without finding it and set out once more without finding it, until my exhausted brain realized that the train didn't go through the little town where I wanted to end up. The tracks had not been laid. True, on that quiet evening when the train comes closest to the town, its roaring can be heard there. Not even roaring, but a single fleeting roar, like an auditory hallucination. This is the only kind of connection there is between the train and the town, so it's important to capture that moment of closest proximity and jump from the train into the night. I had touched on the first pebble of invention. I took away the right to teach—took away a class full of children devouring the colors of history with their eyes. The pebble rolled off down the slope and started a real avalanche—I gave up the wedding beer and later the passport, too, yes, the passport, God forgive me, though it seems to me that the hand of even the strictest government official would not have trembled at using a stamp in a passport to put an end to the cellar time.

I took away his prospects.

He stopped between the cellar and the government offices in Pasvalys, looked around atop the hill with the milepost, across the snow-blown distances, and didn't know what to do. He didn't know what to do as a living thing, as a body. Pasvalys, the large and prosperous city of classical times, was a myth, like the promised land. The body of Gintė's man had no prospects.

But later, as the pebbles of invention came clattering down, this is what I suddenly saw.

Toward evening that winter day in 1950 a horse's head appeared above the hill. The horse slowly rose up from behind the horizon and grew larger. White steam poured from its jaws. It was pulling a sleigh. Two men from a nearby village on the Mūša sat on the seat, and in the straw behind them lay the man who mourned Lithuania, bare-headed, frost-covered, and stiff. At the kitchen table Gintė hardly stirred. The sleigh turned off the road and slid down toward the second apex of the triangle. A small black figure was already waiting there among the gnarled apple trees. Gintė's blood quickly ran dry.

The sun disappeared behind the hill with the milepost as if beyond the horizon.

"Here they come," Gintė's man said to the back of my head.

A group of men were smoking and talking in the middle of the yard. Gintė's man fumbled at the electrical outlet, and two-hundred-watts came on in the apple tree above the white, satiating, intoxicating table. The group fell silent, and everyone turned to look at him.

The head of the collective arrived with pint in hand and wife on arm, and his wife set about getting things organized. She sat Gintė and her man at the place of honor and the youngest couple from Tarpumiškiai at the other end of the table. The man had a coarse, red face. He was cleaning his plate and emptying his glass tirelessly all night—chow down and bottoms up. His wife was full and listless, she poked idly at the marinated peas with her fork and worshipped her husband, his strength and vitality, with bleary eyes. She was pregnant.

The guests ate and drank their fill. The guests danced the latest dances. The guests listened to the sweet songs that sweetened not only the conversation but even the meat rolls from the Pasvalys deli. The cassette tapes were insanely long, and the richness of the deli food was dammed up under the two-hundred-watts. As satiety turned to nausea, a little ghost reeking of tanning brine glided above the table, perched on one then another guest's shoulder, and roared with laughter. The head's wife sweetly asked her husband to come with her. She led him off behind the barn and gave him hell for being too partial to homemade beer and the fairer sex from the neighboring farms.

The thin face of Gintė's man breathed tedium and fatigue. It was dismal in the floodlights for the consul of ancient history of the Tarpumiškiai grade school. What was he thinking about? The fish in the Mūša? Land reclamation, Africa, Thomas Mann? About ancient history, like a child's seesaw? Pericles on one end and Nero on the other. At one moment, Nero weighs his end down, tearing Pericles away from the earth, lifting him up, and look! Brutus is already climbing up the board.

The tape reels kept turning, and angry blood again surged to my head.

Gintė's man and I were maddeningly far from each other. Between the two of us lay a thick, sticky medium in which fish, unable to swim, lay belly up.

In this medium appeared an old man, my right-hand neighbor at the table. His face emerged with its pointed, clean-shaven chin. He clinked his glass against mine.

"Are you still studying or do you work?"

"I work," I blurted.

"Where—if you don't mind my asking?"

"Not at all. I guard a warehouse full of empties at night. I walk along a barbed wire fence with a gun."

"Well, I remember you," the old man said reproachfully. "Don't you remember me? My granddad died then. I even brought over some of the beer from the funeral for the teacher. Back then . . ." and he threw a quick glance at Gintė's man.

Something in me turned upside down. Something fell and shattered. More room for something else appeared. The old man revealed to me the secret law of Tarpumiškiai. He reminded me. I had forgotten it. Finally, I felt the feeble pulse of the story of Gintė and her man in the memory of Tarpumiškiai. Under the snow of 1950 and the rye of 1975 that was practically bursting from its ears.

He reminded me that in Tarpumiškiai there were some underground canals along which man touches man, memory touches memory, rarely breaking through into speech, into word, the way a tree connects with another tree—at the roots, but not at the tops.

Those canals had to reach Gintė's man, too, but he barely moved. His face breathed tedium and fatigue.

I apologized to the old man. He squeezed my elbow with withered fingers.

"As long as we're still sitting here and not going home yet, let's have a drink."

And what was Gintė doing during her silver anniversary? I'm not sure if this has the least bit of significance for the story, but I'll relate it anyway. Just for the hell of it.

I caught a stealthy glance from Gintė. Then another. A third. They fell on the young woman at the end of the table who had covered her big stomach with the edge of the tablecloth. They fell unburdened by envy or suffering, falling, rather, simply out of habit. They were light and empty like worm-eaten nutshells.

The guests having gone their separate ways, the three of us sat a while longer under the two-hundred-watts.

Gintė, the Tarpumiškiai grade-school teacher Gintė, with her exhausted womb, already eternally tired from the effort of nurturing the seed.

Her man, who once upon a time had mourned Lithuania in the cellar for eleven years and later came out of the cellar and started teaching ancient history to the children of that very same Tarpumiškiai, people say he taught well and made it interesting, they say, the university is packed with pupils of his, they say, in Vilnius they never just call him a teacher, they call him an educator.

And I, a man of vague profession and vague vocation with some of the traits of a practicing pickpocket, searching for an elixir of life for the fifth version of their story.

Gintė asked how I liked their farm. I answered that I liked it. She said that when Tarpumiškiai needed a new grade school, and the collective put up a new building, they left the old schoolhouse for their family. I nodded. It was a good brick building, of the old construction.

"How do you know all that?" laughed Gintė. "After all, this is only the second time you've been here."

We discussed the whole family one at a time, like praying the rosary. Then Gintė got up, went into the kitchen, and unplugged the two-hundred-watts from the socket.

Only then did we become aware of the moon shining above us. And only then did all of Tarpumiškiai become aware of it, at the same time all the farms held their breath, and a tired, festive happiness floated away along with the fish in the slow, pure current of the Mūsa.

Gintė's man said, "Who the hell needs anniversaries? The wheel turns fast enough as it is. When I'm sitting in class, I dread the bell."

"Are you afraid you won't have time to tell them about Brutus?" I grinned.

He looked at me attentively.

"Why Brutus in particular?"

"All of history's gangsters are racy characters."

"Brutus was just a cur," Gintė's man said calmly.

"It's Caesar's own fault he went out without a stick."

We were silent for a bit. Maybe he didn't like the tone of my voice. But then he said, "Do you think Vytautas didn't have a stick to chase Jogaila with? The truth of the stick is a temporary truth."

"Vytautas was from a tribe of predators, too."

"And if he hadn't been? While I was still a student, I began to sense that Vytautas wanted to trade something. And then it occurred to me: maybe he wanted to trade the stick for a crown."

I said that this wasn't the Grand Duke's style. It was no longer history. It was another genre.

Now it was his turn to smile.

"You think so? Imagine that you're the first. There were no chroniclers like Dlugosz or Theodore Narbut, no Bychovets chronicle. Not a single patent has been issued for a treatment of history, the stereotype hasn't even been created. You're as free as a bird, and you must answer why, for example, Vytautas had his heart set on being crowned only in Trakai. Why not in Lutsk, or Kiev? Why not in some nice Volynian castle where he could easily have traveled incognito? A couple of Tatars would have been enough to fool Jogaila's scabs and bring the crown. What would have happened if his rival's curs hadn't been so keen?"

"History postulates this moment as unambiguous."

"History doesn't postulate anything. The chroniclers do. You do. I do. But not history."

"And facts?"

"Something that has happened, maybe, though somewhat less often than you think. But something that hasn't happened? History is a storehouse of unrealized possibilities, and a person has to search through them for moral compensation."

"And were you recompensed for thinking about a coronation that never took place?"

"I think I was. I came to think that Lithuania would have returned to her banks. An end to the flood would have come."

"Lithuania, crowned and blessed by the Pope—*and* returned to her banks?"

"Vytautas would have brought her back. He had already achieved that degree of wisdom."

"When did you think this through?" I asked.

"When I had plenty of time to think," answered the man who mourned Lithuania.

It was the first allusion to the cellar. And the only one. A momentary roar, like an auditory hallucination.

"Why don't we get up? I expect Gintė's already made the beds."

I said that I would sit a while longer.

———————

Doesn't history postulate anything?

The night was so quiet that you could hear everything. The Mūša flowing a few miles away. Apple trees growing old in the neighbors' farmstead.

A man loving Lithuania and Lithuania loving him.

And especially the young woman with the big stomach, who, perhaps, was still walking slowly and carefully in the moonlight up the hill with the milepost, overcome by the languid blessing of marriage.

And all the people of Tarpumiškiai were returning to their homes, were gradually returning to their soundless lives—soundless cultivation of rye, soundless adoration of forests and fields, fire and water, soundless understanding of one another, intercession, sympathy.

It was already turning light in the east.

Doesn't history postulate anything?

I started to catch on to what had been bothering me for so long.

I had been searching for a legend here, for the concrete form of a legend, in the object or in the word, I was searching for the Holy Grail, be it forgotten, be it tarnished, lying behind the barn, overgrown with thistles, yet unscathed and intact. I had been searching without ever realizing that the spoils had already been divided—on that morning in 1950, when the man who mourned Lithuania came out of the cellar. When he took off his white monk's habit and appeared before Tarpumiškiai in a striped civilian coat reeking of mothballs. That morning on the hill with the milepost the legend took on another existence. Another form.

Toward evening the worldly form of the legend appeared on the hill. A genius who had spent the fire of his soul—a Renoir with his withered hand, a deaf Beethoven who had already transformed his soul into the Ninth Symphony. Creative genius is a temporary disciplining of the soul. Genius methodically kills itself, blow by blow, until the man who mourned Lithuania becomes consul of ancient history in the Tarpumiškiai grade school. The genius becomes a human being. But could this be the height of the genius's achievements? He pays dearly for a warm night in Tarpumiškiai with a pitcher of homemade beer.

Suddenly it dawned on me that I didn't believe in this. In a deaf Beethoven with a pitcher of homemade beer. Deaf but alive. It occurred to me that this was indeed a hallucination. Real space, real objects, even their dimensions had not changed one iota, but suddenly a tiny angel flew in through the wide-open window. It was as if he flew in from the outside world, but actually, he came from me. The angel born in me covered a part of the world—the deaf Beethoven with the pitcher of homemade beer, and on the hill with the milepost there appeared not a man's head but a horse's. And white steam whirled from the horse's jaws. And lying on some straw in a sleigh is the man who mourned Lithuania—bare-headed, frost-covered, and stiff. And so what if this vision happens to be my treatment of history? I am the one who is postulating it, not history.

Toward evening that day the hero of the legend became a character in the drama of everyday life. Tarpumiškiai had already divided up the Holy Grail among themselves. Tarpumiškiai took to living again, the wolves and the bandits quickly died out in the forests. And an entirely new man appeared on the hill. He married the grade-school teacher. He himself began to teach. He had a good heart—he felt for his neighbors in their time of need, and whenever there was a lot of work, he willingly lent a hand. Modestly and honorably did he live, but children he had none.

Why did Grand Duke Vytautas set his heart on being crowned in Trakai and nowhere else? Why not in Lutsk or Kiev, or in some nice Volynian castle where he could easily have traveled incognito? What would have happened if Jogaila's curs hadn't been so keen?

Is this a question? It's clear to every Lithuanian.

Lithuania would have pulled back from the shores of the Black Sea to her own banks. An end to the flood would have come.

What? Lithuania, crowned and blessed by the Pope, return to her own shores?

To her heart, as hard as the nucleus of an atom.

I came to believe more and more that Gintė's man had discovered the unadulterated truth. This truth was like a handful of grains that no one had ever seen before. They had been scattered in my soul—but only the truest rye sprouted, grew green, billowed, turned yellow. What is it? God's homecoming? God's silent homecoming inside a person, when rye sprouts from what was not a grain of rye? Or perhaps it is the morning when one's pores open up to the divinity of man himself? I saw what lay ahead of me. And once again I decided not to give in. I wound a fresh sheet of paper into the typewriter, and I decided to begin the fifth version, like the earlier ones (except the first and second), with the summer of 'forty-nine, of which I remember only the end—that evening when our whole family suddenly began to look to the North. (Don't get the idea that our gaze flew to the green glaciers beyond the Arctic Circle. No; once it had strayed fifty miles or so from Panevėžys, it got stuck in forests where hungry wolves and hung-over partisans lurked day and night.)

That evening the kitchen table was covered in white, a bottle of store-bought wine stood on it, and fragrant smells from Gintė's garden came in through the wide-open window. What kind of man would come and drink the wine? Gintė came home from the teachers' college. She arrived precisely at nine. It was just time for the cuckoo to come out of the clock, but it waited a little until Gintė had finished crying, then it came out and cuckooed to the whole family to take a long look at the snow-covered forests of the North. For when Gintė had finished crying, she said:

"I got sent to the grade school in Tarpumiškiai. Everyone is so clever, everyone has connections, but I don't have anything."

Grandma didn't turn around but froze right where she was standing at the stove, so I remember only her back. This is my most heart-rending memory, because I don't even remember Grandpa's back, just the door slamming as he went over to see Binkauskas, who was from that North land. Grandpa reappeared later, on this side of the threshold. Gintė was no longer in the kitchen. Grandma was crouching by the stove sweeping the ashes. Grandpa looked ashen. He stayed at the door and stared at the bottle of red wine on the white tablecloth. I couldn't stand it any longer.

"Why are you drooling? Uncork it."

"Who will drink it," said Grandpa as if he were speaking to my father and not to me.

"We'll both drink it."

It was as if Grandpa only then realized what he had come back to, and he yelled at Grandma.

"You're sitting there like you're hatching eggs, and Binkauskas says that there's nothing but wolves and bandits up there, and the local militia are real rabbits."

One wolf (I actually saw him) was sitting in the moonlight on the edge of a ditch, opening his jaws where a bone from Gintė's body was stuck.

"You didn't bring him anything to drink. That's why he said that they're rabbits," said Grandma quietly.

So the white tablecloth was to remain unstained by red wine.

A few days later, Grandpa put the wooden suitcase into the wagon, and he and Gintė set off for the railroad. Grandpa pushed the wagon, and Gintė dragged along behind snuffling. From the gate Grandma made the sign of the cross over the poisonous North tree, which was already sprouting leaves in our family, blooming blue blossoms of menace and spreading its sweet scent everywhere.

It was terrifying and nauseating, especially at night, when Grandma would stand by the window in her white shirt and look to the forests of the North a good fifty miles away. Our family's whole life burrowed deep into the night. At times a complete stranger would suffer for this—someone delivering a telegram toward dawn one morning, perhaps the only telegram at that hour. Gintė wrote that the school bitch had had a litter of four. She wrote that they dug up some potatoes on Sunday. I couldn't understand how you could dig up potatoes that you hadn't planted, but later I caught on, and I wasn't the least bit surprised when she wished me a happy birthday in December for no reason at all.

It was light in the room from the snow, and Grandma was standing at her post like a white monument. The smell of cigarette smoke filled the air. My father said:

"She's alive and well and wishes her dear mother the same. You, dear mother, should go to sleep, it will be getting light soon."

"I don't believe these papers," said Grandma.

"People use these papers to communicate."

"I communicate with her as it is," she said, white as a monument. "I can feel that something bad is happening to her."

In the first and second versions, the Pasvalys episodes did not exist. Nor was there a North tree—I introduced it only in the third version. I mentioned that in the first version I set down only the truth. Of course, not all of it fitted into a dozen or so pages. But truth is a crazy kind of thing: the truth that was put down on paper came to have a completely illegitimate (it seems to me) superiority over the truth that didn't fit on paper. In the next episode I will go to Tarpumiškiai with my mother to ring in the new year. It is here that the first version begins. In time, the image of the trip froze, hardened like concrete, so if it were not for the very nature of the North tree, I would never have transplanted it into the New Year's episode.

The impoverished, though durable, phenomenon of concrete scorned not only invention but also truth, for which there was no room in even a dozen or so pages. It equated these two types of literary material. Grandpa actually did go to see Binkauskas, who came from the North forests. Grandma didn't stand in her white shirt at the window at night. Or at least not to my knowledge. But now these things are equally valuable to me. It set me free because the point of departure was no longer some vague memories but the first version itself, like a solitary rock, like a solitary fallen tree. (Perhaps this was what opened the cage where the little angel was thrashing about—the angel who had covered the man's head and allowed the horse's head to appear on the hill with the mile post.)

Having scorned invention, the concrete legitimized it. Long live concrete! Long live the first version, which began at the very end of '49, several days after the solstice, when my mother set aside a pile of uncorrected essays and said to me:

"It's time for us to see what the Tarpumiškiai grade school is like."

We got on the narrow-gauge train, which shook so much that the herring slipped out of its basket on the rack and fell down on my mother's lap. Gintė was waiting for us at the station in Pasvalys with a horse and a sleigh with a pile of furs in it. Like a real villager, she took us deep into the snow-bound forest, perhaps twenty miles. The day was quiet, and the forest quiet, the snowdrifts under the evergreens as alluring as a feather bed. Gintė was laughing the whole trip.

My mother looked around and asked, "Are you that happy?"

The horse pulled the sleigh to the eaves of the forest, and from the little hill a red stone building could be seen among the bare trees.

I remember well, it was only then that my mother said: "Beautiful forests, aren't they?" and her voice was angry.

"I've never set foot off the road," said Gintė. "I can't stand the smell of moonshine, and it seems like there's an ongoing feast in the forest."

"Or is it the ones with hangovers? Do they ever drop by the house?"

"Rarely. There was one," Gintė laughed again, "promised to wait till Miss Teacher grew decent tits, but people say he met his end, too."

"Are you that happy?"

"Happier than yesterday," Gintė blurted out. Her voice was angry, too.

The red building was the North.

It was the Tarpumiškiai grade school, built under the tsar. In Gintė's room there was a white tile stove with a clay bust of Pushkin in a little niche. The other end of the building was a classroom, roomy and cold during vacation. There was also a corridor full of snowdrifts, and in it, the school's bookcase.

I went through the whole place. I found a barn that smelled warm from animals, hay, and manure. Was I looking, perhaps, for the place where the North tree grew, the tree whose blossoms' scent reached all the way to Panevėžys? The blue forest began here, just beyond the garden. It smelled not of moonshine but of cold and serenity disturbed by neither man nor beast. In the distance a horse was pulling a sleigh with a coffin. In it lay an old man who had lived nearly a hundred years. Behind the sleigh crept a group of little black figures, my mother and Gintė among them. Though I was hanging over the fence straining to hear, I never did hear anyone weeping.

They came straight across the fields, but ahead of them came a man carrying a bucket. He set it on the bench in the kitchen.

"Here's a bit of booze for Miss Teacher for New Year's, " he said and didn't put up much of a fuss when invited to down a mug or two for the road.

He was looking at my mother and didn't want to leave, so he drew himself yet another mug and said cheerfully:

"The places my grand-dad visited. Russia during the revolution, Argentina, too, but he died in Lithuania all the same. Tough, wasn't he?"

I asked permission to go and leaf through the books. They bundled me up as if I were going outside and let me out into the hall.

Even the bookcase there was covered with snow, and groups of great and sad men huddled together inside it. Even now I can see the snow-covered Vaižgantas huddling against Tolstoy, and Maironis against a frozen Goethe. Only Pushkin remained in haughty solitude in the warmth of Ginté's room, but he was made of clay. I didn't know yet that once in a while a time of helplessness creeps up on the classics, when all that's left for them to do is to huddle together, covered with snow and frozen stiff, like surrounded, disarmed soldiers. But I didn't dare touch the books this time. They, too, smelled cold and peaceful.

The red sun set into the forest.

Country sausage, butter, and whole-grain bread were placed on the table, and the clay Pushkin watched the two sisters drink funeral beer and make faces. After we had finished supper, Ginté blew out the lamp. Beyond the window moonlight suddenly shone among the bare trees. It was very quiet. Someone was walking out there, wading soundlessly through the snowdrifts, alone and numb with cold. Or perhaps no one was there. I turned on the battery-powered radio. Chimes rang out, Voroshilov made an announcement, someone trudged closer and closer through the snowdrifts. Voroshilov wished everyone a Happy New Year.

My mother went up to the window and said, "Maybe no one's coming."

"They still might," replied Ginté. "Why don't we each drink a whole mug?"

Beer gurgled into the mugs.

"Things are spinning as it is."

"I'm drunk, too."

"Most likely, no one's coming."

> There stands a saddled steed,
> There stands a saddled steed,
> There stands a saddled steed—
> Reins in hand, I . . .

The scent of the North tree came very close. Someone was standing at the edge of the garden reeking of moonshine. The sisters were singing quietly. I felt completely abandoned. I crept off to the kitchen and drew myself a mug of funeral beer.

> Far away is my sweet home,
> Far away is my sweet home,
> Far away is my sweet home—
> I cannot ride home . . .

Now all three of us were singing. I must have been the loudest, because they kept shushing me. It never did dawn on them that, joyful and giddy, I had survived the night that the government grew strong.

———————

Indeed, my mother said as much while washing the dishes on New Year's morning.

"Maybe they won't come around anymore. The government is stronger. What more can they want?"

Then she said: "Where did you go off to before the sun was up?"

"I was checking on the animals," laughed Gintė.

"What took you so long? Did something happen?"

Gintė laughed again and carried a pail of slops outside.

I tagged along.

The morning was cold and peaceful—the first morning of the strong government. A little troop of redbreasts perched in the apple tree. I hit the trunk with a broomstick, and they flew up. But they didn't go very far, just to the next apple tree—not birds, but little red apples.

"Have you ever seen a little wet calf?"

Gintė stood in the barn doorway in furs and felt boots, holding an armful of hay. What kind of a teacher is she, anyway? "There's one coming soon. Maybe even tonight."

"Why is it going to be wet?"

"And I suppose you were dry when you arrived?"

"I'm going to look through some books," I said.

But one book was clearly missing. The snow had been disturbed in one place, and a black crevice gaped in the group of drift-bound classics. They felt lost with their friend still missing, and they were leaning helplessly. There was an air of expectancy, of uncertainty, in the group—were the classics beginning to mobilize? I remembered the nocturnal "someone" reeking of moonshine. I hurried outside and ran around the schoolhouse, sinking to my knees in the snow-drifts. There really were footprints. They led to a hole in the garden fence, and beyond—across the field toward a distant farm. Smoke rose from a chimney there straight into the sky.

"They did come!" I shouted in the kitchen.

"They who?" asked my mother.

"Robbers. They stole a book."

"They stole what?"

"A book."

"Just a book?"

Ginté went into the other room and began to set the table for lunch. My mother followed her.

"Do you latch the door at night?"

"Why latch it? If they come, they'll just rip it right out."

"Take a good look, maybe something really is missing."

"A book is missing!" I screamed.

"The ones that are left will be enough for you," said Ginté.

At night I was awakened by a commotion in the corner where my mother slept. She dressed hurriedly and went out. I saw her through the window. She went out to the barn. The barn doorway was dimly lit, and shadows of some sort were flitting about. I got dressed, too.

"Don't be afraid of her, she's my sister," in the yard already, I could hear Ginté's voice.

A fly-speckled lantern illuminated the barn. Ginté was crouching down near a cow lying in the straw. A wet, brown thing lay by the cow's muzzle. The cow was licking it. The thing was breathing.

"Isn't it bad for her to lick it? Won't it get infected?" my mother was asking.

"Let her lick, it gets the blood moving," said a bearded man. His arms were bare to the elbow and bloody. He noticed me, and the lantern's flames flashed in his eyes. "And who might this be?"

"What did you get up for?" Ginté scolded me.

"Is this the calf?" I asked.

Ginté's eyes broke away from me and flew to the bearded man. They returned to me. She seemed confused. I looked at my mother.

"Don't be a blabbermouth," she said. I went back to the house, undressed, and pressed myself against the window.

Soon the barn doorway grew dark, and three figures appeared in the yard. One figure headed toward the garden, but another caught up to it, grabbed its sleeve, and pulled it back. The third figure stood and waited. Finally all three moved in the same direction, the door slammed, and voices made their way from the kitchen to my room. Ginté's voice was grating.

"First you wash up, no, this one's clean, dry yourself with this one. What would I have done without you? Verikas explained it to me, over and over, but when the time came, the only thing I would have been able to do was run barefoot through the field and yell.

Maybe you'd like a mug of beer? Another? A third? Will you have a third?"

"I'll be going now," said the man.

"It's still dark," Gintė reminded him. "You still have time. What's half an hour, here or there? We could have supper together."

"I'm going. I have to. Take care."

"Wait, I'll take a look around first."

When Gintė returned, my mother asked her where she had tracked down a grizzly bear like him. I could hear Gintė crying.

"I always used to think about what it would be like the first time he came to visit me. How I would receive him, how I would entertain him. And now he just pokes his nose in in the middle of the night, and back he goes . . ."

"Why didn't he stay for supper?"

"Because he really couldn't."

"That's what I'm asking you, why?"

It seemed to me that Gintė seized my mother's hand, maybe even dug her nails into my mother's palm.

"All right, I'll tell you, but don't let on to mother, okay? He's here, but he's not here."

"What is he, a spirit?"

"You could say that he's a spirit."

"Some spirit. With a beard like that?"

"Why can't you understand? He's a spirit because he's not legit."

"Is he from the forest?"

It was quiet for a moment.

"He's from the forest, isn't he? Have you taken up with one of the partisans? There aren't enough men for Miss Teacher, so she sneaks out to a partisan at night?"

"You're a witch, Stasė," I could barely hear Gintė's voice. "A real witch. He doesn't come from the forest, he comes from his own house. From the cellar."

"From where? Wait a minute, what is he doing there?"

"He lives there."

"In the cellar? What is he? An ex-officer? A nationalist? Was he in the resistance?" My mother was speaking louder now. "Aren't there enough of our kind for you?"

"He is one of ours. Really and truly."

"And he's hiding?"

"He's not hiding from anyone. He shut himself away. He did it himself."

"Long ago?"

"In 'thirty-nine."

"In 'thirty-nine? He's been there for eleven years? He's obviously got a lot on his mind if he's been holed up in the cellar for eleven years."

It was as though they were talking through glass. Gintè was outside, my mother inside where it was warm. Each one saw the other's lips moving but couldn't hear a sound. And then Gintè struck the glass with her fist.

"He's mourning Lithuania there."

"He's mourning what?!"

"Lithuania!" Gintè stamped her feet hysterically on the broken glass. "He told himself: until Lithuania returns to her heart . . ."

My mother burst out laughing.

"Lithuania? What kind of Lithuania, may I ask?"

"Let's go to bed," said Gintè through clenched teeth.

"You didn't answer my question."

"You think you already know all about it, don't you? Stasè— Stasè—you don't know anything yet, but you think you understand everything."

"And do you?"

"Sometimes I sit across from him, and it's like being with a monk. I sense that he is very great. And I think that any minute I'll understand his greatness. It's as if I knew it long, long ago, but I've just forgotten it, and any second now I'm going to remember, but I can't. His greatness must lie beneath the notebooks, beneath my star pupil Kazlauskas's perfect notebooks, beneath the grammar book, the multiplication tables. You know, I always got A's in punctuation at teachers' college, but now I think I need to erase all the commas— they just keep me from understanding things—and the words— they're in the way, too."

My mother yawned loudly.

"What else should be erased?"

"The commas don't bother you."

"If I didn't know you, I'd think that this bearded fellow had driven you out of your mind. Maybe I *will* go to bed. We'll talk when you've cooled off."

This dialogue between Gintè and my mother is copied word for word from the first version. Now I think that the truth of the first version is not much of a truth after all. I could have unintentionally distorted one or another reply, even left one out entirely. I'm more or less sure that this happened unintentionally. It escapes my memory now, but I don't believe that my mother ever elicited from Gintè the precise motives for this man's behavior. Deafened by the very idea (until Lithuania returns to her heart), I tried to save myself with my mother's yawn and let slip the kind of phrase that crunches between the teeth like grit in bread: Gintė stamped her feet hysterically on the broken glass. Yes, she introduced my mother to the man who mourned Lithuania through the glass. Yes, she pounded on the glass with her fist. But a woman's fist is not particularly suited to breaking glass. The glass remained intact. And Gintė stayed on the other side, crouching, perhaps trembling with rage, perhaps crying from rage, while on this side my mother got up. On this side water sloshed into a bowl and splashed.

"So he's never poked his nose out of the cellar until now?" she asked through a yawn.

"He says not."

"Why on earth did he pick today to come out? Was it on account of the calf? Did he feel sorry for it?"

"I don't know," said Gintė.

"Well, maybe you know what it means for Lithuania to return to her heart?"

Gintė didn't answer.

"I thought so," my mother mumbled.

The further course of my plot (the man in the cellar) in no way resembles a pure eighteen-year-old girl, unspoiled and trembling. Rather, she is a woman who is clearly no longer in the first blush of youth, who, in the course of her life, has let more than one passerby out of her door before dawn, and who has set loose into the world several children who were not very good at living. I know this is in my mind, but I don't believe in it. Someone might think that there's about as much use in this disbelief of mine as there is in some hick not believing that there are satellites orbiting the earth. If we could only find a person who believes in the principle of preserving chastity in literature. If such a person is found, let him enter into me, knee-deep in the snow of 1950 by the Tarpumiškiai garden fence, and beyond it, where on a bright morning you can clearly see that man's farmstead with its hopeful vertical white smoke. Let him come into my time, all of which fits into Gintė's time, as she hurries timidly to that farmstead at night. I'm not promising or guaranteeing him anything. But if he has seen despair give off the white smoke of hope, let him come into my time, let him wait in it until the footprints from the fence to the farm become a path. True, it is a path leading nowhere, leading to the man who was but wasn't, who turned to dust like a corpse in Tarpumiškiai's memory and was scattered bit by bit into the fields and forests.

A man can wind up in an uncomfortable position when he's walking along a path that leads nowhere. He might not even notice it himself, but to someone else, like it or not, he looks like a potential suicide giving off a horrifying air of determination. Especially during winters like the winter of 1950 in Tarpumiškiai. They don't make winters like that any more. Nowadays, a man's soul can traverse snowless frozen ground without a trace. But in 1950, I trudged to the garden fence every morning, and I saw the tracks turn into a path, and I kept looking up at the sky. But the sky was clear. And there was no crust on the snow. And the crows were not predicting a change in the weather. They did not foretell a cloud that would fall on Tarpumiškiai in large flakes and would shut the book of a man's soul.

Ginté was left exposed on all sides to the winds and to stares. Though she was afraid to be like this, though she wrapped herself in furs in the middle of the night and tied the thickest scarf around her head, still the roast goose and apple pancakes for him and his decrepit mother gave off steam from her basket, and in the moonlight only her heart, good or evil, glimmered with a captive light. And I thought, everything has an end, Ginté's journeys, too. Someone will stop her one night and question her: It must be something very important, lady, for you to have trampled such a wide path, aren't you afraid of the wolves? Ginté might make excuses, she might say that this is only the first time she has gone out at night like this, but this someone will point to the third volume of *War and Peace* in her basket and say: Lady, who starts reading *War and Peace* from the middle?

I looked up at the sky and prayed for a cloud, and along it came, and large flakes fell on Tarpumiškiai, on the grade school and the church, on farms, on people carrying swill to their barns and on people harnessing horses to go to market, on the government buildings in Pasvalys, on men and wolves in forests. Large white flakes fell on Ginté's path, too. I rolled a dog around in the snow and scratched him under his chin. I tumbled joyfully in the snow, my eyelids sticking together, because I was happy that the sky had plucked out the scrap of paper that marked Ginté's place in the book of her soul.

But later, when the sky cleared up, I waded up to the hole in the garden fence, and in the now featureless field, where no animal had yet chanced to run, I found that same fear and the same sense of menace. The snow was not real. This snow was not the kind that Gintė and I needed. This snow covered the world, but not the memory on which Gintė's path was imprinted. The next morning the tracks again stretched toward the farmstead. They were like the breath of a suicide when he feels a sharp urge to live on a moonlit night in the middle of the lake, when he sees the boat floating away in the distance and surrenders to the force that is pulling him nowhere.

You who are in my time now, you who fit nicely with me into Gintė's time, I think that you have already realized that our time is a piece of clothing that is too thin for us to be able to go back to the cold, clear winter of 1950, to the story of Gintė and her man who mourned Lithuania. Let us surrender, then, to Gintė's time, in which timidity and a suicide's determination strangely coexist. Numb with cold, her time now hurries along the path in search of warmth and shelter in her man's time. He and the two of us are rushing headlong into the time when four Old Prussians, not yet extinct, stand on the bank of a river of blood, when Gediminas, his chest ripped open, moans in pain, and dear old Vytautas waits in vain for the men with the crown.

Gintė's man was once a student of history. But even before that, he was a shepherd, and when he had barely attained manhood, he wrote a work entitled *Lithuania as a Well-Traveled Highway. The XIIIth Century.* The final chord he stole from the writer Vincas Pietaris: Lithuania was still sleeping. But she, too, was preparing to wake in the strong arms of Algimantas, Erdvilas, and Skirmuntas. She was preparing to wake strong and mighty . . . Her own enemies awakened her. But she did not wake all at once . . . She took her time . . .

In the evening his mother would hand him a prayerbook, and he would read out loud: I believe in God, the Father Almighty—but what he saw was not an almighty but an aged, gray-haired Vytautas in Trakai, waiting in vain for the men with the crown. When a man waits long in vain, there comes a time when he no longer jumps from his steed but falls off. Vytautas waited in the great hall of the castle, the nobles waited, too, the faithful soldiers of the Grand Duke waited, the spirit of the strangled Kęstutis waited, the kinsmen murdered by Mindaugas waited, and blood waited. Blood, blood, blood, flowing to the sea past Vilnius, Kaunas, Trakai, past fires in castle towers, past Samogitians sold into slavery, while somewhere on the bank of this red river stood four Old Prussians, not yet extinct. But they were no longer waiting for anything. As a student of history, he was never ashamed of the work he wrote as a shepherd boy, *Lithuania as a Well-Traveled Highway. The XIIIth Century.* Lithuania did open her eyes, just in time for them to overflow with red, for her lakes, swamps, and seas to turn red, for her to kill her own blues and greens. As a shepherd, he sent that time a message calling Jogaila a dog and Queen Hedwig a cat. As a student of history, he once saw four Old Prussians, not yet extinct, on the bank of a red river. He gazed deep into their eyes and saw there the spirit of a dead brother, sadly and helplessly reproaching the living, not for his death, but for him whom the living themselves cry for with all their might.

And he understood what, until then, he had been completely unable to understand: why Vytautas went for the jackpot. Why he waited in Trakai and not in Lutsk, Kiev, or some nice Volynian castle where he could easily have traveled incognito, while a few men brought the crown by way of forests and swamps. It was not that he wanted to startle Europe. The spirit of his dead brother in the eyes of the Old Prussians had said that Vytautas the Great was doomed to fall from his steed. For he had been a centaur all his life. His human half was chained to the spirit of the strangled Kęstutis, to the kinsmen murdered by Mindaugas, to the Samogitians sold into slavery, to the rivers of blood and the bonfires by the Nemunas. But the animal half of him plowed foreign soil, reaping two- and threefold harvests abroad. But the soil it plowed was still foreign. Only when he was old and gray did Vytautas realize that all he had left were his two legs, and they were just human legs. He realized that these legs had rooted him firmly in Lithuania. In a tiny Lithuania. In the heart of Lithuania, hard and impregnable like the nucleus of an atom. This is when he should have sat upon the throne. Not when he fled from the Kréva dungeons in women's clothing, not when he beheld the green expanses between Gruenwald and Tannenberg, but now, now, now, when he finally gazed into the heart of Lithuania with the eyes of a wise, old man.

He cried that night, mourning Vytautas the Great fallen from his steed. That night he went for a walk on Freedom Boulevard. He walked from the Orthodox cathedral to the old town. The sidewalks were full of newspapers shouting about bases, the Soviet menace, and changes in the government.

In the morning he discovered that the nation's leader, Antanas Smetona, had arrived with his suitcase at the Rubicon of Lithuania's border, had declared, "*Alea jacta est,*" as if he were the truest of all Caesars, and then had crossed the ford.

This man, this former student of history, was already standing at the cellar door. We ought to be very careful at this point because it is easy to make a fatal mistake by imagining the threshold to the cellar to be an epochal station in this story, a major railroad junction that opens up the widest variety of possibilities. We have the urge to bring him to the crossroads and keep him there for an entire, hot day, wringing his hands, unraveling the ball of thoughts in his fevered brain. It would seem unprofessional, at first glance, to circumvent any doubts. But what can we do if there never were any doubts, there never was a crossroads or the right to choose? When a train goes into a tunnel, no one screams because darkness has suddenly descended; no one cries out from fright, because that's how the tracks are laid.

This man could already see his cell, could see himself in a white monk's habit. The Saint, gazing into Lithuania's heart, was in his soul. And this man conceived a desire for an actual, physical picture of the Saint before which he could burn an actual, physical Candlemas candle. He searched in Kaunas for a few days. And found nothing. Not one artist saw Vytautas the way he did. No one believed (or perhaps no one wanted to believe) that Vytautas would have the fortitude to declare an end to the flood.

He headed home to Tarpumiškiai, to his old mother. He traveled for a long time, a week perhaps. It was not quite evening when he was coming out of the last forest, so he waited until darkness fell, and only then did he knock.

They spent a very brief night at the kitchen table. He explained to his mother how life would be from that point on, and why. He saw the folds of skin on her neck quiver and felt a stab of pain in his heart, but he said nothing. It grew light. The barn blocked half of the view from the kitchen table, but the other half was free and clear right up to the forest. This was the Lithuania that was set aside for him, that he would see early in the morning for eleven years. A wind came up and tousled the rye. No one had passed through this Lithuania, nothing appeared. It occurred to him that this was how Lithuania looked back then, before Christianity. The train entered the tunnel—

no one screamed, no one cried out. His mother cried out, but in such a way as to make it seem a bit quieter to her son.

There are some things I cannot imagine. For instance, I cannot imagine how anyone could emigrate to Australia. I cannot understand the emigrant spirit. My soul is immigrant in nature, it is constantly returning, and I cannot imagine being trapped in a field of energy strong enough to derail my soul.

The soul of the man who mourned Lithuania was also immigrant in nature, and that is perhaps the most important reason for me to tell the Tarpumiškiai story.

To make everything clear, let's draw two axes. Their intersection marks the equilibrium point of the tendencies toward emigration and immigration, and minus infinity is a steamship to Australia. In the case of the man who mourned Lithuania, the axis of negative meanings denotes only hypothetical movements of the soul. You and I are no more interested in them than in insect life in the jungles of the Amazon. Instead, let's turn toward positive infinity, and perhaps we will succeed in giving it a visible form.

But I say: What if it turns out to be a grave? They buried the man, and a week later they dug him up, and he had turned over in his grave. A living heart beating in the grave is the quintessence of immigrant nature. In the cellar. Eleven years in a monk's white habit. You see, we have circumscribed time and space. The concept is clear, too—until Lithuania returns to her heart. But you ask, all we've got are the limits, where's the positive infinity? I know that you are already tempted to create a literary model of his life in the cellar. But restrain yourself. Consider what it is that you and I would create.

Would we describe the sweetness of an orgasm induced by self-flagellation? Or progressive claustrophobia? Or longing for a woman's body and soul? Would we return again and again, as though to a source, to the gray Vytautas in Trakai? What else? Ah yes, would we then sketch the historical background of those eleven years, as short-lived as the intermediate products in a chain reaction? Would we vary it with a little genre scene or two? We'll have Hans, an envoy of the *Wehrmacht*, squeeze an egg out of a chicken. Hans, like his Führer, is impatient, unlike our man's mother. She smiles patiently, and now she is a quail, luring her enemy away from the nest that holds her young. She is a quail when she cuts a slab of bacon with her knife: a hunk for the bandit, a hunk for the people's defender—just as long as they move the epicenter of their class struggle farther from the nest. What else? And so on, and so forth.

Clearly, in this manner we would reach in our mind a rather high value for immigrant nature. We would look back and see how far we had traveled from the point of equilibrium. We would look ahead and throw up our hands in resignation seeing that we had barely come closer to the cellar. We would reach the limit of our mind, beyond which the actual movements of the soul of the man who mourned Lithuania seem irrational to us, like an infant's wails, like the actions of a madman. We would find emptiness and silence there, ringing in boundless mists, and filtering through these mists, a light emanating from a distant but unusually strong source.

I think that there is yet another way. Our man, gliding freely into these mists, must touch the things that you and I understand. Then sparks will fly, and we will catch at them, take pictures of them, and without scooping up handfuls of positive infinity, we will scorch our fingers on one or another of its properties.

And then will truest rye sprout from a seed that is not rye?

So we give up the cellar story. Let the cellar be for us just a vessel, brimful of positive infinity for eleven years.

When I realized that such a man existed, the vessel was already rocking. Then my mother said: "Why on earth did he pick today to come out? Was it on account of the calf? Did he feel sorry for it?"

Gintė raced down the path for help and brought him back. And what if she had gone to another man for help—to a legal man with an internal passport? And brought him back the same way? Tell me, what, in this case, distinguishes the actions of a man with a passport from those of a man without a passport? Don't the spaces in which they exist have the same properties? Even naked, a man can move from one space to another and remain alive.

But a third person is needed to discover this, a third person who would dare to disturb the hermetically sealed cellar.

Gintė was needed.

Gintė was born at Alaušas Lake. But no one in our family ever said "at Alaušas Lake," they would say "in Alaušas." That's how I imagined it, too—Gintė was born in the lake: one fine morning the lake just washed her ashore. And not all of the lake returned to its bed: a little bit remained in Gintė, a mouthful, or maybe only a drop.

And it never dried up. I know this much is true—a drop of our home lake falls into someone like a beam of divinity. It's not uncommon. Human divinity is not uncommon. Gintė was divine; but it never occurred to me to make this thing concrete, to pray to it. It was self-evident.

To me.

But to him?

For eleven years the optics of the kitchen window determined the Lithuania that he saw. Nearly every morning, as the sun rose, he would sit at the table for a few minutes and look out the window. Perhaps four times during the war their yard had been filled with Germans. They would wash at the well, trample down the white clover, and leave. Once, a few hung-over irregulars wandered by and got a little something "to settle their stomachs" from his mother. In 'forty-two, that's right, 'forty-two, a boy went off into the forest with a basket. And in 'forty-four, before all hell broke loose, a man led a cow away at the edge of the forest. A barn blocked the view of where he led it.

Let's compress all these sights into a minute or so of screen time. The Germans lie down in the clover and pull out something to smoke, the irregulars rush to give them a light, it's a happy day—not one of them got a metal-tipped boot in the behind. Emboldened, the irregulars attack the boy, take his basket of lingonberries, and settle their stomachs after a stormy night. On the horizon stands the man with the cow from 'forty-four. Our man's mother stands by the well like a quail and smiles patiently.

Freeze-frame.

Lithuania under German occupation. A temporary form of the Lithuania that is an eternal and unchanging substance, thinks the man in the white monk's habit as he descends to the cellar.

Gintė is still far away.

Gintė is more than fifty miles and five years away.

But Lithuania's heart is locked up so that the smell of burning flesh will not reach it.

Then everything suddenly became quiet.

Then everything moved.

A man sitting on a train doesn't realize right away that the train is moving. A man living in the cellar comes out into the kitchen at dawn and sees that his Lithuania between the left side of the window frame and the barn has been plowed up. The plowed field is a cliché, and the cliché a skylark, fluttering helplessly inside my shirt, suffocating, for no reason perhaps, because what is a cliché today was not a cliché on the first morning that Lithuania was plowed, when the vessel full of positive infinity first began to rock.

A hint of life in a newly plowed Lithuania. A glimmer of dew on damp earth as the sun rises. It can form any kind of mirage at all at the fringes of the forest, it can even form Gintė, though it's still five years until my grandfather throws the wooden suitcase into the wagon and the two of them set off for the station in Pasvalys. Was that how it happened? Perhaps a plowed Lithuania that stretched to the edge of the forest, perhaps it was Gintė. Perhaps it was not Lithuania that grew green, billowed, and turned yellow, but Gintė. Fearful but self-sacrificing, Gintė became Lithuania, created by Alaušas Lake and by her man.

I do not know the circumstances of their meeting. I have never been interested in them. It is not important to me whether Gintė crept in like a mouse and quietly started to gnaw holes in the thick walls so that the smells and noises of 1950 could stream inside, or whether she rushed in with a gust of wind and dispersed the moldy air in one swoop. The important thing is that she unsealed the cellar. In her weakness, she answered the call of the legend as she would have answered the call of motherhood. A legend will never molder away sealed in a bathysphere because every legend is allotted at least one fearful and self-sacrificing Gintė to come and liberate him.

On the fourth or fifth night after the calf arrived someone knocked at the window. I sat up in bed.

"Lie down," my mother whispered to me sternly from her corner. "Lie down this instant. If it's the partisans, pretend you're asleep, and maybe they'll leave you alone."

Gintė padded barefoot to the door.

"Don't you recognize me?" the man's voice seemed jolly.

They went into the kitchen together. Gintė suddenly exclaimed: "Where's your beard?"

The man from the cellar laughed. "How could I go to the government looking like a caveman?"

"Go where?"

"To Pasvalys."

"Now?"

"I'll wait until morning. The government doesn't work nights, you know."

"You mean, you're just going to up and go?" Terror rang in Gintė's voice. "You're just going to leave as though you were going shopping?"

"Stop this, you're killing me," he said.

Every time I remember that night, I think that they were like the blind people in the story who were feeling the elephant—one touching the trunk, the other the tail. For Gintė's man time was like a train speeding through the last miles of a tunnel: a white patch of day is shining ahead, it's growing, spreading—one more drop of patience, just one more, and you'll come rushing out into free, wide-open spaces, take off your monk's habit and put on a civilian coat. For Gintė, meanwhile, time was roaring like a mountain stream over rocks. The night roared on into the next morning. The darkness into the light whose clarity (of this she was certain) would prove catastrophic for her and her man.

He leaves. Quite simply—like a train coming out of a tunnel. He goes out the way he came in. Now or tomorrow morning. And she knelt devoutly before the night that was madly rushing by and prayed, if not for eternal darkness then for a week at least.

But the man from the cellar said, "You were urging me on for two months, and I kept asking you not to hurry. Now the time has come, and you're holding me back."

"Have I ever said a single word about it?"

"Then why so many words now?"

Things looked bad for Gintė, but she no longer had the strength to stop herself. Proud and merciless, she jumped up and attacked the night, which was impatient for the morning. She attacked her man, demanding that he show her what he had seen outside his window. Was it the night he had seen? But it was night the day before. Winter? But it was winter last year. What did her man think it was that had changed outside the window? He promised to tell her when he returned, and, as if he were her fiercest enemy, Gintė shouted at him:

"You won't be coming back. Tell me while you're still here, so that I'll know."

I strained my ears to hear the spell. And now I strain my memory's ears. That night I heard only silence. And silence is all I hear now. A moment later the muffled voice of Gintė's man repeated:

"You're killing me."

"I'll walk with you as far as your house," moaned Gintė suddenly.

"Tomorrow," he said, breathing deeply.

"Tonight. Right now. I want to have you for the rest of my life."

Her man didn't understand. Then Gintė mumbled something about his life, and he seemed to recoil to the darkest corner of the kitchen. They fell into a heavy silence.

"You're telling me you don't believe you'll come back," said Gintė. "I destroyed you."

"You rescued me," he reassured her gently.

"It's all the same. I destroyed your life, and you destroyed me." My mother was sobbing in the corner.

The next morning the geometric model of the story changed. What until then had been a straight line between this man's farmstead and the hole in the Tarpumiškiai grade school's garden fence became a triangle whose third apex was the hill with the milepost.

The three of us stood at the fence and saw two black figures appear among the bare apple trees. For a moment they merged, then separated, and one little figure turned toward Pasvalys. The other followed it with her eyes. This was his mother. She waited until her son reached the road. We waited until he climbed the hill with the milepost and stopped to look around.

The post once said that it was an infinity of miles to Pasvalys. The shops and the bar in Pasvalys, the streets strewn with horse-apples, and the market square were submerged in fog.

Large and properous, the classical town of Pasvalys was as unreal as the promised land.

He disappeared behind the hill as if beyond the horizon. We all went into the kitchen. Gintė sat down at the table and set her hands, rough and chapped from work, before her. She could see the hill through the window. On it, toward the evening, her man, who had mourned Lithuania in the cellar for eleven years, might appear.

He also might not appear.

Gintė's blood quickly ran dry.

You probably felt the low winter sun turn even colder. You and I are not as comfortable as we once were in Gintė's time. Gintė herself is quite uncomfortable. She is cold and shivering, suddenly undressed in the middle of a field in winter, because the time in which she sought warmth and shelter, her man's time, has disappeared. The last puff of smoke came out of the chimney, turned into a little white cloud over Tarpumiškiai, and gradually, slowly slid across the sky toward Latvia, until it reached the forest in the early evening.

Toward evening two men in a sleigh brought back the man who mourned Lithuania. The sun was still shining. It was red. The snow was also red, and Ginté's path was a somewhat darker red. He was bare-headed, covered with frost, and lay on the straw curled up in an odd way. It was hard to see how a man could have died in such a pose.

But this is how. In the morning he had turned off the road to Pasvalys. He didn't go far, half a mile perhaps, up to a hill covered with birch trees. He trudged up the hill and sat down on a stump. At the time he thought that he would sit there for half an hour or so, not for a whole lifetime.

The valley could be seen clearly from the hill, the Mūša flowing under ice and snow to Latvia, farmsteads with smoking chimneys, and perhaps a man going about his everyday chores—chopping the heads off of chickens by the barn, carrying firewood to the house, the woman of the house calling him to dinner from the porch—sights that couldn't possibly be fatal. It must be that his soul saw a bit more from the hill than his eyes did. Through the ice it saw the fish in the Mūša, alive and free, longing for spring when they would be able to spawn a new life. In the voice of the woman who had come out to call her husband his soul heard the hardness of an atomic nucleus, and in the husband's answer—"just a minute, I'm almost finished"—was that same hardness. Who knows what it was that he wanted to finish—but if he was carving wood in the shed, then it was probably a cradle, not a coffin.

He didn't know that he would need a coffin as well.

When he came out of the shed and shook the wood chips from his knees, that man who had climbed up the hill with the birches that morning was still sitting on the stump. Maybe he's drunk, the man thought, maybe he wants to sober up before he goes home. He was almost right. Our man had wanted to sober up and go to the government building in Pasvalys.

But the farther he got, the more intoxicated he became. Intoxicated from the idea that he had survived everything, that he had persevered and could now come out into Lithuania in peace. After he climbed this hill, he was very careless. He was even more careless in thinking that soon fish heavy with roe would be swimming into the rocky rapids to spawn. When he imagined that all this was his, his heart swelled much more than a man's heart is meant to when it lacks oxygen at the very summit of the hill of hope.

The farmer came out of his house toward evening, glanced up at the birches, and immediately ran over to his neighbor's house. They climbed up the hill together. Get up, you'll freeze, they said to the man sitting on the stump. Get up, they repeated, then knelt in front of him and carefully examined the frost-covered face, the open eyes, fixed in blessing. His gaze was straight and concentrated. The men crouched on either side of him, hoping to make out what his eyes were seeing before they became fixed. Off in the distance stretched the valley of the frozen Mūša, the farm chimneys were smoking, there was nothing there that could make a man die. The men exchanged glances, then one stayed by the sitting man, while the other went off to harness a horse.

You and I have to stand by the garden fence one more time. We still have to wait out the death of Gintė's path. White death will fall silently from a dark cloud, and the path won't even have time to make a sound before the low, cold sun rises and begins to shine in blue crystals for the passersby. The cloud is already over the forest. It is rising, slowly encircling Tarpumiškiai, in no hurry to collect the spoils that heaven has given it. The doomed path must receive its last rites. One more man must walk down it: a man in light city shoes, wearing a leather jacket and a cap that doesn't cover his ears. You and I see this man walk away from the farmstead, where the white puff of smoke is missing, and head toward the school, blowing warmth into his bare fists and hitting one against the other. This is the government man from Pasvalys. In the course of three days he has managed to leave city-shoe footprints in all the yards of Tarpumiškiai, has eaten his lunch wherever noon came upon him, and stayed overnight wherever he happened to be.

"Don't be afraid of him," my mother told Gintė after she had seen the government man going from yard to yard. "He's sniffing around because they told him to. He didn't have blood on his hands, he wasn't a *kulak*, or an irregular, so why would they take you in?"

"I don't care anymore," said Gintė, all the while sitting at the kitchen table with her hands stretched out on the print oilcloth.

She was wasting away. Her blood was drying up.

The government man came just in time. The first snowflakes were settling on his cap as he crawled through the hole in the fence. It was already snowing in earnest as he stamped his city shoes up the school's porch steps, and when he took his shoes off in the kitchen and stood by the stove, you couldn't even make out the barn through the window anymore. The path died swiftly and silently, with no time to make a sound.

The government man stood by the door, his white big toe poking out through a hole in his sock. He looked at Gintė. I looked at him and waited to see what he and his government were going to do now. Gintė wasn't looking at anything. Her hands were on the oilcloth.

The government man said, "I'm sorry I came uninvited, but I came to tell you that you're very beautiful."

Now Gintė turned to him.

"What is it you came to say?"

Having heard her reply, the government man took off his jacket and hung it on a nail. He sat down at the table opposite Gintė and stepped on the bare toe with his other foot.

"Not beautiful as a woman. When I came here, I didn't even know what you were like, although to tell the truth, I wondered what the face of a person with such a beautiful heart might be like."

"I suppose you didn't come here just to tell me something, but to ask me something as well," said Gintė.

The government man smiled. He wasn't much older than Gintė.

"Do you know what I would have done if he had come to Pasvalys?"

"Would you have locked him up?"

"Maybe," he said. "Until I found out what I did today in Tarpumiškiai."

"And then?"

"Then I would have sent him to get his picture taken."

"For Siberia?"

"For a passport."

Gintė's hands slid off the oilcloth and disappeared beneath the table. So much of her blood had dried up that this was the only way she was able to express her horror.

"What kind of passport?"

"An internal passport. What other kind is there?"

"I don't believe it!" Gintė screamed.

"I give you my word of honor," said the government man, looking her straight in the eyes.

His word of honor was like yesterday's date on a document signed today. Yesterday, it would still have had force. Today, it becomes something like a deed that is the single thing carried out of a fire-swept house.

Is there any joy at all in holding a paper like that in your hand when all that's left of the property is a bread oven and a chimney?

"What could you possibly have found out from them?" asked Gintė (not so much asked as folded up his word of honor and pushed it aside). "They didn't know anything. They only saw his grave. Some saw it in America, others in Australia."

"You're not from the village," said the government man. "If you want to become a villager, you still have a lot more education ahead of you. They know everything."

"Even why he stayed in the cellar?"

"Everything."

"And that he kept telling himself that he would only come out when Lithuania returned to her heart?"

"That is the most important thing that they knew."

"But how?"

"Maybe from his mother. Or maybe there was another person who was close to him."

"There was no one like that," Gintė started.

"Then it was his mother. It doesn't matter to me. What matters to me is that they knew, and that they managed to protect him until such time as he could come out. It was for themselves that they protected him."

"I don't understand what you're so happy about. That he died?"

The government man laughed.

"That he returned. Tell me, did you understand his life?"

Gintė was silent for a while.

"Somewhat," she said.

"I do too—somewhat. And I only understand you somewhat. You probably understand me somewhat. But maybe we don't need to be so precise. You understand with your heart, but the mind—God knows!"

"He died like a saint," said Gintė.

"That he did," the government man nodded. "It's strange. You put out a homespun tablecloth. You set out a decanter of the purest water, speak from the depths of your soul, but as long as their saint is in the cellar, they're all in the cellar, their souls are in the cellar. Now everything has been written down and added up, and in a week or two there won't be any more partisans, and life will begin again."

"Do you have a wife?" asked Gintė.

He stepped even harder on the bare toe.

"My wife got tired."

"Did she die?"

"She left me."

"Bring me the sewing kit," Ginté told me.

And facts?

"Something that has happened, maybe. But something that hasn't happened? History is a storehouse of unrealized possibilities in the sense that a person has to search through them for compensation."

"When did you think this through?" I asked.

"When I had a lot of time to think."

It was the first allusion to the cellar. And the only one. A momentary roar, like an auditory hallucination.

"Why don't we get up? I expect Ginté's already made the beds."

I said that I would sit a while longer.

He went across the yard. The consul of ancient history in the Tarpumiškiai grade school. A deaf Beethoven intoxicated by home-made beer. The cast-off skin of the everyday version of the legend.

He disappeared in the dark doorway.

Twenty-five years, I thought. That's the cycle of our meetings. At this moment the end of the current cycle seemed unreal and un-defined in the dark opening of the door. Should I say good-bye? Shaking his hand now would be like pressing my lips to a dead man's forehead. I suddenly felt empty, and I thought about the woman with the big stomach who was going home wrapped in languorous bless-ing. I put a piece of fat Pasvalys meat roll on a slice of bread, stuck it in my pocket, and walked away after that woman.

The sky behind the old farmstead was bright orange. I lingered at the third apex of the triangle, leaning against the milepost that now said it was twenty miles to Pasvalys. Under this sky, the rye that had overgrown the triangle of the Tarpumiškiai story seemed even yellower. Twenty miles? I felt empty and disappointed. It's only twenty miles, so I'll drink them up this morning like a glass of old wine, in small mouthfuls, savoring them.

But, like the man who mourned Lithuania, I didn't get very far, half a mile perhaps, just up to a hill overgrown with birch trees. I climbed it and sat down on a stump. I'll sit here for half an hour or so, I thought, looking at the valley, the Mūša, still making its way to

Latvia through thick clumps of reeds. People were getting up after last night, the chimneys of the farmsteads were already smoking, the door of a house on the opposite bank slammed and its owner walked across the yard to the shed. I heard his plane slide down a piece of wood, return, and slide down again . . . His wife stood on the threshold and called him to breakfast. The man came out of the shed and, I saw it clearly, glanced up at the birch trees. I took out the sandwich of fat Pasvalys meat roll.

I don't remember if he went back to the woodshed after breakfast. If he did, then he must have glanced up at the birches again, maybe he even stopped and looked for a moment, otherwise I would have heard his voice, very close, barely fifty steps away, at the foot of my hill. Two middle-aged men were climbing up.

"This one is alive," I heard. "This one is alive."

"What is it you're doing here, sir?" asked the one who had walked from the house to the shed.

"Sitting," I said.

"There was a guy like you sitting here years ago. He was already stiff when we found him."

I laughed.

"You didn't find anyone. I made it all up."

"And did you make us up, too? Did you make up me, Wolff, and him, the other Wolff? And maybe you made up our village, Wolverton, too?"

The other Wolff was silent, looking angrily at me from the corner of his eye.

"But he's alive," I said. "He's alive and well and teaching in Tarpumiškiai."

"There's something here you don't understand. You're getting something confused. I'm talking about the one who spent eleven years in the cellar."

"So am I. He celebrated his silver wedding anniversary. He was drinking beer all night. He's alive."

"Were you drinking, too?" the first Wolff interrupted me.

Now both Wolffs laughed heartily. Both of them wiped tears from their eyes. They both stopped at the same time. The second went back to looking angrily at me from the corner of his eye while the first one said:

"Why don't you go now? Go on. We haven't got time to drive dead men around."

It was the same tone of voice people use to chase you out of their garden.

There's something here you don't understand . . . I walked down the hill and thought angrily (angry at who knows whom): what are the facts, then? Who can tell me?

In which version will I find out what the facts are?

In the sixth?

In the seventeenth?

The hundred thirty-first?

1981
Translated by Gregory M. Grazevich

Juozas Aputis

The Author Looks for a Way Out

It's like this: on a hill alongside Garspjaunis's marsh there's a large silage pit. It's the early part of June, which means that summer has begun. The larks hover in the air a long time because their nests are already empty. At each end of the silage pit there's an incline, made so that small tractors with trailers can easily drive in one end and out the other. It's not a big job, it seems, and there's enough help: two tractor drivers, one of whom is very stocky, has a knotted neck, quite stubby perhaps because a year ago another guy who's also in the silage pit—a second-year college student who has large, rather bulging eyeballs—pulled some stunt on a cross beam; the driver, who was drunk at the time, wanted to do the same thing, but he couldn't pull it off. He plunged from the beam head first, cracking his neck; the driver let out a thundering bellow, but as we can see he's quite recovered, the roughneck's just acquired more backbone.

The other driver is such a shorty he's not worth talking about, his eyes are incredibly blue, a real pansy, but that's not so: his whole head is covered with leathery scars. Not a Sunday goes by that he doesn't get into a fight, and someone cracks his head open with an iron bar or a rock.

So we don't have to repeat it later, we'll come out with it now: he's the one who'll be holding the legs of the tallest one here, that tall, timid kid whose neck is pale and very long and who's always gazing off somewhere. He doesn't eat anything during the break, either he doesn't have anything to eat or he doesn't need much. He just chews on a thick blade of grass. The other one—the roughneck—gobbles down his bacon with bread, smacking his lips.

Five men are needed for this incident to take place, so there's also a fifth man: together with the tall wimp and the naive-eyed student, he helps spread the grass that the tractor drivers bring and then drives the two horses back and forth to stomp it down. Stomp it down—these are the words used in the silage pit, and no one uses any others. The fifth guy is as thin as a stick, but his hands are made of iron. His big pleasure in life is to squeeze some kid's hand in one of his iron fists and tighten his grip slowly so the kid starts groaning. The stick then says, "I'm gonna keep squeezing till it runs down your leg . . ."

Soon this guy will be twisting the student's hands and digging in with his iron nails.

And then there are two broads helping them out. Out of respect for the female sex we could even mention their names: the swarthy, taller one is Jogasė; she's probably best known for saying to any man looking at her the least bit intently: "When you looks at me yer eyes lights up . . ."

The second one is the older one, her name is Vincė, she has four kids by four different fathers. She's noted for a scheme she carried out against an accountant, one of her kids' fathers, when he was fired from work and had to leave the meeting hall. Vincė lined up her assistants along the walls to prevent the accountant from jumping out the windows so that, whether he liked it or not, he had to leave by the door, where Vincė stood waiting with a piece of stovewood. That he got soundly thrashed wasn't so bad; what was worse was that word of the way she "made the sign of the cross over him" was on the tip of everyone's tongue and followed him far and wide.

So it's lunchtime. Vincė and Jogasė are done eating and are sitting facing the men; Jogasė is laughing and looking around to see whose eyes are lit up; Vincė is calm and content as a cat.

The roughneck guy crammed the last bite into his mouth and glanced at Jogasė, then the wimp who was still sucking on the blade of grass and standing off to the side suddenly got on his nerves.

"Why don't you ever eat lunch?" asked the roughneck.

The wimp turned red. The guy was so damn shy!

"Don't want to . . ."

"Why don't you want to?"

The wimp shrugged his shoulders.

"Maybe you don't like women either?" The roughneck spat it out as if he were getting rid of a blob of grease.

The fellow turned even redder.

"Maybe you're not even a man?" The redneck didn't let up and now stood up.

"Don't . . ." Jogasė tried to intercede.

"Maybe his eyes lights up too?" the redneck shot back, becoming even more enraged for some reason.

"Hey, maybe you're really . . . ?" He approached the wimp and grabbed him by the arm. The latter tried to get away, but the roughneck, caught by a blind fury, threw him down on the silage not far from where the horses were standing, their heads hung low. The fellow jumped up but was angrily flattened again.

"So, you bastard, we'll have to inspect what you're made of, since you won't eat lunch."

It seems that it was only now that everyone became aware of the student, who rushed over to the roughneck, grabbed him by his shirt, and wanted to pull him away. The two girls turned their backs, even though they were secretly watching.

With one swing the roughneck flung the student aside. He jumped up again, but once more he was sent headlong by a strong blow. The roughneck now yelled to the bean pole, "What the hell do you have iron fists for? Hold that idiot down, while you," he motioned to the scar-faced truck driver, "you, help me." He rushed over to help, and the other guy with the iron fingers bent the student's arms behind his back and twisted them so hard that the tears began streaming from the student's naive eyes.

The driver with the scarred head straddled the wimp's legs, and the roughneck pinned his shoulders to the ground leaving his own hands free. The boy groaned, grunted, and squirmed under the two bodies that reeked of gasoline.

The student tried to break loose, but the fingers of iron were twisting his hands so painfully that the pain made him fall to his knees. He still tried to crawl closer to the roughneck, but now they twisted his one arm so hard that he broke out in a cold sweat and turned pale. With bulging eyes he looked at the green marshes in the distance, and only one thought resounded in his head, "What can I do now? What am I to do in this silage pit?" At this thought he tried with all his might to crawl over to the smelly roughneck, but the stabbing pain forced him to yelp for the first time. "What am I supposed to do now? What is my place in this pit?" Cold sweat streamed down his face and now he was thinking, "I've only one way out—I've got to lock up and chain my eternal hatred . . . That's the only way out . . ."

"Everything's okay, just as it should be," said the roughneck, panting as he raised himself up from the wimp. The other driver also got up. He released the student's hands. The wimp retreated to the side, turned his back to everyone, and as he straightened his clothes, he was laughing insanely. The three inquisitioners dully stared each other in the face.

Jogasė tried to giggle, but Vincė slapped her face.

The pale student came up to the girls and in a voice that somehow didn't sound like his own voice said, "Take off! . . ."

And that's the whole story. The author simply couldn't find another way out: What do you do when you meet up with iron-fettered villainy empty-handed? The author supports the student's thinking, but doesn't necessarily force his ideas on other people; everybody's free to decide on his own.

1978
Translated by Rasa S. Avižienis

Rimantas Šavelis

In the Autumn Rain

A horse stopped by the bar one day.
"Give me a double," he said.
The bartender poured it; the horse drank it and ordered another. On his way out he suddenly turned his head and said:
  "Aren't you surprised to see a horse drinking whiskey?"
  "Not at all," answered the bartender, "I drink sometimes myself."

"Aren't you surprised to see a horse talking?" asked Bėris, the bay horse. The harsh autumn night glowed in his big, sad eyes. "No," I answered, "I talk sometimes myself."

"Well, what do you know . . ." Bėris shook his head. "Bored?"

"Hell, yes," I said, rubbing my wind-burned face with the palms of my hands.

"Heck, yes," Bėris corrected me and yawned broadly.

"I've never seen such weather. It never used to rain like this."

"You're right," I told Bėris. "It used to rain much less . . . Are you cold?"

"A bit." Bėris tried to shake the mane from his eyes and pushed his behind windward to make himself more comfortable. "You're probably soaked, too."

"To the very bone."

"It's a dreary time of year," sighed Bėris. He bit into a tuft of grass and spat it out in disgust. "I'd drown myself if summer weren't just around the corner."

"Summer's still far away. October, November . . ." I counted on my fingers. "Eight more months. That's the hell of it. Until then we may have to wait in the cold for a miracle. But this rotten fall *may* bring a miracle yet, just wait . . ."

"It's sickening!" Bèris shook his head, "Just sickening. Though, to tell you the truth, miracles do happen, even in the fall."

"They do," I agreed. "Wasn't it like this three years ago? It rained and rained, and then suddenly it stopped."

"I'm not talking about the rain," said Bèris after a rather long pause. Only then did I notice that he was staring off into the distance, morosely, his head bowed in unhorselike sadness.

"What are you thinking about?"

"I just remembered a story," answered Bèris after a moment. "You're right, it's damn cold," he shook himself and looked at me mischievously. I could tell he was up to something.

I'm not that gullible. I caught on to his horsing around right away. Still, I was the shepherd! I had no right to leave my post.

"Nothing doing," I said and grudgingly glanced at my herd, snorting and stomping in the pestering autumn rain. "Nothing doing," I repeated, getting angry at myself. I pulled a wad of tobacco from my breast pocket and began to lick the rolling paper. "All right, tell me this story of yours . . ."

Bèris sighed scoldingly and fell silent for a long while.

"I was in the field one day," he finally began. "Do you realize there was a time when no one was tending us?"

"I sure do. Those were the days."

"Well, let's see . . . I was in the field one day. And the weather was just like today: the rain was beating on my face, the wind whipping my back, the grass so wet that I couldn't lie down, or even rest my head. I wasn't so much standing as leaning. My mood, you understand—was gloomy, to say the least. I'll go and find myself a barn or shed somewhere, I thought. Enough of this. I was angry, you know? I thought of all the people, asleep in their warm houses. Even wild animals have caves. But there I was, alone, huddled up in the rain like a dog. I was already heading toward town when I heard some footsteps nearby. I turned my head and almost snorted in surprise. In front of me stood a mare. A small white patch glimmered on her forehead. I swear, I've never seen a mare with such a beautiful white spot."

"What are you chewing on?" asked the stranger.

"Nothing, there's nothing to chew on here," I didn't particularly like the stranger's tone.

"Then why are you hanging around in the middle of this field?"

"I don't know," I said. And I really didn't know, although I had been standing in this field all evening and could easily have found shelter nearby. But you know yourself. In this kind of weather nothing but profanities pop into your head.

"It's lonely around here. And bleak," sighed the stranger. "Does it always rain like this?"

"Almost all fall. You're not from these parts, I take it?"

The stranger didn't answer. She walked around me and stopped very close to me. Then she gently touched her lips to my neck. I have never felt such soft, passionate lips. I melted. My entire body felt whipped. Back then I wasn't this old. But I was no spring chicken either. Maybe that's why the earth trembled beneath my feet.

"What's your name?"

"Bèris."

"And I'm Whitestar."

"That's a strange name," I said.

"Yours is too. But I like you, anyway. Would you like to escort me home?"

At this point my blood boiled. All my good feelings for the stranger vanished into thin air. I was pretty popular then, but to go off with the first mare that comes along?

"What are you afraid of? Wolves?" I said, ready to call it quits. I was chilled to the marrow, and more than anything I was longing for a warm barn or shed.

"Who?" asked Whitestar.

"Wolves," I said. Do they frighten you?"

"What kind of fowl are they?"

Lion, king of the jungle! The shock almost knocked me off my feet. And to this very day I don't understand how she made it there all in one piece. Do you remember how many of those bloodthirsty creatures were prowling our forests that year?"

"I remember. It was a living hell."

"Probably worse," Bèris corrected me. "You know, after that kind of answer, I couldn't leave the silly mare to her fate. It was probably the first time she'd ventured away from her mother and run into this fierce world, about which she apparently didn't have a clue. On the other hand, as I mentioned earlier, I was at the age that, after one soft caress, I could forget the whole cold, tiring week. You should also remember that I was rather sick of being alone.

"Well?" asked Whitestar impatiently.

"We could trot for a while," I said.

We trotted at a brisk pace. The heavy, rain-soaked earth sloshed under our feet, the rustling forests flew past us, while the farmhouses appeared and disappeared in the darkness. I felt the blood in my legs reviving and my numb muscles reawakening. A long-forgotten warmth was filling my body. I no longer regretted accepting the stranger's invitation, especially when, to my great surprise, the rains stopped and the skies cleared. Above the glistening trees a big clear moon sailed into the sky. In disbelief, I looked at my friend, trotting half a pace ahead of me. For a second time, the earth swayed under my feet. At my side, with her jet black mane flying and her head thrown back in the wind, was the princess of the forest herself. I had never seen such a young and elegant body. Her graceful legs overrode the dangerously slushy meadow and the slippery forest path. Under the moonlit sky, with her feet on the ground, soared the most beautiful swan in the world. A swan as black as coal. Never had I seen such a mare!

"Tired?" Noticing my gaze, Whitestar turned her head. Her white patch was mocking me.

"Are you kidding"?" I answered, but I realized that in a few more minutes my lungs would be finished.

Fortunately, Whitestar slowed her pace, and the road started to descend. In half an hour we found ourselves in a deep valley, at the very center of which a wreath of trees encircled a lake. A warm mist, fragrant with sweet flag, floated above, and moonbeams crossed the lake like a silver bridge.

Steam was coming out of my nostrils, sweat poured from my sides, and my lungs were wheezing like a punctured bellows. I shuddered, warding off a sudden deadly fatigue. Whitestar was standing among the cattails, her head high and proud. Tall and graceful, she was poised to leap across the lake.

"We're home," she said. "You may go for a swim, if you like."

"A swim?" I asked, astonished. "Who on earth goes swimming in the fall?"

"Give it a try," she gestured, and her patch seemed more openly mocking than before.

I dipped my nose in the water. It was as warm as in midsummer! When I raised my head, I was dumbstruck: there was no trace of autumn! Not in the cattails or up in the trees. Everything was flowering luxuriously, as if the winds and rains ravaging the other side of these hills had completely forgotten this hidden corner.

The lake rinsed away my fatigue, and for a long time I splashed and snorted in its waves. When I waded across the hard gravel bottom to the shore, I felt such a fierce hunger that I completely forgot my manners. The grass was succulent and sweet, and it smelled so temptingly of summer that my stomach, starved from the fields, wasn't satisfied with just a little. I ate till I could eat no more, and only then did I lift my head sheepishly from the ground.

"Isn't it wonderful here?" Whitestar asked, without concealing her pride. She still looked ready to leap across the lake. The moon shimmered and flickered through her mane.

"Wonderful . . ." I said and gently touched her neck with my lips.

When I awoke, the eastern skies were ablaze with red light. Freshly bathed and glowing with dew, Whitestar came wading from the lake. Water splashed from her muscular legs and splattered all around, smoothing the flattened grass on the bank into waves. Her neck arched high and chest thrust out, she resembled more than ever a black aquatic swan.

"Time to head back," I said, suppressing a strange shudder in my heart as her legs touched the shore.

"You want to go back?" asked Whitestar, the white patch on her forehead sincerely astonished.

"Of course, what else am I to do?"

"You're going back? To the cold and the rain?"

"That's the way things are," I said, and I was seized with terror. Wasn't she going to say "Stay"? Could she have forgotten our night of love? I held my breath and watched Whitestar, completely absorbed in her black eyes as black as her mane.

"You don't like it here?"

"I like it. Very much."

"Then why are you leaving?"

And then I understood. It was I, a visitor from the gloomy and barren lands, ravaged by the cold and rain, that had to say it.

"My fields are back there," I said.

Whitestar pulled back her head, the white patch on her forehead mocking me again.

"Then go back. Go back to your fields."

But I couldn't tear my eyes away from her. I knew, I knew with all my heart that I would never meet another Whitestar—not in the greenest forest clearing, not in a barn overflowing with sweet crunchy hay. So bow your head, visitor from those cold wretched lands, and say it.

"Take care of yourself," I said and walked over to the hill, the lake, red from the bright morning skies, and Whitestar's dumbfounded patch, raised high, shimmering in my eyes.

Halfway home, when clouds darkened the sky and the damned rain began pelting my back once again, I realized my mistake. But there was no going back. I had said the wrong thing entirely.

Bèris was silent.

"And she hasn't shown up in these fields since?" I asked.

"No," answered Bèris, staring off into the distance, his head bowed in unhorselike sadness. "I tried to find the path back to the lake but had no luck."

We were silent for a long time. The rain pattered on the clover, my herd, huddled together, stamped and snorted, swatting the wind with their tails.

"It's so damned cold," Bèris tossed his mane and squinted at me again.

A cottage stood in a quiet glade in the forest. During the long autumn nights the village men would meet there, some to play cards, some to watch TV, and others just to kill time. The owner had once worked in a distillery and knew a bit about blood-warming beverages. We opened the door and were immersed in smoke and the ringing of voices. No one paid the least attention to us. They were busy enough with their own affairs.

"The usual," I growled at the bartender and sat down in an empty corner.

"You sit, too," I pushed a bar stool toward Bèris. "Tonight you'll be human."

"I won't," said Bèris. "But I will sit down."

After we had our third round of the usual, and I began wondering about the meaning of life for the second time, Bèris looked at me again with his big, sad eyes and said:

"By the way, what I told you earlier never actually happened. I made the story up myself . . ."

I felt something somersault inside my chest.

"I feel like crying," Bèris said and smiled.

I must point out that a horse's smile has never been known to cheer things up.

"Let's sing instead," I said.

"I've never tried to sing in my life. I doubt the guests here would appreciate my voice. Let's go back outside."

"Okay," I said.

But halfway out the door I stopped. A strange thought had occurred to me.

"Hey, buddy," I cornered the owner as he hurried past. "Don't you think it's strange to see a human being walking around with a horse?"

"Not at all," answered the owner, "I walk around sometimes myself."

"Thank God," I said, relieved, and followed Bėris out into the autumn rain.

1980
Translated by Jūra Avižienis

Ričardas Gavelis

Handless

For Gražina B.

Winter in that land lasted eight months. Four were left for the other seasons.

But the river never froze completely. As if alive, its current had to breathe air and be able to see the world. It surrendered to no frost, it was invincible, as if it were the current of the lives of all the people who had been relocated on its banks. Tens, hundreds, thousands could perish. But there was no power that could destroy every single one of them.

A solitary raft of rough logs floated down the river. It made its way forward slowly, as if it were dead tired. Driven by the cold, wild animals stopped on the river bank and followed it with fearful glances. But the raft did not care about them, it was looking for people. And still there were no people.

The raft was bare. Only by looking extremely carefully could you make out something pale and crooked on the middle log—perhaps a small frozen animal, a sign, or perhaps just an unclear mirage, the reflection of the boundless snows.

The desire came on suddenly. It took over not only his soul but also his entire body like a disease that long had secretly lurked inside and awaited its hour of triumph. Vytautas Handless thought about why it had happened just now. Perhaps his retirement was to blame, endless spare time and a sweet kind of vacuum that had enveloped his life in a few weeks. Both his daughters concerned themselves with the separate apartments they had longed for, and when he went to linger by Ona's grave, he could find nothing to say to her, he couldn't explain anything or describe the unquenchable desire that was oppressing him. Smoking by her grave, which was encircled by a chain, he awaited some sign, Ona's ghostlike reply. But no sign came. The dead tend to be silent, they don't speak even in dreams.

For eight years now he had been writing her a letter every week and reading it out loud every Saturday in the empty living room. He wrote about everything: the scent of the lilacs, the neighbor's hook nose, the contours of the clouds, the St. Bernard that he had wanted all his life but had never had except in his imagination. He would tell Ona everything, the way that he was used to doing, though sometimes it occurred to him that he would write her a good deal more in these letters than he would have admitted to her had she been alive. He would confess to her his sadness and frailty; had she been alive, he would never have revealed them. Without any shyness he would tell her all his quirks and little manias: that all his life he'd been desperately afraid of fish, that he read relatives' letters only in the bathroom, that he swore by all that was holy that this childhood friend Martin's soul had been reincarnated in the neighbor's cat. He didn't even hide the fact that he had been unfaithful to her twice. In the letters he revealed much more of himself than he could have earlier, he almost came to believe that he could tell her absolutely everything in them. But he never forgot that it wasn't really so. He couldn't find it in himself to write about what was perhaps the most important thing, that lost period of four years. He never spoke of it, anyway— not to her or to anyone else. Not even when every year Aleksys came on the fifth of March and the two of them would light a candle by the portraits drawn from memory—even then he didn't speak of it. Aleksys, who worked at the theater, would complain that it had been simpler at the old theater, but who the hell could understand the caprices of current fashion. Vytautas Handless spoke of the shortage of parts, the outdated machinery, and the hysterical director of the shop. One might say that they communicated in code, thinking and wanting to say something entirely different. They never spoke about the most important thing, the reason why they actually got together here; they never spoke, otherwise they would have been forced to remember that only the two of them had survived from the entire twenty-six.

"The message, the message is the most important thing," Bronys kept repeating with his eyes shut, "I'd make up the kind of message so the whole world would drop everything and come running to us. But I have nothing to write with and nothing to write it on."

The men's heads drooped to the ground, although they were light as feathers. All their faces looked the same, and their eyes were the same—all they revealed was the effort to force out at least one idea.

And the clouds kept floating and floating in the same direction as if showing them the way, if not to freedom then at least to life.

To speak would have meant to remember at once that which had been forgotten only with the greatest effort, that which had been exiled from the memory, chained and thrown into the deepest hole, perhaps the abyss; it would have meant to see again that rambling brown stump like a bull's head that had gripped his hand with its teeth, the frost and the blizzard, or first the blizzard and then the frost, the men continuously falling into the snowbanks, their faces, all the same, all equally ashen and expressionless, quite unlike the ones that Aleksys had drawn, though once upon a time they, it seems, had really looked like that, they had really been like that: Valius, Zenka from Kaunas, the two foreigners, Pranas, and all the others, flat, sketched with a blunt pencil (Aleksys always drew with a hard lead), standing in a circle around the thin, solitary candle on the table in his room. He and Aleksys did not want to remember, to remember them and the others clearly, and still others, all the nameless and the faceless. They did not want to, they did not dare to and could not. In silence they would down a shot, then another, they would empty the ritual bottle neatly, and sighing Aleksys would say: I'm off to feed Elenyte. (His wife hadn't left her bed for several years now. Little Elenyte, one more forbidden memory: the womb frozen by the black snow, the hands that had made fabulous sausages, Elenyte, the ant with her legs pulled off.)

Aleksys and his Elenyte disappeared; Ona did not reply, she gave no sign. Vytautas's daughters daily fought with their husbands and made up again, sometimes they asked if their father needed anything, if he could use some help—what did he have need of, he was sturdy and not especially old, he could even help others, even them, if the need should arise. Summer was at its peak, but Vytautas Handless liked Vilnius, the old, hot streets were dearer to him than the quiet refreshment of the lakes at home.

The desire ambushed him, stung him like a snake biting a naked, unprotected leg, the poison dispersed throughout his body immediately, fogged up his brain, disturbed even his dreams. The poisonous desire pulsed in his heart together with his blood, maybe the blood itself became the desire, his heart became the desire, his kidneys and liver, and his entire body became it. The strange temptation to conquer himself burned like an icy fire, Vytautas Handless suddenly felt that all of his life he had not dared to admit to himself who he really was, he pretended to others and tried to fool himself, he had devastated an important part of his soul, without which he was not the real Vytautas Handless, he went on existing like some other person—someone with a different face, a different name, a different soul. The cock having crowed scarcely three times, he had denied himself, he himself was Jesus and the apostle Peter. He had to recover himself, return to himself at least before he died.

The thought struck him that perhaps Ona didn't answer because he had kept his essence from her, he hadn't told her about his hand, wandering the world, or perhaps the heavens. Now the hand was calling him.

His grandfather Rapolas had once advised him: if you're ever confused, cast a spell, or better yet wait for a sign, but not from this crucified God, instead wait for one from the oaks, from the altar place, from the current of the sacred river, from the cry of the sacred wolf; simply go on living, he'd say, don't be afraid that you'll miss seeing it or hearing it, no, when it appears—and it will appear— you'll recognize it right away, it will speak to you in a loud voice and you'll know everything, you won't be able to deny understanding it, choose a holy place and wait. Vytautas Handless did just that, he wandered the Vilnius streets (after all, Vilnius is also a dreary kind of temple), looked at the moldings on the cornices of the old roofs, inhaled the odor of the city, which perspired gasoline, secretly listened to the conversations of passersby; he wasn't in any hurry, he knew the fateful sign was looking for him, was searching with equal tenacity, and that inevitably they would run into each other.

He found the booklet with hard covers in a passageway, he flipped through it, his hand quivering, he stuck it in his pocket, and suddenly felt the urge to run away from himself, to hide in a gloomy forest, dig himself into the ground, burn the book, because he already knew that this booklet was the sign, he knew this with certainty, just as that other time, between the barbed wire, when he had picked up a ring of sausage from the damp ground, genuine sausage, it smelled so good, Lithuanian sausage—without any hesitation he had recognized the smell of home wrenching his soul, he looked around (then, back in the zone, and now, by the dilapidated passageway) and cursed his fate abominably, feeling that any freedom of decision or choice had disappeared, that now he was being guided by the ring of sweet smelling sausage (the booklet with faintly damp hard covers); it was leading him into the unknown, into perdition, or maybe even into nonexistence. His fate was always decided by the strangest or most shockingly trivial things.

Winter in that land lasted eight months, but the river never froze completely even in the depths of winter. As if alive its current had to breathe air and be able to see the world. It surrendered to no frost, it was invincible, like the common current of the lives of all the people who had been relocated on its banks. Tens, hundreds, thousands could perish. But there was no power that could destroy every single one of them.

They brought the twenty-six of them to the abandoned logging camp. There were to have been twenty-five, but at the last minute the supervisor of the zone had shoved Vytautas Handless over by the others.

("Your odor gave you away, boy," he said, almost friendly. "You smelly thief, you."

Handless was still aware of the bitter taste of garlic and rosemary, the scent of juniper smoke, the smell and taste of home, when the zone superintendent crept along the row like a dog sniffing each one of them. He had nothing doglike about him; rather, his appearance was that of a tired history or geography teacher. But he was approaching Handless like death, like Giltinė, the mythological goddess of death, instead of the scythe he grasped a polished riding crop.)

The guards swore out loud, wading those few kilometers from the rusted out tracks of the branch line. No one had cut timber here for several years perhaps. The file of men dragged along silently; only Aleksys, when he first got off, muttered:

The sausage was mine. Elenyte is only in exile, she sent it to me. And as usual they filched it. Did it taste good?"

Here the snow didn't crunch at all, people's voices momentarily froze into ice and fell into the snowbanks without a sound. Trees that you wouldn't see even in a dream stood around them, probably a number of them were on their second century. They were painfully beautiful, yet at the same time they were somber, as if they were in a frightening fairy tale that had no happy ending. Looking at them, they were overcome by the fear that nothing else existed in the universe, that these stern and soulless trees had overtaken the entire earth. (They have no soul, Bronys was to shout later. Oak has a soul, ash can have one, even aspen—but not these ghastly giants.) The men clambered over the snow banks, each with his own sign, his own angel overhead. Bronys was being followed by his gaunt Dzukish muse, Aleksys by the image of his Elenyte, while above Vytautas Handless's head floated only the spirit of fragrant Lithuanian sausage, shining like a halo.

Finally, the abandoned logging camp lay before them. Satisfied, the guards stamped their feet, shaking the snow from their boots as if they had arrived home. One could barely take the camp in at a glance; in this country everything was inhuman, you would think that once upon a time giants had lived here. But the giants had long ago disappeared. Only the guards remained, they kept stamping their feet as if testing the ground's durability. But the ground here was harder than steel, a steel earth.

"Tomorrow we'll bring the rations," said one in a hoarse voice.

"By tomorrow we'll escape!" snapped Zenka from Kaunas, he was the only one who felt good.

The guards didn't bother replying, They didn't even shrug their shoulders. In winter no man could move more than twenty or so kilometers in this country—not even on skis, not even with a gun, not even stalking prey. Even seasoned hunters didn't stray too far from their cabins. No one could escape from here, not even the animals, not even birds—except perhaps the clouds that kept drifting and drifting in the same direction.

"Are they going to leave us alone?" said Bronys in amazement. "It can't be."

"In the Land of Miracles anything can happen. Anything!" shot back Zenka.

For some reason everyone called that part of the country, the valley of that river, the Land of Miracles.

"We'll bring food tomorrow, food for the whole two weeks," boomed the guard, walking away.

He played with the hardcover booklet like a cat with a mouse, even though he understood perfectly that it was the book, the book itself, that was playing with him, making him suffer, hypnotizing him like a boa constrictor hypnotizes a rabbit petrified with fear. It burned his fingers, but as soon as he would fling it down, he'd pick it up again, open it, for the hundredth time look over the face in the small photograph. It reminded Vytautas Handless of Ona's face: the rather wide lips, protruding cheekbones, the large, dark eyes. The woman in the photograph looked kind and tired, she was probably a champion milker, or perhaps a weaver. For some days he debated with incredible seriousness which would be more convincing, as if this had any meaning at all. Only the document itself was important, the miserable little book whose owner gazed at Vytautas Handless with kind, sad eyes, Ona's eyes, understanding him and justifying him, allowing him to act as he saw fit. She offered her help without his asking, she didn't begrudge him the booklet with hard covers, that respectful testimony, giving its owner rights and privileges—after all, she was an ordinary woman, a milker or weaver, maybe she wasn't even aware of the privileges that he needed so much, needed briefly, not forever, just for the trip there and back, a journey into the past, forbidden, dangerous, and probably inevitable. He had to find his past and look it in the face. A man who has forgotten his past and renounced it is nothing but a windup doll.

He didn't ask himself anymore why the desire, he only wanted to comprehend why it arose now of all times, feeling with his heart that his retirement had nothing to do with it, the spare time had nothing to do with it; after all, painful thoughts had always tortured him, taken away his breath and suffocated him, had howled in the deepest closed off subterranean passages, knocking at the iron door. But he had never broken down the door, had never even attempted to break it down. Why now in particular? His life had finally settled down quite nicely: a job in an enormous workshop, even responsibilities of a sort; certificates of merit and a medal of seniority; two beloved daughters, relatives and friends. Nothing reminded him of that which he himself didn't want to remember, if anything it helped to clench shut the subterranean door. Why now in particular? Why not right after Ona's death? Why not some other day or week or minute of those thirty-five years?

Having thought it all over calmly, he decided that there was no reason for it, but he felt that the pressing desire would still win, had already won over him. It seemed to him that some other Vytautas Handless had occupied his soul, but a different one from the one who all those years had lived, worked, and made an effort, harmoniously and correctly. The other one always knew how to force the world to be the way it was supposed to be, he could put his things and thoughts in their proper places, while this one, the new one, sowed confusion and ruin not only in himself but in the whole world; in his mind, the sun didn't rise in the east and set in the west, two times two was by no means necessarily four, odors changed to tastes, ideas to clouds, always drifting and drifting over the frozen earth. Suddenly the world lost its harmony, each item existed separately, by itself, and it could mean whatever one wanted, now this, and in the blink of an eye, that. But what was worst was that this new one could remember that which had been forgotten for eternity, that which perhaps had never even existed. The world fell apart and would not go together again. Vytautas Handless had felt this way only once in his lifetime—during the great council of the nineteen men (that's all that was left of the twenty-six). Once he caught himself talking to the hook-nosed neighbor's cat, asking for his childhood friend Martin's advice. He realized that the unquenchable desire had overcome him for good. He had to commit himself (he had already committed himself, only he was stalling) or go out of his mind.

"It's like a desert in my head. Camels are grazing, nibbling the sand."

"The raft won't hold two. It won't even hold one. It won't hold anything."

"Did Elenyte's sausage taste good? Did it?"

"Men, the famine and cold have shocked our spirits. Our thoughts don't belong to us anymore. Men, pull yourselves together, think of something very

ordinary. Don't do it, don't do what you've decided to do. Come to your senses! How are you going to live afterwards, if you survive?"

"It's the voice of God! Whatever comes into everyone's head at the same time is the voice of God!"

"I have many heads. And they're all so empty, so light. Men, listen, I have many heads. And each one of them talks in its own way."

"An idea of the greatest lucidity. Of the greatest clarity. A mighty idea. Great lucidity. Great clarity. A great raft. The great message."

"Do you agree, Handless?"

"Did Elenyte's sausage taste good? Tell me, was it good?"

"I'm a doctor. Everything is going to be okay, no pain. I have a medical degree."

Carefully, Vytautas Handless tore the picture of the kind and tired woman off the document, previously having apologized to her out loud (his grandfather Rapolas had always taught that at least a tiny part of man's soul was hidden in his image, it could hear, understand, and sympathize). He kept repeating to himself that he was making the document over for himself, wishing only to find himself. He wasn't aiming to become another person, or to steal anything from the woman he didn't know. The honorable certificate was only a key, a magic phrase like "open, sesame," only in the cave that was about to open (that was perhaps going to open) in reality neither gold nor emeralds were waiting for him, nothing awaited him there—unless it was he himself: gaunt and malnourished, thirty years younger, he himself in the shape of a dragon, his jaws open wide, greedy for victims, the last of twenty-six men. Vytautas Handless, the last of twenty-six men, holding in his hands the document with the feminine last name, while in the pocket next to his chest was the picture of the real owner of the document, so similar to pictures of Ona.

Suddenly it struck him as incredibly funny that he was setting off on the most important feat of his life under cover of a woman's name, he laughed choking, laughed till the tears came, tears that turned into the most real bitter tears under his gaze, although Vytautas Handless didn't understand for whom he was crying—for himself, for the woman, for Ona, or for the future journey, he only knew that no one would notice the feminine name; from previous times he knew that there, far beyond the Urals, in the former Land of Miracles, no one recognizes or remembers Lithuanian first names or even last names.

The snowstorm stopped raging just as suddenly as it had come in roaring. And all at once an eerie freeze set in. Not one of the twenty-six men could remember such a freeze—not even those who had wintered here before. The storm released its fury for two or three days, not one of them could say how many nights of terror there had been in the shaky shed—two or three. Several of the men became totally confused; this country had different arithmetic than the rest of the world.

The frost pressed down relentlessly for several days, it seemed that soon even the air would turn to ice and start to crack. The entire world froze, only the river did not surrender and the twenty-six shabby men. They kept the fire going day and night, as only a few matches remained. In that land fire and life often had the same meaning. The men mostly kept silent, only Bronys constantly repeated that they were little male vestal virgins, that they would survive if they threw even the tiniest piece of oak into the fire. But oak had not grown here since time immemorial. Bronys kept getting up to search for the holy wood, and the men would hold him down sullenly but without anger.

The last leftovers of the January rations were running out, when some of them returned from the forest with bark and pinecones and tried to bite into them. Others shoveled snow, kept the fire going outside, and attempted to dig out some miraculous roots. But the frozen ground here was stronger than human patience. At least twice a day volunteer scouts would wade out to look for the train tracks without any luck. There were no tracks, they had disappeared forever together with the guards and their dogs. All that was left were waist high banks of snow and the ethereal frost, which caused the trunks of live trees to crack. Then there was the river, as if alive its current had to breathe air and view the world. It refused to surrender even to this eerie frost, it was invincible, like the common current of the lives of all the people who had been relocated on its banks. Ten could die, all twenty-six, thousands of others could. But there was no power that could make every single one of them disappear.

They came up with the idea of building rafts, but the ghostly tree giants did not wish them well. The axes and saws crumbled as if they were glass, though the men constantly returned to the shelter, by the fire, and patiently heated the helpless iron. The iron of the trees was more durable. Even the most patient ones, sacrificing almost all the axes, produced only a small raft; it wouldn't have carried even the lightest of them.

Toward the middle of the second week the men started to rave. One of them, screaming at the top of his lungs, would constantly rush out of the shed into the unknown. Some of them never returned. Those who retained at least a little common sense were still able to comprehend that one should not leave the fire. In that country fire and life often had the same meaning. No one knew any longer in which direction to proceed, where to seek help—all directions had long been the same. They had only one good ax. Only a few matches remained, each one was secretly afraid that even those might not light. The men chewed on pieces of their clothing, bark, and woodchips. In the far corner of the shed a few had collapsed into a heap and were raving

deliriously, as if they were communicating in a secret language or were sing-
ing ghostly chorales. Pranas knocked out Vaclovas's remaining teeth, when all
he had done was mention that someone was bound to come looking for them—
after all, they were human beings. Valius held up the most steadfastly. If it
hadn't been for him, the men would long ago have waded out into the un-
known, in the direction of an indifferent death. Valius wouldn't say anything,
he'd only glance at those who'd gotten up with his fathomless eyes, which
were sculpted into the shabby face of a saint, and the men would suddenly
become anxious. But there were some that even he could not restrain. And
there were more and more of them. The men's conversation had long since lost
its meaning. One of them claimed to be flying, another told the same story
about a fox hunt over and over again, a third was possessed by naked women,
tempting enough to drive him mad, who then took to their heels. This
couldn't go on. Something had to be done.

Somehow they had to send a message to the world of men, they all re-
alized this. The only route was the river. The only messenger was the meager
raft, which would probably get caught in the first bend of the river. The men
argued and raved. They couldn't write anything, uselessly they tried to en-
grave something on the wood of the raft. They had to think of a sign that any-
one would comprehend at a glance. The men decided to call the Great Council.
This idea, which had struck Bronys, united them all for a moment, even the
delirious bunch fell quiet and crept closer to the fire. Chewing on chips, bark,
and the ends of their felt boots, they all tried to think of something with their
frozen brains,

Only the two foreigners didn't join in the general to-do, they didn't go
searching for the spur tracks, they didn't run over the snow banks screaming,
and they weren't delirious. Five times a day they scrupulously washed their
hands and faces, and even their feet, they always faced the same corner of the
shed and intently began to murmur a prayer. They were the very happiest.
They didn't care about the great message, or the raft, or food, probably not
even about life. They were the happiest.

Only after he had gone there, after he had descended into hell
and climbed out of it again, only after he had written and sent out the
first letter, did he understand what it was he had hoped for all along
and secretly awaited. He did not expect to find anything there that
had been there before, then he could turn around and go back with
an unburdened heart, paste the photograph of the tired weaver or
milker back into place and settle accounts properly with himself; he
tried, he did everything he could and even more, but fate itself erased
the evil nightmare from the surface of the earth.

Fate had no desire to help him, it was probably sitting comfort-
ably in a soft easy chair, with its knees crossed, carelessly watching
to see what Handless would do and how he would behave. Now,

when everything (by no means everything) was over and done with, he could remember it, even though it was with shyness, always convincing himself that nothing terrible had happened, everything was simple, it hadn't shocked him and wasn't driving him crazy— he was most afraid of this. The hangover helped also—it had been a long time since Vytautas Handless had had occasion to drink pure alcohol.

He wrote the first letter just after he arrived in the familiar town, which had turned into a noisy city over the years: bulldozers buzzed around, construction crews in trucks sang songs at the top of their lungs. The weather was beautiful, he was constantly taking off his coat and carrying it over his arm, always fearful that he'd lose his money and papers. It seemed to him that everyone he met was looking at him suspiciously, but soon he realized that no one was paying him any attention, that he wasn't in anyone's way, he was simply unnecessary. All the gazes said: what did you come all the way here for, what are you looking for, come to before it's too late.

But it was already late. He said as much in the first letter, still naively rejoicing that the city was so big and noisy, completely different from the muddy town with wooden sidewalks that had remained in his memory. Everything had changed here. Carefully, Vytautas Handless went over his address on the envelope, he didn't think then that there would be many such letters, letters to Ona. Being so far from home, from the chain enclosure of her grave, he suddenly felt that she was still alive. Thanks to her he had survived more than thirty years ago, he'd survive now too, for his Penelope had repulsed the young men and was waiting, was waiting for his return from the wide and somber banks of the river.

A solitary raft of rough logs was floating down the river, it was making its way forward slowly, as if dead tired. Driven by the cold, animals stopped on the river bank and followed it with fearful glances. But the raft did not care about them. It was searching for people who could receive the message. But still there were no people.

He climbed into the bus whistling fitfully, looked out the window at the skeletons of some kind of factories or power stations, having no doubts that he was performing only a formality. A bad presentiment stirred under his heart only after he saw the swamp where they used to dump piles of sawdust in those days. Even now their stench was exactly the same. It was even harder to see the barbed wire fence.

But it was hardest to go inside, step into the living past, to open the zone superintendent's office door; but, no, the hardest was putting on the mask, making a proper face: a face both solid and in-gratiating, conspiratorial but insistent. Hardest of all was to speak out—up to that second it was still possible to retreat, to flee, to pre-tend to be lost. The zone superintendent pierced him with his glance for an infinitely long time, took him apart bone by bone and inves-tigated each one separately, squeezed them, smelled them even; he spent even more time squeezing and looking over the document. To Vytautas Handless it seemed that he would never get out of there; in a moment he'd end up behind the barbed wire for falsification of doc-uments. But finally the superintendent slowly and unwillingly got up from his chair, came around the table, and gave him his hand. From that second on everything had to succeed, he understood that he had attained victory, that he'd calculated everything correctly, that the current of destiny had caught him and would carry him forward itself like the frozen river had carried the mute raft of rough logs. Vy-tautas Handless's insolence knew no bounds, but he had calculated correctly: everyone here was seeing the certificate of a Supreme So-viet deputy for the first time; it acted like a magic password, right away the secret door opened slightly; the zone superintendent, who resembled a tired teacher of geography or history, immediately went to pieces; he was afraid of only one thing: did it not perhaps reek of some dangerous inspection here. But Vytautas Handless didn't allow him to collect himself, he had learned his part well, he had rehearsed it in front of the mirror a hundred times, even though now he was doing everything differently. He had intended to speak matter-of-factly, but he poured out an entire monologue about old age, the desire to retrace the paths of his youth, said that he'd worked here once (after all, he had really worked, only it hadn't been that kind of work at all), he related an enormous number of details, pelted the chairman with questions, made idle jokes, asked that his visit not be made public, pulled out the grain alcohol and cognac as well as the snack he had brought (the host's eyes lit up), and kept calling the su-perintendent "my good colleague." Afterward everything took place as if in a dream, the kind of dream where nightmare landscapes are more real than real ones, monsters are more alive than the most alive of men, and meaningless words have much more meaning than all the wisdom of humanity. But it wasn't a dream, it was far from being a dream, it finally dawned on him that he was caught in a horrible trap. Everything here looked different than it had in the old days, but this had absolutely no meaning. Vytautas Handless visualized the old barracks anyway, the old paths, he saw the hill that had now been leveled, the holes had been filled, he recognized every tree that had been felled long ago, he smelled the old odor that had dispersed heaven knows when, the odor of injustice and despair that could not be covered up, which had enmeshed the zone more tightly than barbed wire. And the people now looked quite different: gloomily staring creatures and insolent kids wandered around, but he didn't see them at all, while he was watching the kids, their faces kept changing, they became completely different, they became the faces of others, familiar and unfamiliar.

"What're you in for?"

"For the cause," said Valius. "It's okay, good times will come for me, too."

" And you?"

"I don't know," replied Handless. "For nothing. It was a mistake."

"They accused me of aiding the guerrillas," said Pranas. "How are you not going to help them? Did they ask my permission when they showed up at night?"

"Me, I'm in according to the plan," said Zenka from Kaunas, grinning as usual. "This Schwabian shows up, we were buddies in school, he says, take off for the country and hide—according to the plan your turn's come up. You can hide out in the country, they'll take someone else in your place. By the time I got my stuff together and all that, they got me the same night."

Vytautas Handless finally figured out why there had to be two of him, who needed the second Vytautas Handless, who was doing everything differently: now the other one was cracking jokes and looking around with an eager eye, he was acting the way he himself, the real Vytautas Handless, never could have managed to act (he surely could never have pretended to have been his own caretaker here once, to have sent himself out to work through the snowbanks, to have left himself and twenty-five more men to go out of their minds slowly in the eerie permafrost). He made the zone superintendent laugh and made fun of the prisoners, and then courageously drank the undiluted alcohol, inventing ever new detail; he allowed the real Vytautas Handless time to recollect everything leisurely, let him cry quietly and honor the men with a minute of silence, an endless minute of silence, while the other one carried on and drank and almost fell down the steps and was brought back to the hotel in the zone superintendent's car. But at one point he couldn't take it, he suddenly grabbed his host by the shoulders and roared: give me back my hand, return my hand! But no one caught the gist of his words, thank God, no one understood. And later he spoke out to the bare hotel room walls, to the stars, hidden by the clouds, to the ghosts who had gathered in his room; he wrote the second letter, then the third and the fourth, perhaps even the thousandth, or perhaps none at all. He tried to write on behalf of all twenty-five men, tried to carry within himself twenty-six souls; he heard the men's voices, saw their faces, felt himself to be all of them at once, but this feeling could not be described in any letter.

The Great Council lasted until evening, without reaching any decision. They had the puny raft and the single ax. They could stick the ax into the middle log and send it off downstream. Would this be a sign?

With their brains frozen, the men's heads wouldn't stay on their necks and kept falling over. Their thoughts turned to ice and had to be thawed out. The men bent their heads closer to the fire, scarcely able to bear the heat but the ideas didn't want to come.

The men continually glanced at Valius, but all they saw in his eyes was helplessness and torment. They looked at Bronys, begging, but he only raved on, first more quietly, then more loudly, murmuring lines, his own and others'. Vaclovas was unceasingly counting his broken teeth, he raked them in the palm of his hand like bits of gravel. Pranas for some reason got the urge to take off his clothes and run around naked. Aleksys was patiently chewing on Ele-nyte's sausage that long since had disappeared in someone else's stomach. It was the Council of the Great Silence. The silence of each of them joined with the general silence, and the latter flowed into the silence of the indifferent century-old trees, the silence of the blinding snow, the silence of the clouds floating across the heavens. It was a council without debates, without suggestions. No one could find a sign that all people would understand at once. Perhaps such a sign didn't exist. To announce that they were here, that they were slowly dying in body and soul, only a living person could do that. Before he began to rave, Bronys had suggested that one of them turn into a dwarf so that the raft could support him. Finally Valius spoke and said that in such a freeze even a dwarf would turn into a piece of ice within the hour.

No one was aware when and how the great idea dawned. No one knew who was the first to utter the words out loud. Suddenly it seemed to the men that each of them had long harbored this thought. They burst into conversation, each one talking louder than the other; they didn't even need to vote. Only Valius tried in vain to make his voice heard over the din of the others. No one was listening to him, they all kept glancing at Handless. He had to be the one to agree. They all waited for him to speak, although there could be only one reply.

"I agree," Handless finally said, "I agreed long ago. It's my destiny. My grandfather warned me a long time ago."

"Come to your senses, you madman!" Valius was the only one to exclaim.

The two foreigners, having understood not a word of the entire Council, sadly nodded their heads and started to wash their hands with snow. It was already midnight, the hour of the final prayer.

The stump had already been hurting for a long time, it had already started hurting in Vilnius, as soon as the miserable, insane desire had overtaken him. An oppressive sick feeling troubled his heart too, and periodically everything would get confused: it seemed to Vytautas Handless that his tortured heart was beating somewhere beyond the confines of his body, in place of his lost hand. It seemed that he wanted to recover not so much his hand as the heart he had lost. He didn't blame the men then or later—he never thought about the horrible council at all, he didn't even dream about it (this amazed him most of all); the nightmares were quite different, but now the awful council appeared as if from underground; again he was sitting in the shaky shed, by the fire, and he couldn't run away anywhere because beyond the thin board walls there was the eerie frost and there was no road leading to people. Vytautas Handless wandered around the buzzing, reeking city, he saw the dirty streets, the holes in the foundations, people's pale faces, but at the same time he was there, at the council, he heard every word, saw everyone's eyes. Periodically he would stop, lean helplessly against a tree or a wall, concerned passersby would inquire if he felt all right, and he'd just nod his head. How could he explain to them that just now, right by this tree, he heard Pranas's voice and saw the distorted face of Zenka from Kaunas, that he already knew what his decision would be and was trying to concentrate, summon at least one clear idea? But there was only one idea: if the enemy takes away your hand, this at least is understandable; if your own people tear it off—it means the end of the world has come. He was just waiting for the angel of perdition to trumpet and for the book with the seven seals to be brought.

Vytautas Handless could long since have gone home. It wasn't easy to get out of there, but with the miserable falsified document he could have bought a ticket at any time, even without waiting in line. It had been a week since he had gone anywhere, but every day he would write a letter and mail it. Only the dead could read letters like those without feeling fear.

He felt that he had to understand that which was not to be understood, had to feel that which couldn't be felt, had to explain that which was not to be explained. He convinced himself that he wasn't going home because he was waiting for Ona's answer. But in reality he was detained only by the pain in his heart, the heart beating beyond the confines of his body, in place of the lost hand. He couldn't return without having found the hand—which meant his heart. On the evenings of his letter writing his grandfather visited him, smoked his curved Prussian pipe, and nodded his head sadly.

"My child," he would say in a longing voice, "that's our family emblem. You can't influence it, it's been that way for ages past. Even our family name is that way. My hand was torn off by a shell, your father's chopped off by the Bermondtists. I've said many times: prepare yourself ahead of time, child, say good-bye to it. It belongs to you only temporarily."

"*If we send his hand off, anyone will recognize this kind of sign. You understand, if Handless really becomes handless, the secret will of the gods will be fulfilled. You understand? The gods themselves call for it.*"

By the middle of the second week he had made up his mind. Now he gave up hope of finding anyone there, in the deserted logging camp, anyone from those times. If he tried with all his might, he could visualize a vast area of stumps, piles of trunks, and the rotten shed. He could make out the gigantic stump that looked like a bull's head, he could feel the hand hopelessly pressing the handle of the last ax. Grandfather sat beside him in the shaking four-wheel drive and for the last time tried to talk him out of it. However, Vytautas Handless knew that he would go there, in spite of everything he'd go there, he had already gone—it was an accomplished fact, even though it was hidden in the future. The future, the current of time didn't mean anything anymore, he knew well what was to follow, he could relate everything in the greatest detail to anyone ahead of time and then take them to the logging camp so that they would see that in reality everything will be just as he said.

Just when he gets out of the vehicle, he will suddenly get the urge to turn back, but his muscles will not obey him. Finally, he'll comprehend that he can't leave his hand, his heart, to the will of destiny because at the same time he will be leaving the twenty-six souls imprisoned here. He'll be taken aback because the spot will be exactly the same as it had once been, even the remains of their fire will be untouched. Without anger he'll kick at the rotten skeleton of the shelter, with a firm step he'll walk over to the stump that looked like the gigantic head of a bull (now it is looming quite close to the shed—but then they spent a good half hour crawling to it), and he'll fix his eyes on it. The stump will glance at him, and he at the stump, they will battle it out—who will outstare whom; they will contend for a long time, oblivious of time, or perhaps, turning the clock back some thirty years; they'll try to trample each other because this will be the most important thing in life. He wasn't afraid at all, he knew he would win just as he had won back then, he knew that he was invincible, he had always been invincible, especially now, when he had twenty-six souls; he was invincible like the river's current, like the sunlight, like the eternal patience of Ona waiting for him. He knew that in the end the stump would surrender and would shake with its death rattle, when he put his right hand, the good hand, on it resolutely and firmly.

Four of them went out into the freezing weather. The doctor was carrying some bandages, torn up from some filthy underwear, soaked with sweat. Formerly he was called Andrius, but for several days now each time he ordered them to call him by some other name. Sometimes he would secretly admit to having several heads. Zenka from Kaunas and Aleksys went with them. Zenka said he'd seen everything there was to see in life and therefore he had to see this too. Besides, once upon a time he had worked as an orderly. Aleksys came along just in case. If Handless should happen to faint, he promised to carry him back in his arms like a baby. Aleksys knew well that now he was the strongest of all—while the others had been starving, he had kept eating Elenyte's nonexistent sausage. They hurried along so that the ax, which they had heated in the fire, wouldn't get cold and crumble. They thought that they were going along at a good clip, one after the other, though in reality they were only crawling and staggering, each off on his own, like gigantic snails, letting out a roar now and then. The doctor wouldn't stop repeating out loud that this kind of freeze kills off all germs. Zenka from Kaunas kept telling the same anecdote, which no one was listening to.

They went behind a small hill so that they couldn't see the dilapidated shed, which was enveloped in puffs of steam. Handless wanted it this way. He was silent even when he had approached the large stump, which resembled a bull's head, he only pointed at it with his hand. He flourished the ax three times but each time he didn't chop. Zenka from Kaunas muttered that the ax would freeze and offered to hold down the hand stretched out on the stump so that Handless wouldn't pull it back involuntarily.

"I'm not going to wait for others to take it away from me, grandpa," said Handless to the empty space. "I'm going to do it myself."

The ax bounced back from the stump without a sound. Aleksys caught Handless, who was falling, while Zenka from Kaunas grabbed the ax and slipped it inside his coat. The doctor finally shut up, quickly holding the bleeding limb tight and bandaging it. Separated from the body, the hand moved its fingers as if in surprise, then fell on its side and froze. There was almost no blood dripping from it.

The linden trees in Vilnius had finished blooming, the pavement gave off an almost imperceptible unhealthy steam. He fetched the letters, which the neighbor woman had collected, and counted them diligently, even though he could not remember how many he had sent. His home seemed totally alien to him, he didn't go to visit his daughters, only went to the store and back and filled his refrigerator full of canned meat and eggs, bought some fresh potatoes, and locked himself in, opening the door to no one, not answering telephone calls.

Vytautas Handless had to think. He had to get used to himself, a quite different Vytautas Handless, a man who had dared to open the forbidden door, to descend into hell and return, a man who had gotten the urge to experience for a second time that which it is possible to endure only once, a man who was carrying twenty-six souls. He found it strange that he wanted to eat and drink, and later urinated and defecated. He found it strange that he fell asleep and dreamed of himself without a hand. All his life he had dreamed of himself only with both hands. Hopelessly, he tried to get a sense of whether his victory was really a victory—a victory over whom?—his mind was of no use now, his mind had long ago forbidden him to leave Vilnius, it could explain neither the ill-fated desire, nor the journey, nor the return. Vytautas Handless couldn't understand what forced him out on the ill-fated journey, what he expected to find or experience. Yes, twenty-five men had mournfully invited him, the last of them all, but he didn't have to go, it wouldn't have been a betrayal. He could feel nothing with his heart, all the feelings he had experienced during those two weeks didn't belong to him, they were someone else's. Yes, he had won the battle, he could calmly recall any moment of those days, the memories that had long been imprisoned broke out into freedom, but they had no power to overcome him. The stretch of life that had been torn from him once upon a time again was in its place, everything was in place, but Vytautas Handless himself had disappeared somewhere, he didn't exist and had to be found or perhaps created anew.

For four days he read his letters (the letters of that other Vytautas Handless), forced his way through the tangle of words wanting to understand at least a little the other Vytautas Handless (to understand himself), the one who had never broken away from that freezing land, who had remained there for all time, who sat on the banks of the river that didn't freeze solid, constantly waiting for the raft of log ends to appear with the sign, who kept hoping that his hand would come slowly floating on the black waters. He read and kept asking the paper out loud why all that had once been experienced and forgotten had to be experienced one more time. Could it be just because man can't live without a memory? But can he go on living, now that he has become the living memory of twenty-six men?

The fifth morning he placed the letters in a neat pile and tied them with a ribbon. The day dawned bright and clear, the partly empty city hummed quietly, several times the phone rang irritably. Vytautas Handless put some water on for tea and carefully ate his breakfast. He wasn't terribly hungry, but the tea seemed excellent. Shutting himself in the bathroom, he rinsed his mouth and returned to the kitchen because he had forgotten the matches. The phone rang again, it rang endlessly and obstinately—this was the last sound that Vytautas Handless was to hear.

If his soul (all twenty-six souls) had been able to glance from a distance at his bust, the dead body, in a few days it would have seen how, together with the men who had broken down the door, the neighbor with the fat lips sidled in and curiously, showing no disgust, looked over the blue, bloated face, the black tongue hanging out, the greasy, shiny rope, scarcely to be made out on the swollen neck, the bathroom full of ashes from burnt paper. With sincere sorrow she said:

"There you are! And I would have bet anything that Vaciukas from number forty-six would go first."

The men who had broken down the door prudently flipped through the document with the feminine name and the picture of Vytautas Handless pasted in and reservedly asked the neighbor if recently he had not started acting a little strange. Had he, for instance, shown any desire to turn into someone else, or had he commented that life was better in the world of the dead? The neighbor woman proudly shook her head and said that Vytautas Handless had been the calmest and most sober of all the neighbors and had never talked any nonsense. He had cared for nothing, she added, except for his daughters and the neighbor man's cat.

Winter in that land lasted eight months. Four were left for the other seasons.

The frost overcame everything—that which was alive and that which was inanimate. Only the river never froze completely. Its current was invincible, like the common current of the lives of all the people who had been relocated on its banks. Tens, hundreds, thousands could perish. But there was no power that could destroy every single one of them.

A solitary little raft of rough logs floated down the river. It was empty. Only by looking extremely carefully could you make out something pale and crooked on its middle log. A man's hand had been attached to the icy bark with a rusty nail. It was white all the way through, not even the contours of the veins could be seen through the dull skin. This hand was the sign that every man had to understand.

The raft made its way forward slowly, yet obstinately. And still there were no people.

1987
Translated by Violeta Kelertas

Ričardas Gavelis

A Report on Ghosts

Events of the past few months compel me to take pen in hand. This creates certain difficulties. I don't remember the last time I held a pen for any length of time. Pensioners rarely get the opportunity to write unless it's filling out tax stubs. I decided not to write my memoirs, although I do have something truly valuable to leave for humankind. I have always considered diaries a pastime for sentimental girls. Besides, it's dangerous for a person of my profession to keep a diary. For whatever reason, I have lost the habit of writing. Please pardon any flaws. I will attempt to set everything down as accurately and clearly as possible.

I was born in 1923 in Rokiškis county. My father was a carpenter, as were my grandfather and great-grandfather. There has always been an abundance of carpenters, wheelwrights, and cabinetmakers in our family, and our women excelled at milking cows. Whenever anyone's cow started mooing because it hadn't been milked enough, mother would immediately put her scarf on and be off in that direction. She knew she'd be called out anyway. Now the family has scattered. When I hear the name Šukys, I can't even tell if it's a relative or just someone with the same name. I think that every true Šukys is a master craftsman, no matter what kind of work he does. It need not be planing shelves. A master director can make directing a craft. Let's just say that the women of our family were masters at milking cows.

I've always stuck out from the rest of the family like a sore thumb. Even as children, all my brothers and cousins were carving, whittling, and gluing things. But for as long as I can remember, I have been obsessed with two passions: ethics and zoology. I plunged into the problems of good and evil from the very moment I could think. After I'd barely learned to read, every day on my way home from school I'd make a long detour to the Kamajus library—hoping to find information about animals in the newspapers. I would snoop around the forest for hours on end looking for rabbits, deer, foxes, and badgers. I couldn't get enough of them. My idol was Baranauskas, the famous zoologist. My father enjoyed hunting—that's why I almost ran away from home. But I never became a naturalist. I dedicated all my intellectual energy toward the problem of good and evil, it torments me even today. Obviously, there weren't many philosophy books in our little village. I couldn't find any in town, either. My only source of information was the teacher, Kalvaitis, and no one's quite sure how such a dandy ended up in our provincial high school. He smoked pungent cigarettes in a long cigarette holder. Naturally, his knowledge was incomplete, and I had to fill in many facts myself. In 1948 we were forced to ostracize Kalvaitis. Fortunately, by that time I had already amassed quite a collection of philosophy books and could continue my research on my own. On the other hand, one draws essential information from one's own life. Abstract problems were what interested me the most. For example, where do the concepts of good and evil come from? I discarded the concept of god immediately. The god that created the world that we perceive must have been either a lunatic, a sadist, or a human being. The latter case is the most credible. The townspeople wouldn't listen to one word of my convoluted talks. It's very possible that most of them considered me insane at the very least. In 1940 I helped organize the elections, that's why during the occupation I was almost arrested. Ever since I've been fascinated by the morality of informers. Ever since it was first reflected in my consciousness, the idea has created many problems for me. What motivated Judas? Was it money or honor, or did he betray Jesus out of simple envy? Did the traitors of pillaged Lithuanian castles act on political motives or personal ones? Do informers spin the wheel of history forward or do they stop it? Later I analyzed informers more carefully. I almost succeeded in understanding their souls.

Vingelis, the mayor of the village, protected me from the occupation army. He knew German and had a very nimble tongue. He was a very clever and a truly dear person. It was especially regrettable that he was deported to our country's eastern regions in 1948. But the fate of one person is irrelevant in the process of history. I quite understand that the same is true in my case as well.

After the war my brothers scattered in all directions, while I stayed behind in the village to help establish order. The summers

were not too bad, the wheat harvest was good, the potatoes grew bigger than normal. I was a grown man already, but I was still interested
in the wildlife of the forest. Some beavers had settled near our village. I spent a lot of time observing them: how they felled trees, how
comically they tiptoed around. They did frighten me a bit, though:
every time they slammed their tails against the water, I thought I was
being shot at again. During the operation I found myself a girl named
Julè in the next village. That same night she became my first woman.
I was completely naive in matters of love, but the masculinity of my
shotgun propped up against the bedpost inspired me. I've never noticed any aberrations in my sexual behavior. My first woman im-
pressed herself upon my memory more than any other. Julè's eyes
were an amazing cornflower blue. I would lead her around the meadows, I would tell her about the beavers and about good and evil.
Somehow, I felt responsible for her: she had lost her father and two
brothers on that night. She was always silent, even during the sexual
act. In 1946 I was finally called to real, serious work.

At first I had difficulties adapting to my new job. I hardly had
any time to enjoy the wildlife of the forest because I was up to my
ears in work. However, I found plenty of time for practical investigations into good and evil. And abundant sustenance for generalized
conclusions. I was virtually enslaved at that time by the problem of
responsibility for one's actions. And the problem of guilt. Every case
was uniquely subtle. My colleagues envied me because everyone I
took on confessed to being guilty. Every single one. No exceptions.
Of course, the confessions didn't mean much, but at that time I had
already begun to formulate the outlines of my ethical theories. There
were things I had to prove to myself. I broke no bones, nor did I kick
in any kidneys. They all confessed their guilt on their own. Each one
of us is guilty, but people under suspicion are doubly guilty, and people in custody are triply guilty. One simply has to realize this for oneself. I remember one case in particular. An elderly man was accused
of writing leaflets. His only defense was that he was illiterate, and
therefore *could not* write leaflets. And he truly was illiterate. I don't
know how my colleagues would have handled this case, but I demonstrated great perseverance and will. I taught him how to write,
thus proving that he *could* have written the proclamations. He himself understood that he was guilty. He truly was guilty. Like everyone
else. Just like myself. If, let's say, they had apprehended me, I would
have become guilty, too. I had committed numerous small infractions. Tiny, tiny ones, almost intangible, unnoticeable ones. Tiny as
ants. As microbes. Yes, but the sum total of tiny infractions is very
tangible. Mathematical analysis teaches us this. From my first glance

into a person's eyes, I could see his guilt. I very much wanted to meet just one innocent person, but I never did. In 1949 I was transferred to Vilnius as a reward for my good work.

At that time I was especially tormented by the problem of recompense. Although I had discarded the concept of god, I still believed that life compensates us for our works. I all but proved this mathematically. The balance of good and evil requires it. I waited impatiently for my recompense, but no concrete answer ever came. I became especially distressed after a secret business trip to the eastern regions, the purpose and results of which I still cannot reveal today. For the first time in my life I began to doubt the correctness of my chosen path. Worse yet, I began to doubt some of the claims of my ethical theories. I had to have a clear answer—how would the world reward me? Prestige, good living conditions, and respect were not enough for me. I wanted more for my efforts. I began having trouble sleeping at night, and I wandered the streets aimlessly. The city oppressed me. I missed the beavers, the foxes, and the rustling of trees. Foxes, at least, appeared on women's shoulders, in the guise of collars. Vilnius was full of dead foxes. I couldn't stand this city, not until I met Marija. Everyone had told me she was the most beautiful woman in Vilnius. She seemed the most beautiful woman in the world to me. Even when I was absorbed in the problems of good and evil, I had always worshipped beauty. I realized that she was my appointed reward. Shortly afterward Marija ended up in our office by mistake. I couldn't allow them to accuse her of antigovernment activities without evidence. I told her this myself and she understood me. She became a wonderful wife. Our family was ideal. Not every woman will understand and support a husband who doesn't come home for days at a time and, when he does return, tumbles into bed and doesn't want anything—just sleep. She felt for me, and I felt for her. Together we raised two wonderful sons, born a year apart. We were truly happy. I even put my ethical theory aside. I couldn't theorize when life was so wonderful. As I watched my children take their first steps, my eyes filled with tears. The world bestowed on me everything I could possibly desire. My path was one of victories, of large and small blessings. I had an enjoyable job, a woman I adored, handsome, intelligent children. I was formulating a theory that would leave a mark on the history of philosophical thought. The world loved me. At that time I was interrogating a doctor named Ginzburgas. He had all the marks of a poisoner. Unfortunately, he didn't know the slightest thing about poisons. I was obliged to teach him, thoroughly and tediously, but he could never remember anything. Perhaps he was pretending not to remember. My task was clear and concrete. I was to prove beyond any doubt that he was a poisoner. He had to understand this himself. But he was as stubborn as a mule. It was very difficult, and only my sons could keep me calm. I watched them play for hours on end. They had just started learning to talk. We had a veritable zoo at home: two parrots, a hedgehog, a turtle, three marmots, and a dog. I was very disappointed that we couldn't keep a fox or a beaver. Nonetheless, by interacting with these lesser animals, my children learned to appreciate nature. While I was meditating about nature and ethics, it occurred to me that Ginzburgas also had two sons. He would not have been able to bear it if some kind of accident were to befall them. It's really too bad that my victory over Ginzburgas was totally unnecessary.

I remember that case especially well because immediately after it I started to devote special attention to my ethical theory. It doesn't tie in with this report directly; therefore, I won't expand upon it here, although a few aspects of it unintentionally find their way into the sentences of this report. It was taking up almost all my time. It practically pushed all other thoughts from my mind. I even neglected my job, that's probably why I was transferred to a lower-level position in 1956. I was never promoted again. I ended up farther away from actual people and closer to paperwork. This, of course, had its own advantages. I was able to generalize from more than just my own personal experience. As I leafed through the dusty papers, the people described would appear before my eyes. I enjoyed imagining their past and present. In the course of time I would understand them inside out. I would know them better than they ever knew themselves. I liked to imagine the rest of their lives. I sometimes think that I could have been a writer, more than likely. I tried to imagine what they were doing now. This nourished my theory of moral compensation. I often remembered the experience of the aforementioned business trip to the eastern regions. All these thoughts, as they appeared in my consciousness, would provoke all kinds of new questions. When a person ceases to be a person, can one accurately describe the limits of this change? Is the predisposition to give up one's ideals, goodness, and beauty at the first sign of danger innate or is it acquired? Were there many nameless Giordano Brunos, or did they go to the fire knowing that this was the only way to make it into history? Were all the great inquisitors converts like Torquemada? Is "The Grand Inquisitor" a profession or a vocation?

Things went well for me for a while. Only my theory was taking shape with difficulty. I worked day and night, risking my health. All my life I was in perfectly good health. Preventive check-ups were a waste of time. I think that my good health was also the world's recompense. If the world wants to get rid of someone, it makes them sick or just simply does away with them. My own sons prove this presupposition. The older one grew up with strong convictions and excellent health. The younger doubted everything; he would question everything, that's why he succumbed to many childhood diseases and grew up rather sickly. Doubt eats at a person more ferociously than cancer. Order heals better than any medicine could. That which upholds order and destroys doubt is moral. My whole life I acted altogether morally. I succeeded in learning that my younger colleagues secretly called me "Mole." I think that the etymology of this term is clear: moles dig deep. It's the absolute truth. I've never coasted along the surface. The same name-callers frequently asked my advice. Even my higher-ranked colleagues. They'd often say, "What would we do without you?" In 1976 I was retired.

Marija was not only an ideal wife but also an ideal mother. After I'd arranged for apartments for the children, she moved out to live with our younger son. He needed help with every step he took. Marija visited me once a week, conscientiously performing her wifely duties. Although I was still young and bustling with energy, I did not look for another job. I rejoiced in the opportunity to dedicate myself exclusively to my ethical theory. As a retirement gift, I requested a new apartment. My old one was very good but too much out of the way. I didn't have any neighbors. I requested an apartment in a bigger building. My request was granted. I acquired abundant neighbors and was able to continue my investigations. I was seeking interesting, extraordinary individuals. Unfortunately, I was disappointed once again. All my neighbors were guilty and fearful of their recompense. I could see the guilt in their eyes. But I am forgiving, and besides, this no longer concerned me—I was retired. All my life I had searched for the innocent person, someone whom upon our first encounter in my office I could have released immediately. Unfortunately, I never found such a person. It's possible that such a person doesn't even exist. The neighborhood soon found out about my past profession. Immediately I sensed respect and even submissiveness in my neighbors' behavior. Whenever I passed by everyone would fall silent out of respect right away. This disturbed me a bit—I have always been democratic. I was living alone, my sons hardly ever visited me. It must be a family trait to be so independent. One thing still baffled me. My younger son, for some reason, took his wife's last name when they were married. Nor could I understand a certain neighborhood expression—I learned that the teenagers secretly called me Muravjov. I don't understand. Neither my actions nor my surname have anything to do with *muravei*,* the Russian word for ant. The other phenomena in the neighborhood were pretty much clear to me. People will be people. I missed active work. My mind, of course, was occupied with my ethical theory, but my body longed for activity. I was forced to take long daily jogs in the nearby pine grove.

My calm, orderly life lasted until the past few months. This spring a baffling nostalgia took me by surprise. I began to long for something. This is a very unhealthy feeling. I have heart symptoms and something like heartburn, my fingertips sweat, and my right foot feels numb. No logical analysis helped me get a grip on what it was I was longing for. I visited my old workplace, I socialized with my old colleagues. But it didn't help in the least. I argued with my sons and turned to drink. That didn't help either. I visited my birthplace and wandered along the paths of my youth. Not even a hint of the beavers remained. The badgers had also disappeared. The only deer I managed to find was lame. Perhaps I am getting old. The nostalgia weighed on me even more. I even considered a trip to the eastern regions where I had gone for that secret business trip. I discarded the idea immediately as impossible. It's not easy to decipher the world's structure. Theories spring up from practice. And theory can sometimes have practical applications. I concentrated on my unfinished ethical theory to see what it would advise me.

A long and painful contemplation helped. My theory dictated that I continue to administer good. Bring goodness to humanity. My theory affirmed that I was actually yearning for goodness. Unfortunately, I hadn't adequately defined goodness. I attributed this shortcoming to the conditions at my old job, but in my new surroundings my ideas became somewhat muddled. Good is relative. I began seriously to doubt whether it was right for me to be good to the guilty. A myriad of questions got confused in my head once again. Is it right to watch helplessly as your friend dies of gangrene? Might it not be better to kill him? Is it right to convince a person that the course of history is unalterable, to prove to him that he is destined to disappear, so he might as well get out of the way of history's machine right away? Is the life of an innocent child as valuable as Dostoyevski said?

That's when children happened to catch my attention. Unknowingly, children frequently help solve the most difficult problems. I

---

*Mikhail Muravjov, known as the Hangman, was sent to Lithuania by the czar to put down the 1863 rebellion and was notorious for his bloodthirstiness—trans.

noticed that our neighborhood's younger generation lacked interesting games. I decided to help them. Apparently, the knack for craftsmanship still lay dormant in the Šukys family genes. I had never before tried my hand at carpentry, but in eleven days I had built a lovely storybook house. Actually, during the last four days two neighbors helped me. My nostalgia subsided immediately. Nevertheless, the next day I felt sick. Unfortunately, this did not arouse my suspicions. I thought that I had simply overextended myself. This was a dangerous naïveté and a disastrous mistake. Four days later I was quite ill. For someone who has never been sick every illness seems horrible, but mine was truly strange. My temperature would not go down for seventeen days. My physician only frowned and shrugged his shoulders. My liver, kidneys, and bladder hurt. My head was fine, but somehow it did not connect events. Most likely because, although I was ill, I had never been so happy. I felt blessed, fortunate. Through the window I watched the children crawling in and out of my little house. I felt even better than I had in my youth watching the beavers. I convalesced slowly, yet my wife visited me as usual—only once a week. For that reason, for the fourth time in our lives we quarreled. Unfortunately, I did not attach enough significance to this, either.

After I got better, quite unexpectedly I began to take pleasure in looking in the mirror. Certainly, I had always combed my hair and shaved in front of the mirror, but I would look only at my hair, my beard, and perhaps my face. I had never looked carefully at my eyes. I came to the conclusion that they were really beautiful: gray irises with tiny golden dots encircling them. But it wasn't the beauty of my eyes that stunned me. While looking into the mirror, I realized something amazing. The expression on my face showed that I was innocent. I, myself, was the innocent person that I had been searching for all my life.

For six days I could not come to my senses. I kept going to the mirror and staring into my eyes. There was no longer any doubt. I was innocent. There was no need to worry. I could relax and end my days with my head held high. Aristotelian logic and my gray eyes with the golden speckles confirmed this. But for some unknown reason nostalgia began to gnaw at me again, stronger than before. It ate at me like a beast. It ate at my chest and left a bitterness in my mouth. It coiled itself into my veins and crawled to the very tips of my fingers. It gnawed on several parts of my body at the same time. At night I couldn't sleep because it rolled around in my stomach, nauseating me. The calmer I tried to to feel, the more I believed in my divine innocence, the more furiously the creature devoured me. I became determined, come hell or high water, to find Julė, my first woman.

For twelve days I felt like a real detective. It wasn't easy to find Julė. I had to muster all my talents. She had changed her name three times. Her traces had totally disappeared twice, and then they reappeared in a completely unexpected place. I found her in a remote old folks' home. Julė looked quite withered away, although she was only sixty-three. Her gaze was still the same cornflower blue. She didn't recognize me. She called me Monsieur Bureau. Her eyes continually oozed pus, and the corners of her mouth leaked saliva. She chattered endless nonsense, at times breaking into French. I don't know a word of French. But I did everything I could. The home was filthy and smelled. I found a place for her in a reputable retirement home. It didn't seem like a good idea to leave money with her, so I arranged for a trustworthy doctor to take especially good care of her and to bill me once a month. Human ruins are not a pretty sight. I took care of everything and hurried home. The world had repaid Julė for her life, it was not right for me to meddle. I realized that I had behaved inappropriately. Nevertheless, the nostalgia disappeared without a trace. I felt peculiarly relieved. My arms and legs were as light as feathers. I felt as if I could fly. But I didn't rejoice overly much. I was secretly waiting for a new illness to overpower me. A mysterious intuition appeared, perhaps a kind of understanding of the very essence of things. I wasn't wrong. The nameless illness assaulted me within three days. This time it made my bones ache, my pancreas and spine hurt. My body was protesting against my behavior. True, my temperature didn't rise. My blood chemistry was as normal as could be. Tests exhibited no pathology. Nevertheless, the severe illness lasted for thirty-two days. I began to question seriously whether it was my body that was ill and not my so-called soul. Suddenly I got well. After this illness I quite unexpectedly became impotent. My wife practically stopped visiting me altogether.

My naive blindness ended. I began to understand the connection between phenomena. I was overcome with horror as I watched the storybook house that I had built. The house represented the beginning of all my troubles. It was responsible for my intermittent liver aches; once they subsided, my kidneys would begin to hurt. I had made a horrible mistake. I wanted to knock down the house, hoping to cure myself this way. After long meditation I discarded this idea. The little house itself wasn't to blame, it was the fact of its construction. Julė wasn't to blame, it was my efforts at helping her. I had made a major mistake. The foundations of my ethical theory were shaky. I had made a mistake, and the world turned its back on me immediately. All my energy evaporated, I could no longer jog through the pine grove. Contemplative analysis did not help one bit. Sheer coincidence saved me. An old colleague came to visit me. People of our profession never visit one another unless it's for a good reason. My colleague had come to inquire about my younger son. He intended to appoint him chief administrator and to send him on a trip abroad. Like it or not, I was forced to remember that my younger son no longer called himself Šukys. I didn't catch on right away as to why he was asking me about someone named Staugaitis. I told him the truth about Staugaitis—that he had strange convictions, and he had never given me any reason to trust him. Besides that, he was the silent type, and still waters run deep. I couldn't lie. All my life I had been extremely honest. My ethical theory dictated that I act this way. My colleague thanked me sincerely. After he left, I was overcome with remorse. I knew well that my younger son would not be offered the prestigious position. I knew well that his career was finished, and he wouldn't understand why. All his life he would not understand anything. And so he'd go to his death without understanding. He'd probably blame fate. I worried more and more and went to bed quite ill. In the morning my health suddenly improved. Neither my liver nor my kidneys hurt any more, I even breathed easier. The next night I dreamed about two enticing young women. For a long time I tried to choose one of them, but they fought ferociously over me. Neither would give in. Frustrated, I gave myself to both of them together. In the morning my sheet was stained with spots of indubitable origin. This inspired me. I was determined to complete my ethical theory at once. There was plenty of material. The events of the past few months had crossed the final t.

Unfortunately, there are at least two sides to every story. My nostalgia—my so-called nostalgia—swept over me again like a wave. It knocked me down, it covered me with salt water and suffocated me. I felt as strong and healthy as ever, but at the same time I was half-dead. I couldn't sit. I couldn't lie down. I couldn't even stand— all I could do was pace from one corner to the other. I felt as if an outsider were pushing me out of myself and grabbing my skin for shelter. I realize that sounds vague, but how else can I express it? I wracked my brains, what to do? I knew that I was killing myself, but I couldn't do anything else. I wanted one thing only—to escape from this nostalgia, this alleged nostalgia, as quickly as possible. I suspected more and more that this was not simply nostalgia.

A young couple had caught my attention long ago. They were renting a room from a fat, quarrelsome landlady. It was painful to watch them. In the evening the tall, slim man would rush to the yard every fifteen minutes for a smoke. Regardless of the weather. His wife's girlish, golden-haired, and full-breasted beauty diminished daily. It was clear that their living conditions were destroying the family. I considered the matter for two days, but I couldn't stand it any longer. I invited the young man over and presented my suggestion. There were two extra rooms in my apartment that I hardly used. The other two were quite sufficient for me. I suggested they move in with me. No conditions. No rent. I promised to convert the apartment into two in the near future and to give one to them. Listening to myself, I could hardly believe what I was saying. I never thought that I would have done something like this. Like Job, I was determined to give away my only overcoat. I was prepared to settle them in my apartment and to sleep on park benches myself. To my surprise, the young man declined my offer. Categorically. And he glared at me with wolf's eyes. He left without saying good-bye. I thought my nostalgia would completely suffocate me. I went to bed in a cold sweat, but I awoke light and happy. The so-called nostalgia was gone without a trace. This bolstered my assumption that what's most important is the intention and the deed, even if it's not carried out. Anxiously, I awaited my recompense. I was prepared for anything: a heart attack, kidney failure—but not for what befell me.

That day the ghosts made their first visit.

They came at twilight. They were male. One was terribly large, approximately two meters, fifty centimeters in height—it practically touched the ceiling. The other was terribly short, not even one meter in height. I knew immediately that they were ghosts. Perhaps it was because of their abnormal height. Right away the small one rushed to rummage through my drawers impudently. Thank God, I keep my ethical theory in my head. The large one behaved relatively modestly, he just grabbed a crystal vase and went to the kitchen for a drink of water. Both were dressed in ordinary work clothes. I felt as if I'd seen them before. For the first three minutes I was in shock. Then I began to wonder whether I wasn't dreaming. The minute I had that thought, the ghosts hastened to assure me that I wasn't dreaming. Until that moment they had been silent—I was stunned again. The midget pushed the drawers back into place and mumbled that a true ethical theory must be valid in the afterlife. He also babbled something else about the dead and the second coming. I finally came to my senses, but I didn't utter a sound, I just aimed the ashtray at the midget. I must have thought that it would shoot straight through him; instead, it bounced off his head and shattered into bits. The large one pleaded with me phlegmatically not to start shooting with the pistol engraved with my name because the bullets might harm the apartment. But they wouldn't hurt the ghosts. The whole time the midget was making faces. At first I couldn't figure out what to do. Then a way out occurred to me. I stood up and went out into the yard. The ghosts did not follow me. I smoked four cigarettes and went back into the apartment. The ghosts were no longer in my house.

It is worth noting that I was less dumbstruck than might be expected. I suppose I was unconsciously expecting something like this. My tired brain, little by little, began to make sense of things. I had invited this response by single-handedly attempting to correct the inequalities of this world.

The reasons for the wicked world's response could be the following:

1. my altruism must have disrupted the world's stability: there are no storybook houses in other yards, other looney lady pensioners go on living in their filthy rooms, it is forbidden to take on the work of God the order-maker;

2. the so-called good that I was doing was actually evil; once they've gotten their storybook house the children will want God knows what else; Julė, after being cared for so diligently, will come to her senses and understand her situation—it's better to have nothing and to know nothing;

3. strictly regulated good is indeed good; until I retired, life blessed only me;

4. people like me are rare; the ghosts, too, wanted goodness from me;

5. I suffered for my innocence; the world detests the innocent; if you are innocent, you should pretend you're guilty anyway;

6. people of my profession are not allowed to retire;

7. my ethical theory is flawed—this can't be, I add this point only out of respect for Aristotelian logic.

So a new stage of my life began, my war with ghosts. First I tried to stop doing good deeds, but I couldn't. Lately I've been spending all my time letting women go ahead of me in line, and I carry shopping baskets for old ladies. Good deeds appease my nostalgia, my alleged nostalgia, which still starts to gnaw at me around noon. I rush out into the street, hurriedly carry a few old ladies' shopping baskets back and forth, and return home to await the ghosts. It's getting too cold to dawdle in the yard. Usually, all kinds of invalids come to visit. Their colors are often quite pleasant—blue, green, pink. They come carrying things under their arms: an arm, a leg, and sometimes even a head. They don't say anything, they just sit down in front of me and fix their quiet, vengeful eyes on me. I recognize some of them. Sometimes I offer them cigarettes. I pleaded with the young couple four more times to move in with me. Each time the fellow grew more and more enraged, and last week I learned that they had suddenly moved who knows where.

The nighttime ghosts are completely different. They chatter incessantly, interrupting my sleep. Mockingly they call me Jerry. My name is Jeronimas. They often drink all my beer and smoke all my cigarettes. And still they taunt me: "Why, Jerry won't miss them." I have no concept of how to behave toward them. I've grown somewhat disillusioned with my ethical theory: it doesn't really analyze ghosts at all. Nevertheless, I continue to pursue my research. I think the theory can still be expanded. For now I have established a few incontrovertible facts. There are never more than seven ghosts at a time. Once I asked them to bring along a few of the beavers from my childhood. They were not able to bring any beavers. Their external appearance is very normal. To make sure of this I bored a hole in the bathroom door: the ghosts urinate and defecate often. It's not only the dead who come to visit. Occasionally, the ghosts of my current acquaintances come by, although they themselves are as healthy and alive as can be. The ghosts can do me no physical harm. They just appear, that is all.

In the incomprehensible scheme of things in the universe the ghosts also have their place. This I understand. What's more difficult to understand is why they appear only to me. I don't feel like such a distinguished or unique personality. I am an ordinary worker bee. It remains for me to prove that, quite the contrary, the ghosts do not appear only to me. Perhaps others hide this fact. Someone must be the first to speak out. For this reason I am writing this report.

I've succeeded in documenting that the ghosts appeared when I began doing the so-called good deeds of my own volition. The world, which until then had loved me, suddenly began to try to undo me. Apparently, unrestrained good threatens the world's balance. True good is predetermined and substantiated from the beginning. No anarchy is allowed here. It just invites illness and ghosts.

Regarding the ghost situation, I have a few more observations:

1. because the ghosts inevitably appear not only to me, someone must have discovered a means of defense against them; I humbly request that after evaluating my circumstances, such a person might introduce me to his methods;

2. absolutely everyone hides their ghosts; therefore, my report will expose a completely new aspect of life after retirement;

3. the presence of ghosts has been established; however, a means of defense against them remains undiscovered; in this case I am prepared to continue analyzing their lives and behavior, thus serving the common good;

4. my so-called nostalgia attracted the ghosts; it is crucial to examine it; perhaps some concoctions already exist to cure this malady;

5. my innocence is entirely to blame; I need to become guilty.

For now it is difficult to add anything more. Two male ghosts are playing chess in the living room. A female ghost is standing behind me, she keeps looking over her shoulder and tittering. She bends down and presses her breasts against me as hard as she can. I feel the so-called nostalgia returning again just beneath my heart. I have been writing this report for four days now—that's why I haven't done as many good deeds as I should have. I am beginning to suspect that people who spend their lives sincerely worrying about the more progressive part of humanity are completely unnecessary to the world. The chess-playing ghosts eye me suspiciously, and once in a while they insolently discuss the most secret facts of my biography. I feel as though I've been stripped naked. Impatiently, I await the day when I can exterminate them all. I'll exterminate them for the second time.

Thus my report is complete. I don't know if it will end up in the right hands. The chess players glare at me more and more suspiciously. Apparently, the female ghost is signaling to them. There is one other possibility, in which case my report will not end up in the right hands, either. It's only a remote possibility, but once again I turn to Aristotelian logic. Theoretically it is possible that I, too, am a ghost.

> With warmest regards,
> Jeronimas Šukys
> Reserve Pensioner

1987
Translated by Jūra Avižienis

Saulius Tomas Kondrotas

The Suspended House

The most beautiful and happiest time in Germanas's life coincides with the time when at some point his father, following his own set of rules, lifted the house built by their barbarian ancestors off its foundation and, on the model of civilized nations, turned it to face the sun. The work took all summer. Quite a few clever devices were used, the foundation was rebuilt, and while father was working on it with the help of his closest neighbors, the house, raised above the ground by ropes and pulleys, hung suspended in the air for a week, swinging and creaking quietly at each breath of wind. Those who saw the house at that time could not get the picture out of their heads for years; the suspended house inspired belief in the set order of things and in the order of the world since its very creation. Beggars passing by broadcast the message along the dusty summer highways to the east and to the west, to the south and to the north. This work of Germanas's father was his last. Later the season of autumn storms came, foul weather obliterated the distances, and evil spirits started lying in wait for people by the roadsides. The earth began to decay, people's health as well. Every day it became harder and harder for Germanas's father to wake up. And he knew that the morning when he would be unable to accomplish this feat at all was not far off. He would wake up, but it didn't seem like waking up; instead, it was like the slow release of an embryo from the womb where it had spent many days and months. It was as if a large and wrinkled embryo, warm and damp, were hatching from an egg, the egg of night itself, as if a soft, gentle silkworm were emerging from a cocoon, a cocoon made of black wefts, issuing from the night and the bed, contradicting the will of nature and God, which holds that silkworms don't issue from cocoons in this particular shape. There were days when father no longer rose from his bed at all. He was lying there left in peace, his eyes becoming ever clearer and bluer, he gazed at the wall, waiting for all that surrounds us and comes into our field of vision, for all the reality in our lives to burst at any moment like a soggy newspaper, he kept waiting for the hour when he could reach out his arm and tear the newspaper and find beyond it the Real World opening up, we had always suspected it existed, secretly, we had always wanted to enter it or dreamed at night that we had, the world of real colors, real forms and sounds, the world of real happiness. From time to time Germanas's father would already be reaching out toward it . . . But he would always pull back because there's no way of knowing whether what he wanted was really out there. It could well be that there was nothing there. Winter came, at first an ordinary one, then it kept getting deeper and frostier, but father still lay there, getting no better, no worse. He took to watching the snow fall from the sky, hour after hour, day after day. He was waiting. Finally, one day he saw the snow, instead of descending, begin to rise. He called for Germanas's mother and told her to give him paper and ink to write his will. While he was writing, he happened to glance at the west wall of the room. He saw a swarm of some kind of insects flying toward the wall, sticking in it as if it were a denser kind of air and disappearing. For some time he watched the insects flying through the wall, until suddenly he became excited. Excited because this unusual circumstance seemed neither strange nor unexpected, as if he had long awaited it. Objects lost the stability and constancy of form that they had patiently retained for more than sixty years. His age had used up its share of the stability of objects that had been allotted to it. Hurrying to keep paper and pen from evaporating, and ink from turning to black steam, father wrote his will. In his hurry he made a mistake; he noticed it right away but had no time to correct it. By the time he had finished, not only could he see snow out the window, but he could look right through the ceiling at it as if through a dense cobweb. His chair heaved a sigh, the desk, its joints creaking, stretched its limbs, the inkwell yawned. Germanas's father's heart started to beat in time to the Boston waltz, then stopped. Father abandoned this world fearing only one thing, namely, that after his death he might be resurrected naked. When day came, they found him dead, leaning back in his chair. He froze in such a position that they were unable to straighten him, no matter how hard they tried.

That day Germanas had gone to the forest for logs. As dusk fell, a snowstorm came on, the snow came tumbling down from the sky so wildly that you couldn't tell which way was up. In the space of half an hour the roads were clogged with snow. People, horses, and sleds sank in the snow, they were afraid that the horses would break their legs because they wouldn't see the snow-covered ditches and potholes, that people would lose their way and freeze to death. Germanas toiled to help the horses pull the heavily laden sleds, he sought firm ground, he held the logs that were about to spill out when the sleds listed dangerously. All of them had only one desire— to escape from this hell somehow. They felt themselves beyond the law, it seemed that just anyone had the right to kill them. The battle with the snowstorm for his life didn't allow Germanas to realize that this was a fateful night for him, that afterward life would change. Germanas was one of those people who can't imagine that things are happening right now, that the world is constantly moving and incessantly changing from its foundations up. He surrendered to this change passively, as if he were sitting in a train car, constantly surrounded by the same faces and seats, he wasn't looking out the window, he wasn't noticing that the train was rushing headlong; by the way, he did feel the rattling of the wheels, but he ascribed no meaning to it, he knew the train was moving, but he didn't see that it was already rolling along different ground, in a different time, Another Country, Another World. Both intuitively and from ill-fated books he knew and felt that in spite of everything the world was changing, but since he couldn't visibly perceive this change, he tried to discern it in places where in reality it scarcely existed at all: in people's souls.

Around midnight the storm's fury ceased, a white moon appeared, and there was enough light to see the steam rising from the sides of the exhausted horses. Germanas and his friends could figure out where they were. Now they had no trouble finding the road, and giddy from fatigue, they headed home to the sound of the runners crunching and the horses snuffling.

When he heard what had happened, Germanas went to his father's room, took the old man by the shoulders, and clenching his teeth, he straightened him out. Later he laid him out on a bench and did everything that had to be done. Only then did he undress, wash his face and hands, and lie down to mourn. He remained in bed the rest of the night and all the following day, and when mother stroked his forehead and said it was time to get up and get ready to honor the deceased, Germanas just mumbled without opening his eyes:

"If it weren't for him we'd be doing up our clothes the wrong way and speaking an inferior language."

Germanas's father was a direct descendant of those stubborn Samogitians whom Ksaveras Bogušis had observed in 1803 and about whom he wrote that supposedly they attended school when they were already grown and often asked the teacher to whip them so it would be easier for them to absorb an education. Germanas's father read books, he also was in the habit of kissing people in greeting and was convinced that the world moved according to principles and laws that even the stupidest of men can understand intuitively, but that the mind was given to man for the very reason that he should make reality more complicated and varied and fill it with human faith and charm. He had broad shoulders and a small waist. His arms and legs were proportionately long. Looking at him, you could sense a certain energy exploding from within him, exploding body and soul, and when people felt this energy and natural force acting upon them, it excited them, compelling them to admire him and to fear him. When he didn't like someone or didn't want to meet them, hatred flared from him like the flames when you get too close to a hot stove, a fire, or a hearth. At times it seemed as if his energy and will were too much for any one man, and observing that he went to bed early, people decided that he was a werewolf. In his youth he fell in love with a woman, Germanas's mother. He had a difficult time seducing her because she was an exemplary girl who came from a Protestant pastor's family and his bestial physicality offended and depressed her. At first she couldn't believe that he could be a good man, then she couldn't believe that matters of the soul, which she had been trained to respect above all in the world, could take precedence for him over physical ones, later she couldn't believe that he could manage to be faithful to her all his life. This kind of threefold disbelief hastened the union, which with regard to its happiness was equal to all other marriages and differed from them perhaps only in that their life was more diverse. Thus, when in his youth Germanas's father fell in love with his future wife and felt her dissatisfaction with his body's mysterious enthusiasm, he ascribed this dissatisfaction to disgust with corporal life and bodily functions in general. So he resolved never again to urinate and defecate, but this was the one instance when he met failure.

Wisdom was and continued to be the most important thing in Germanas's father's life. He studied it constantly and found it everywhere: in old penny newspapers, in books and reprints on cheap yellowing paper, in conversations and customs. All kinds of wisdom. The wisdom that comes from life. The wisdom that comes from marriage. In reality he was a wise man. He never lost his wittiness and bright outlook. He was upright in body and soul. One Christmas (this Germanas remembered), when a lot of people had come over,

Germanas's father decided to entertain them with a lottery. He cut up enough paper for all the guests and wrote out a wish for each of them. He put them all in his pocket and at the height of the celebration he had everyone pick from it. You learned your future by reading what was on your slip of paper: one person would marry so-and-so, have so-and-so for a wife, this year or that year a son would be born to them, one would live to such-and-such an age, etc. (the fortunes rather exceeded the expectations of their owners). The drawing was the source of great fun, jokes, and laughter and was immediately forgotten, but it was remembered again in a few years, when everything that had been foretold started coming true word for word. There was no end to the amazement caused by Germanas's father. But this time he wasn't so happy and joyful as he had been during the first holiday, he sat staring straight ahead into the fire in the hearth. Germanas remembered him clearly this way, lit up by the fire and conversing with it. His old age was coming, and father feared it, afraid he might become worthless and malarial, that he might start living merely by habit without savoring life. He was aging, doing his utmost to hold onto the remnants of his youth, which were being scattered more and more by the winds. Old age made the skin on his face look like a toad's. And when he was asked how he was, he would say:

"I keep getting older and older."

Many things caused him dissatisfaction because they had appeared in the world only recently, when his life was drawing to a close (that is why he refused to acknowledge the present as progress). He was unhappy with the spirit of the new times, "the cold and bony soul of man," as he himself used to put it, that had no essential spontaneity, a soul in which any kind of unexpected emotional departure from common sense had been poisoned at its very inception. In father's opinion, a man with that kind of soul could never act unpredictably, he could not say "I don't" at the altar, he could not get up one morning and for no apparent reason board a train and take off for parts unknown, he could not start crying for no reason. Besides, he did recognize that the imagination of this kind of person, the play of cold reason, could on occasion get caught up in astonishing convolutions, in perpendicular vortices, and the person would feel intoxicated by life, but this was not real life (which was physical and not always sweet-smelling), like that of people cut from the same old cloth, to which father felt he belonged; this was more of an inner life, a synonym for pure reason.

By means of his mind and memory father attempted to adhere to external things so they would help him maintain the shape of his past life, but this proved difficult for him, and at times his mood resembled that of the infants during the massacre in Bethlehem. And in his speech and thoughts he kept returning to the worthless mind of the new times, which was lucid, precise, mechanical, logical, and coherent, without any surprising twists in the chain of reasoning, unless the very substance of the reasoning determined the surprise, something in the layout of the chain of thought, but certainly not some outbursts or unexpected discoveries whose cause happened to be emotion. "There's no room for the brain or heart in that kind of mind," Germanas's father used to remark. "This is a mind of the brain but not of the heart."

Germanas would object. He was offended by his father's contempt for the era, which was his era, full of unimaginable possibilities, a time that, contrary to his parents', wasn't polluted by world wars and rotten traditions (traditions rot like vegetables). Germanas would object and wave his arms while arguing with his father. Father would then shut his eyes, a barely noticeable smile dancing on his lips, and to the impartial observer it would seem that his soul had become a feral cat with sharp claws and a sleepwalker's eyes. "Love?" he would test Germanas's words. "What can you expect of people who believe that love is possibly the only truly animal trait remaining in us?" And when Germanas claimed that the world was a happier and better place now than in his father's time, the latter replied: "Tell me, do you seriously believe that the world can be made cleaner and purer without washing with tears? And happiness? Can this happiness even come close to the happiness that we dreamed of? All you want is to have no worries, have enough to eat, and be able to stay drunk." And again they became angry and quarreled. "Don't talk to me about science and superstitions," father would say stubbornly. "How do you know that contemporary man, your man, isn't or shouldn't be superstitious? What do they have in common, your technology and superstition, your science and superstition? Are they so interchangeable that you think that the one is capable of destroying the other and taking its place? You don't find it strange that the scientists of my youth were superstitious, but this contemporary man of yours, who, by the way, is much further removed from real science than the others, considers contradictions unworthy of him. But, after all, science does not destroy superstition, just as the songs we sang and the songs you sing, the stories we heard on winter nights and the ones you hear, do not disappear on account of it, nor everyday sadness in the final analysis. We might even take pride in our superstitions because they play a rather important part in making us human, they give color to our daily lives. Perhaps I'm wrong, perhaps science and superstition are one and the same. However, even then you have no grounds to think that your contemporary man can't be superstitious, since at this point your science is just as far from ultimate knowledge as it was in my day, as it was a thousand years ago. This contemporary man of yours vainly believes that he knows enough to be able to renounce superstition. This kind of belief is itself a superstition, only it's ten times worse and more harmful than a black cat calmly stepping across our path."

"You are things," father would say to Germanas. "Intelligent things, but that's all."

After a while father started to avoid these arguments and discussions, he would respond to Germanas's questions with silence, and this hurt Germanas even more. Father became more and more withdrawn, he spent many days and nights of solitude going quietly crazy because of the new world, because of his age and helplessness. He was suffering, and this made his palate turn black, and his eyes become clear.

More and more often Germanas would catch his father standing or sitting, his eyes fixed on the hills in the distance or on the edge of the forest, but he wasn't looking at the hill, or at the clouds, he was looking at his own past. In these nature scenes he was searching for something that could look back at him with a loving gaze, something that could give him warmth. He still felt the desire to laugh, but amusing things were long gone. When father suspended the house to swing on the creaking cables, Germanas envied him: he himself yearned to do something like that someday. It seemed to Germanas that his father had already done everything and now there was nothing left for him to do. He felt the maturity of his body and his heart, but was hampered by his father's existence.

Suddenly his father was no more, the arguments and disagreements ended for good. While there were the two of them, the world seemed too small for both of them. But when one of them was gone, the world suddenly became too large and spacious for the one left behind, it was too empty, the horizon receded, the sky rose, the earth sank lower. He walked around in vain with his eyes half closed, hoping to reduce the range of his vision, make the space that he could see narrower, make the world more comfortable for himself. In vain his eyes sought objects to rearrange, to make life more comfortable. Always in vain. A house can be raised, but a well can't.

Shortly after father's funeral Germanas went to live with Zakaras, an uncle from his father's side of the family. In his will father asked Zakaras to care for Germanas for a while, to teach him the code of morality, to instill in him once and for all those things that the father had begun instilling but hadn't had time to finish.

Zakaras was a few years younger than Germanas's father. He was a veterinarian; by day he took care of cows, horses, and angry squealing pigs in a yard, smelling of manure, while evenings or early mornings he liked to walk along the edge of the forest with a single-barreled twenty-two-caliber rifle and lie in wait for some animal or bird. Zakaras was a different kind of person than his brother, Germanas's father. Initially, Germanas couldn't understand what he was supposed to learn from Zakaras. Zakaras seemed a totally worthless person whose entire business was conducted in the trampled farmyard mud, half-mixed with manure, and along the forest, full of oriole voices. But in time Germanas realized that Zakaras was an inner man. That is, that his worth lay in his soul and not in his exterior. In his thoughts and not in his deeds. Father was valuable because of his visible efforts to change something, because of his activity, while Zakaras's worth was in his efforts to comprehend life by pondering on it. Zakaras could even be funny when he tried to do something. Until Germanas got to know him better, he found him repulsive because of his hair, stuck full of hay, his muddy feet, stuck barefoot in his cracked rubber boots, his nicked nails and runny eyes.

Shortly after Germanas's arrival Zakaras decided to entertain his nephew, who found the new place rather gloomy and miserable. One time after supper he brought out a rusty rapier and performed for Germanas the show that had earned him a good deal of popularity in his youth at the academy. For a time he stared intently at the sharp end of the rapier, then he stuck it in his mouth and swallowed the blade inch by inch so that only the handle stuck out under his nose. Then, grasping the handle, Zakaras carefully removed the rapier and let out a wet belch.

"Take a look," Zakaras stuck the sword under Germanas's eyes, "it's a real rapier. No fooling."

There was a time when Zakaras performed his act during festive student celebrations; enveloping his stunt in mystical and theatrical secrecy, he would come out on stage dressed as a fakir, trying to make the expression on his face suit the occasion—it had to be dignified and mysterious and yet happy and befitting a feast. The young veterinarians, red in the face from the beer and boar testicles, roasted in cream with marjoram, would choke on their enchantment and the smoke of cheap cigarettes. It was a completely different time now, a different audience, and Zakaras with his greasy lips and unbuttoned fly did not much resemble a starving fakir, so his trick did not seem funny but pitiful and sad instead. Nevertheless, since Germanas did not wish to insult his uncle, he would, naturally, have smiled and clapped, if not joyfully, then at least loudly, if he hadn't gotten sick at the sight of the macaroni, which they had eaten for supper, stuck to the damp blade of the rapier. Germanas jumped up suddenly, ran outdoors, and for a long time stood leaning against the log house, feeling a chill in his stomach and rocked by convulsions. The next day, and even a few days later, Germanas and Zakaras were embarrassed to look each other in the face.

So in the beginning Germanas found it unpleasant at Zakaras's house. Then he got used to it, and later yet he came to like Zakaras. Zakaras won him over with his conversations during the long winter evenings or during the hunt, when, lying in wait for a bird to appear, Germanas inadvertently learned to be patient. He would have found Zakaras's reasoning tiresome, for the latter thought out loud all the time, if it hadn't been for the fact that he was interesting and strangely altruistic somehow. Some of his arguments seemed totally meaningless, it seemed that no one else could get anything out of them, others were quite sensible and necessary. Germanas learned to listen to all of them without interrupting them or disagreeing, the reverse of how he had conversed with his father. His ears were receptive to Zakaras's voice, which had a light ring to it, being a trifle pensive and musical.

Zakaras's favorite topic was gypsies. For him they were something abstract, not a real nation or class but a spiritual nation of some kind of phantom, sometimes good, sometimes evil, like chimeras, figments of our morbid mind, though they were still people, colorful men with earrings and women in motley dress. Zakaras did not call a person who had played some harmless trick "a rogue," but would refer to him kindheartedly as a "gypsy." A dishonest person whom Zakaras disliked he would also speak of as "a gypsy." Sometimes, lying in ambush, Zakaras would suddenly sit up in the grass, light a cigarette, momentarily illuminating his face, and quietly say:

"We see right through the gypsies. They live among us but they're totally alien to us, our gaze has no point of reference for judging their appearance, their speech or thought, their lifestyle, it can find no familiar point of departure, and therefore it wanders off without fixing on anything. The gypsy world is a world apart."

Other times, supping always on the same macaroni, or returning in the early morning hours from some cow that had just calved, Zakaras would speak differently. Wiping the dew from his shoes in the moonlight, he would begin explaining that every nation, besides its main representatives, has its own Jews and its own gypsies. For example, Lithuanian gypsies are marked by no special features, their ancestors always lived here, no one can tell them apart from non-gypsies, and it's only because they are gypsies by nature that over many centuries they've learned to speak the gypsy language, dress like gypsies and think like gypsies, walk like gypsies and smile like gypsies.

"I myself am a gypsy from the Labanoras bogs," Zakaras used to say. "Gypsies are not a nation nor a race, gypsies are a separate and special breed of people. Parents who aren't gypsies themselves can still give birth to gypsy children."

There are nations, continued Zakaras, where all the women are gypsies, while not one of their men is a gypsy. There's also the opposite. Finally, everyone is a gypsy at some stage in his life.

Germanas would listen, and it seemed to him that he hadn't reached this stage in his life yet. He didn't quite understand what Zakaras was saying, but he sensed that gypsies had or would have some kind of meaning for him, they would somehow be connected to his life, and therefore, he tried not to miss any part of Zakaras's discourses.

But it wasn't just gypsies that Zakaras held forth on. The veterinarian with the uncombed hair also spoke of other things. At one point he and Zakaras competed to see who could think up a better poem. On hearing what Germanas had come up with,

> The sky is a wasteland:
> the bird flies,
> with his back touching
> the blue sand,

Zakaras joyfully admitted defeat. Sometimes Zakaras related stories he had heard somewhere or made up himself, in which people would find themselves in difficult situations, their interpersonal relationships would get mixed up, and then he would ask Germanas to evaluate each person's morality or to solve some complicated problem. He never praised Germanas, nor did he censure him, when he did what he was asked, he only remarked "you're a gypsy," either in a gloomy or a happy tone. They spoke of animals and of the songs of distant countries, which they heard on the radio, songs in which you could hear longing for days gone by, when the world was embraced by love, when everything thrilled with the fever of love, when passion poured from the sky and soaked men and women through and through, forcing them to make love. When was this time? No one knows. Maybe it's already happened, maybe it's yet to come, maybe it's now, Zakaras used to say. It's prominent in all folk songs, the songs are saturated with physical love. But the peoples of different nations imagine love and themselves in relation to the world of love differently. For some nations it happens more openly and bodily, more feverishly and naturally. It was as if Zakaras was preparing Germanas for some kind of suffering that he couldn't avoid ("If the father has suffered, in the course of his life the son will have to experience at least a moment of his father's pain. That's why we are sad sometimes for no reason"), he even spoke out about death ("Sometimes you feel you're immortal. At times like that it seems to you that your decisions can be undone or that you may regret them. It's wrong to think that. You have to know that you will die"). Zakaras never talked of himself or his past, he didn't look to his past for arguments to support what he was saying. It was as if he had no personal history, he was always the way he was at this particular moment, he spoke only about other people and things. In this sense he was a wonderful teacher, and Germanas knew this. It's the worst thing for a teacher to base himself on his past, his personal experience. Nevertheless, Zakaras did not appear to be a vain eccentric. A strange kind of gentle bitterness, a dissatisfaction with himself and his life would slip out in his speech. One time he said:

"When we are unhappy, we grieve because happiness passed us by. When we feel happiness, we often grieve because it's different from that of others. We envy others their happiness, though we understand very well that they envy us ours."

Zakaras was not a strong-willed person. His will would not have sufficed to give Germanas's thoughts and feelings direction if the latter had not himself been inclined toward this. However, his words had a will of their own, they acted on Germanas, and in the course of a year he went through a great change without himself realizing its direction.

One morning when Germanas had been living with Zakaras for a year and three months, he woke up at the break of dawn to see Zakaras bending over him, his eyes the color of watered-down beer fixed on him. He was not surprised, almost as if he had been expecting something like this.

Throwing their coats over their bare shoulders, they went outside.

"You can speak of evil only as long as good exists," Zakaras began in a roundabout way. "My life contained no evil in just this sense. There was absolutely nothing good in it, and therefore for a long time I have been unable to comprehend it as evil. There weren't any moments when I felt happy or felt capable of happiness, there weren't any days like that to compare to the rest of my days, so that I could see that there was little or no goodness in my life."

"I'm not curious about anything, uncle," said Germanas and again remembered the rusty rapier with undigested macaroni stuck to it, but this time he did not get sick because he had come to love this man with the crooked legs who had nothing left to give him.

Ever so slowly the time came when Germanas, sitting by the fire in the evening, patting the dog as sleek as a glove and listening to the chatter of food cooking, began to long for a woman. He felt warm, sweet blood flowing around his heart. Life is like a spider web where everything is connected and intertwined. The world too is like a spider web.

Albas Lukšas was obese and drank like a fiend. When Germanas got to know him, the idea that Lukšas was only a barbarian whose language barely resembled Lithuanian and whose clothing wasn't cut the way it should be wouldn't leave him. In Lukšas's flabby body lurked an evil power that ordered his life, ordered it even against his will. Lukšas was very nervous. He was one of those people who continually expect something without knowing what it is, who speak and laugh rather naturally, to all apearances, but on closer examination reveal hidden in their voices and laughter a kind of anxiety, heartache and a scarcely noticeable anger that what they're expecting just isn't coming, and everyone and his brother is to blame for preventing this something from happening. When he encountered Lukšas, Germanas felt stimulated by the unpleasant energy that Lukšas radiated, he felt that there was something that he hadn't done to help him, he felt an irritating itch in his body and in his heart. In time, after careful observation, Germanas partly figured out Lukšas's character and nature, but the mysterious itch never ceased.

Germanas understood that Lukšas liked whiskey not because it tasted sweet, as it did to other drunks, but because it intoxicated him and made him oblivious to everything. What was it that tormented him so persistently? There were two things that gave him no peace. Above all Albas Lukšas wished with all his heart that his life would change, that one day it would turn upside down. Everyone has moments when the thought strikes them that it would be good if those closest to them died. And even though they are immediately ashamed of this thought and chase it away, saying "no, no" to themselves, the fact remains that it was thought. Perhaps this rises inevitably from the implacable desire, hidden even from oneself, to start life anew. Lukšas desired this a great deal more than most people. He believed that something was bound to occur in the world, some change, after which people like himself would be especially valued, people with veins enlarged precisely this way and hearts exhausted by the effort of pushing blood into the furthest reaches of their fat bodies, cirrhotic livers, dimmed gazes, dirty necks, and indefatigable expectations to become somebody they're not and probably never will be. He imagined that the change would occur in the blink of an eye, the way the invention of gunpowder had attached a new value to people. A weapon that fired raised up some and demoted others. Strong, stupid men with the power of bulls, knights in chain mail and raving lunatics, to whom a heavy ax was nothing but a toy, armed in endless self-confidence, became worthless. All those who until now could only dream of manhood with their crooked, envious smiles now fought their way to the top. Now all the weaklings with a marksman's eye became men, they took on the lunatic shield of confidence and, kicking the knights aside, stood like men (feet apart, thumb hooked in belt) in front of the women, who before could have become their wives at best, but never their mistresses. Never.

Lukšas also expected something of this sort. He wanted to become renowned as a shamelessly courageous man. And he was shamelessly courageous when, sitting patching the crotch of his pants, he became lost in visions. Streams of images flowed from his brain, fragments of nebulous plots, as if his soul had separated from his body, taken off over the world of men at amazing speed, and could catch only fleeting bits and pieces of life. At times like this Lukšas felt better than others. But so far it seemed that way only to him, Albas Lukšas. It was necessary, however, for the world to recognize this too.

Another thing that gave him no peace was the passage of time. Time kept flying, and Lukšas's life didn't change, every day bringing him closer to . . . Lukšas didn't dare to think about it. He was in a state of desperate fear. His teeth ached at the very idea of it. Consequently, he was always joking. He was acquiring a reputation for being a jovial man. Lukšas's jokes were desperate, he joked and made fun of everything because he was afraid of serious matters, all of which were connected to the temporal and death. He made fun of sad funeral music and of funerals themselves because he was afraid of the one thing than which there is nothing more serious or more temporal.

Sometimes after a bender, and in due course this was all the time, people would hear Lukšas talking to objects. He gave tables and chairs, fences and sawhorses first and last names, asked them

things, and answered them himself with a smile. From time immemorial people thought this was due to too much drink, but soon they
became accustomed to this behavior of Lukšas and began to look on
it as a peculiarity of his. But Germanas understood that this manner
of Lukšas stemmed from the same fear, from the desire to see the
world wholly alive. Lukšas could experience more happy hours from
a chair called Marta, or from an ax christened Johnny Clang, than he
could from him, Germanas. In other words, it seemed to Germanas
that if Albas Lukšas was a madman, he was a very clever madman.
The Clever Madman.

Germanas met Lukšas accidentally. Once, when he had come to
Raseiniai for some laxative for the pigs, he saw standing in the middle of the bus station square an old man with cheeks so flabby they
made his face look tearful. The old man stood in the center of the
square, failing to yield way for the cars, and the drivers were honking
their horns, making an awful ruckus. The old man appeared oblivious to everything, he was looking kind of sideways, concentrating, as
if he had stepped outside on a stuffy night to listen to the nightin-
gales. Germanas went right up to the old man; at that moment, the
driver of the first bus that came along, losing his patience, jumped
out and ran up to the old man, pushing him aside. The latter fell
right into Germanas's arms, obediently and quietly, and as he was
falling, Germanas heard the sound of a tree snapping.

The buses drove off, the square emptied, only Germanas was
left standing in the center of it, with the sleeping old man, his face
buried in Germanas's chest. Germanas pulled him over to the station,
intending to leave him there, but then he thought better of it and
started asking people if anyone knew the old man or knew where
he lived.

"Everybody knows him! That's Lukšas," said the first ticket-
taker he met. "When he gets drunk, he comes to the station. He asks
all the drivers to take him somewhere so he can be happy."

She pointed out where the old drunk lived, and Germanas,
leading him home with much effort, surrendered him to some
woman working in the yard. He felt a little uncomfortable, he was
afraid Lukšas might die, having imbibed so much alcohol. Thus,
when in a few days he again happened to be in Raseiniai, he stopped
in at the old drunk's house. He found him quite cheerful, sitting
there mending his pants, which Germanas later learned Lukšas always tore when he was drunk. Entering the house, Germanas
greeted them, saying:

"Good day."

"These are mysterious words," replied Lukšas. And now Germanas noticed that Lukšas wasn't as old as he had thought. Lukšas was about the same age as Zakaras.

They chatted for a while, then Lukšas's wife, a quiet, elderly woman, came in, bringing some boiled meat and cucumbers. From that day on, whenever Germanas was in Raseiniai, he would visit Lukšas, sometimes they'd drink together, but most of the time they would just chat. They developed somewhat of a friendship. Two or three times Germanas stayed the night at Lukšas's, and they slept in the same bed after talking half the night. Lukšas had only one bed, and there wasn't anywhere else to put a guest.

Albas Lukšas had a daughter named Aleksandra. Germanas met her. She was a young spinster with a slim waist and hair cut like a man's. One of her traits was a certain air of concentration. Germanas noticed it right away. She really was different from other women who thought it cute to behave like a child, believing that this suited a young woman. She was like the sad girls of Siberia. Something unknown, perhaps the severe Siberian climate, took away their warmth and feminine gentleness, the softness of their motions and speech. Oh, those sad, mannish Siberian girls! Aleksandra's skin was of just the right gentle roughness so that when you were stroking it with the palm of your hand or touching her in some other way, you could feel how soft and smooth her skin was. If it really had been gentle and smooth, it would have appeared just barely moist, but on touching her, the impression of gentleness vanished.

When Germanas met her for the first time, they sat down in Lukšas's room, which reeked of wet rags, and spent a long time talking about everything. She was intelligent. And Germanas noticed this immediately. At the time that they met she was twenty-three and had two lovers. She had already gone through twelve of them. Not one of them was happy.

Aleksandra wasn't promiscuous, only damaged somehow from birth. She wanted love and to be loved. And when someone did fall in love with her, she surrendered body and soul to him, and it seemed that that was how it should be. But it was quite the contrary. At some point she would start to feel boredom, irritation, even hatred, her clever and innovative mind would start creating all kinds of complicated intrigues and set up various snares for her loved one, more accurately for her former loved one, because Aleksandra felt no more love. Some other young woman might have left her beloved then and there and that would be the end of it, but unconsciously Aleksandra would start to grind her teeth, a desire for revenge would seize her. Revenge because he hadn't altered her nature, because he hadn't been able to attach her to himself, because he hadn't been able to force her to love him, because . . . etc. She would devise all kinds of ruses, even very cruel ones, to bring more pain to her lover, to make him suffer, to break his spirit in the end. She didn't want, as other young women did, for the unloved men to disappear from her sight; no, quite the reverse, Aleksandra needed to have them in her proximity, have them nearby, so she could constantly see them and control them, as if they were her belongings, so when the need arose, she could use them as a tool for some new intrigue.

Back then, talking to Aleksandra for the first time, Germanas did perhaps feel some attraction to her, but only a very slight one. He had no idea yet that his bed at night would soon be strewn with the pine needles of love. But the better he got to know Aleksandra, the longer he sat in front of the fire in Zakaras's house, lacking the resolve to go to bed, thinking and thinking about what was happening to him. It felt as though the floor were rocking under his feet like the bottom of a boat.

Germanas tried to find more and more excuses to go to Raseiniai. Not wishing Zakaras to find out about his friendships and to feel betrayed, he would think up business in Raseiniai that was supposedly important to Zakaras rather than to him. Germanas was even ashamed to admit to himself that more often than not, making for Lukšas's house, he was thinking of Aleksandra rather than Lukšas. When he found Lukšas at home, he'd be quite disappointed because then he would have to talk to him. But when the host was out somewhere or lying drunk, Germanas would feel his spirits lifting—he could see Aleksandra and talk to her. Now Aleksandra was usually at home, as if she were waiting for him. In the beginning, when he had first gotten to know Lukšas, Germanas would almost never find her home. If Lukšas wasn't home either, then he'd go into the kitchen and see Lukšas's old wife sitting all by herself with some knitting in her hands. But now it was as though Aleksandra didn't go anywhere, and he found this pleasant. They would sit down facing each other. Germanas would tell her about his father, about his work and opinions, about the house he had suspended, about Zakaras. He didn't especially enjoy talking about himself. Aleksandra was glad to respond, she expressed her opinions about the world forcefully, and Germanas liked the fact that she didn't care about handicrafts or clothes, and that she wasn't overly critical, but formed her impressions of people not on their physical appearance but on their essence, on that which was secret and true in them. She didn't like to talk about herself either, so Germanas knew nothing of her past or about the tyrannical defect in her character, but even if he had known, he still would have liked her. He only suspected that most of her opinions were based on personal experience because she defended them stubbornly, with such conviction that they couldn't have been shaped by just books or education. Once Aleksandra spoke some daring words that Germanas took to heart and that he would later remember often: "Still, there's a place in each of us which the other will never learn the entire truth about. We'll believe what we're told, but it won't make any difference whether it's real or invented because we'll never be able to know the truth. Once you say something that isn't true, it has the power of the truth forever, no matter how much you try to deny it later. These things shouldn't be discussed at all, or else you should get used to the idea that as soon as you say them they will burn themselves into your consciousness. And even if it's something totally absurd, nothing will be able to erase them from there. Not argument, not persuasion, and not logic."

Germanas didn't know exactly what kinds of things Aleksandra was talking about, but he felt the truth of her words, and that he too possessed the kind of knowledge that isn't based on any order in the world but is right and certain for him, and that he himself had supplied others—his father, Zakaras, Lukšas, Aleksandra, and even himself—with that information.

Immersed in himself, in his own impressions and experiences, he failed to notice the changes occurring in Aleksandra, which would have granted him some respite. Day by day he became more and more attracted to Aleksandra, he tried to resist, realizing intuitively that the bond between a man and a woman is full of suffering that strengthens the feelings but clouds the mind. He failed to note that Aleksandra's eyes were ever more radiant, that her skin was becoming paler, ever more luminous and clear, transparent even—she had already fallen in love with him. But no matter how hard he tried to resist and banish the persistent ideas and images of Aleksandra, time passed, bringing closer the day of the dog, when you love without any resistance or will on your part, you love like a dog, with open heart, you would even crawl on the dirt floor and humble yourself just to please the one you love. Germanas's inexperienced eye didn't note the changes in Aleksandra, but the changes in him could not escape her gaze. She knew that the day of the dog would come, that he couldn't get away, she wanted to know this, she wanted it to be that way because she herself was already overcome by the powerful black night of love, she felt dependent on Germanas. People begin to

control themselves only when they start to depend on someone un-
conditionally. Usually it is the most independent people who are the
ones to be dominated.

Too bad that Germanas did not understand this, too bad that the
ones we love, perceiving the doglike quality of our love, very often
behave toward us as if we really were dogs. Germanas's arms were
made of wood when he embraced Aleksandra for the first time. Quivering with happiness, she thought with a smile that he hadn't the
least idea of how to enjoy a woman's body, that there was an area in
Germanas's soul that she could still create and shape according to her
tastes and desires. Then nothing would obscure her joy, no thought
of the future. She wanted only to belong to him completely.

They came together naturally somehow, as if by chance, as if
they had encountered each other naked in Lukšas's bed by accident,
and Germanas felt happy, just like the time that he had been sleeping
on the ground on a warm summer night, filled with the chirping of
grasshoppers, and had listened to the creaking of the ropes holding
up the suspended house. They made love quietly, without speaking;
only once did Germanas feel Aleksandra's palm clamp over his
mouth that burned with his cries. It seemed to Germanas that it
wasn't he who was experiencing something extraordinary and beyond compare but that the world was changing as it experienced his
passion. He lay with his eyes closed, with the surface of his skin he
felt the stars stray from their paths in amazement, the moon become
brighter and illuminate the whole world, the rivers begin to flow up-
stream, and the wind hug the earth and lose itself in the grass. The
words uttered by Zakaras on some occasion came back to him:
"When Eve was in Adam there was no death. Death appeared only
when she separated from him. If she enters him again, and he accepts her, there will no longer be any death."

"I accept . . ." whispered Germanas, "there will be no . . ."

But perhaps he only imagined that he was whispering something because not one muscle of Aleksandra's body moved.

For half of an entire year Germanas felt as if he had learned
what it was like to dwell in heaven and be immortal. It seemed to him
that he could absorb light, that he could command objects and all of
creation. It seemed to him that all misery had ended, and all the insects, trees, and plants that carried evil had become extinct.

One evening Zakaras asked Germanas:

"What's the matter with you? You haven't been yourself for the
last six months or more. Don't you like staying here with me? Lord
knows life here is dull . . ."

"I want to get married, Zakaras," Germanas replied.

He was sitting in front of the fire and playing a harmonica to the beat of the dancing tongues of flame. Up till now the idea hadn't occurred to him, he hadn't discussed it with Aleksandra either, but as soon as he pronounced those five words, he felt as if he had been considering it for a long time and had firmly decided on it. It was a sudden decision, but the right one, unsullied by doubt.

"Whom have you chosen?" asked Zakaras.

"Aleksandra, Lukšas's daughter."

Zakaras made a face as though he were pronouncing the word "hatred."

"That's those people from across the river," he said, lost in thought. "From across the river."

And after a moment he said:

"They're not like us."

And after another:

"I don't know if you have made a good choice."

And then:

"They're different. We won't know what to expect from them."

Zakaras said nothing more on the subject, and although Germanas didn't like the fact that Zakaras hadn't approved of his idea, he was satisfied that he at least hadn't rejected it.

It was a Saturday morning when Germanas knocked at Lukšas's door, wearing his best suit, which he had brought from his native home but hadn't yet had the opportunity to show off. Fortunately, all the Lukšases were home. They were sitting in the kitchen drinking coffee when Germanas stepped inside, smelling of toilet water and starched shirts. He was unusually happy, and even Aleksandra's eagle eye discerned not the least unease or shyness. Germanas said hello, patted Aleksandra on the head, kissed Lukšas, then he picked up his wife, who was already wasting away, and set her on his lap.

"I've come to propose," he said. "It's a good thing we're all here. I'd like to ask you, Lukšas, to give me your daughter's hand in marriage."

Lukšas's wife looked at her husband; Aleksandra kept her eyes fixed on Germanas.

"Should I leave the room?" she inquired.

"Stay," Lukšas stopped her. "You're an independent young woman. I don't ever want to hear you say that we decided things behind your back."

Germanas glanced at Aleksandra, but he could read nothing from her face.

"What do you think?" asked Lukšas.

"It makes no difference to me," she answered, "whatever you decide, that's how it should be."

A chill went down Germanas's spine at the tone of her voice. Judging by her voice, it really didn't make any difference to her whether she'd be his wife or not, and Germanas wasn't prepared for this. He was in love, but he also felt loved in return, so he hadn't hesitated even an instant as far as Aleksandra was concerned, but now he heard indifference in her voice, why, he couldn't figure out so quickly.

For a time there was silence in the kitchen, only an insect rustled in the pile of wood by the stove.

"So what's it going to be?" Germanas broke the silence.

"I don't know," pronounced Lukšas, "you never know what to expect from her. I won't keep it from you, Germanas. We noticed it when she was still a child, she sometimes seems removed from the world and the people in it."

Germanas suddenly turned his head toward Aleksandra and thought he managed to catch her eye, even though she was sitting turned away from him, almost facing the other way.

"I don't care," she said.

"Well, then we don't care either," said Lukšas, and Germanas's calves started to itch at his smile.

They decide to put off the wedding long enough for Germanas to let his mother know and for Lukšas to get ready.

Germanas continued to visit Lukšas's house as if nothing had happened, his love for Aleksandra seemed to grow stronger every day, but something started to change, too.

When Germanas got to be friends with Aleksandra, he started to spend more and more time with her and less and less with Lukšas, and the latter suddenly became lonely. Germanas scarcely noticed that Lukšas was acquiring other friends and drinking companions, and once when Germanas came to the house, he found some near-sighted hunchback with bright red hair and bluish hands sitting there. Gazing off somewhere over the top of Lukšas's head, the hunchback was telling a tale about how some female fish in the Red Sea slowly change their sex if there is a shortage of males. If males are present, he said, they act aggressively toward the females and don't allow new males to appear. As long as the male keeps the females under his control, not one of them turns into a male.

Germanas didn't join in their talk, but while the hunchback was speaking, he examined him closely. Brown hair in long, shining curls lay on his shoulders, one of which was higher than the other. His face was oblong, he had big eyes, a narrow nose, and his skin was white and without blemish. There was a kind of hemorrhoidal beauty lurking in this holy face. A short trunk, a large, pointed hump on the right shoulder blade, arms that were too long. As he talked, the hunchback walked back and forth, waving his arms. One foot was bent inward and when he walked, he waddled sideways.

It was as though Lukšas had only now noticed Germanas, sitting in the corner. He got up, took the hunchback by the arm, and led him over to Germanas and introduced them. Lukšas's proximity again caused Germanas to start itching. The hunchback looked Germanas over from head to toe insolently, without a bit of decorum, smiling the smile of a man who is superior in every way.

Afterward during almost every visit Germanas would see the hunchback in Lukšas's room or hear his gentle, even voice. Germanas was satisfied that Lukšas had a friend and that he could spend all his time with Aleksandra.

Once Germanas asked Lukšas who his new friend was and where he was from. Lukšas laughed angrily:

"He's probably not human, but what do I care."

Germanas's love grew stronger and stronger. He felt that if this continued, he'd be strong enough to eat rocks. But he felt that after the morning of his proposal Aleksandra's caresses had cooled, that she was freeing herself from her fascination, and her behavior became more and more calculated. Although her eyes looked brightly at Germanas and hadn't yet lost their loving gaze, his spine tingled with a mysterious fear. He was ashamed of his caresses, his calflike gentleness, so persistent and smelling of mother's milk. But love, the infectious disease that he had contracted, made him shut his eyes and chase away his doubts.

Germanas had the feeling that Aleksandra couldn't stand the hunchback, who sat for days on end with her father or was off somewhere drinking with him. The hunchback did not drink as much as Lukšas or get as drunk. In that respect the hunchback was even useful: he wouldn't let Lukšas bounce around the station or marketplace or sing at the top of his lungs at the post office, the pharmacy, or the grocery store. You couldn't really say that the hunchback disliked drinking. No, it was as if he avoided getting drunk, as if the obvious example of Lukšas had had an influence on him. He was careful in his drinking, and it seemed not that whiskey or wine were his goal but that drinking with Lukšas was his means to some secret evil end.

Germanas continued to think as before that Aleksandra was re-
volted by the hunchback, that his handsome face nauseated her.

Until one day he entered the room with a bunch of wildflowers
he had picked on the way. The first thing he saw was the dog, drunk,
lying by the bed, its jaws open wide and Aleksandra's beautiful arm
almost up to the elbow in the dog's mouth. The dog did not seem
unhappy. Germanas's gaze slid along the arm, passed over the naked
feminine shoulder, then over the other shoulder, twisted, covered
with brown hair, masculine. Aleksandra turned around, looked at
Germanas with turbid eyes, and smiled at him.

Once when he had been lying on the ground, staring at the
starry sky and listening to the cables of the suspended house creak,
Germanas had felt a strong chill of fear that the cables would break
and the house would fall and shatter into bits. Now he experienced
that same feeling of horror that he had felt once before, he could even
hear the cables rattling, unable to bear the weight any longer, but it
lasted only an instant. Germanas pulled himself together and the
house remained suspended. Putting his flowers down on the table,
Germanas smiled back at Aleksandra. He smiled sincerely and simply, looking her in the eyes with his own eyes bright and clear. Before
leaving he noted that the smile had left Aleksandra's face without a
trace. As he was stepping over the threshold, it occurred to him that
he'd like to be buried alive now, his head pointing west.

No one knew what was going on in Germanas's soul at that
time. Not Zakaras, not Lukšas, and not Aleksandra, who liked to
think that all men are the same, that over the centuries all people are
similar, that one man coming home from a long journey is always
similar to another also returning from a journey, it didn't matter
whether the dust that he shook from his feet at the threshold was ordinary highway dust or cosmic dust. The belief in the similarity of
human beings was the real assumption that allowed her to love men
and then to betray them and scorn them. In reality Aleksandra was a
moral woman after her own fashion. In loving men and then leaving
them she did not violate her own moral code, because in reality she
loved only one man and never once betrayed him. This man was an
abstract composite image, formed by the assumption that all men are
alike. Aleksandra always felt this. But this time something unfore-
seen happened. She couldn't understand what was different this
time. Germanas's smile, which proved that he hadn't cracked up,
gave her no peace. But he should have cracked up, thought Aleksandra. He should have. This drove her crazy. Aleksandra gnashed her
teeth in anger, but the strange thing was that this time it wasn't Ger-

manas who exasperated her, but she herself. She was a burden to herself, she felt the weight of her muscles and bones, the weight of her heart and even more—the weight of her soul. She was tortured by doubt, which was vague like the contours of unseen animals deep in the forest. As long as you do things without hesitation, you can do things that other people find terrible, inner conviction carries you through. But you're in trouble when this conviction falters and disappears. Then you feel your knees buckling, you start to fall, and from then on everything you do starts to feel unreal somehow, you begin to think that you've been deceived, in the end you don't know what you can or cannot do. The hunchback began to irritate her again, he followed her around crying until finally he realized that she was thinking of Germanas and then he stopped whining, retreated into himself, but even when she didn't see him, Aleksandra felt persecuted by the hunchback. In three days she was overwhelmed by the feeling that thirty years had passed.

Only Germanas knew what he suffered during those three days. Afterward, when Germanas appeared at Lukšas's house as if nothing had happened, he had a hardened heart. He felt free, he had no ties to any living creature, and this time a chill ran down even Lukšas's back—Lukšas, who thought he had seen everything in his lifetime. He was cheerful and playful, his step was as resilient as a panther's. He talked and joked with Aleksandra, he even kissed her on the forehead, he joked with Lukšas, and with the hunchback, who cowered at the sight of Germanas, as if an extra hump had grown on his back. Not one of them understood what had happened, why in his presence they were overcome by the feeling that a rush of wind had roared between them. They had never before seen such freedom because they could not have seen it. Only executioners and idiots ever are this free and independent. They couldn't tell what was happening to them, all they felt was the horror creeping down their spine while he was joking, even though Germanas's tricks were funnier and wittier than ever. None of them—not the experienced and wily Lukšas, not the treacherous and clever yet weak hunchback, not Aleksandra, intelligent but beset by doubts—knew that any kind of cruelty perpetrated against other people is an unbearable burden to the executioner as long as he feels like one of them, a part of some society, some whole. It's hard to lift your hand to cause pain to the body to which it belongs. And vice versa: the one who is causing the pain feels no suffering when he can think of himself as separate from other people, *completely different*, when he's able to look at the world of this moment from a bird's eye view, from a historical perspective, in which all individual passions and torments dissolve easily and quickly like a drop of ink falling into a stream of swift, foaming water.

They felt uncomfortable, and when Lukšas suggested they drink some whiskey, the hunchback was quick to agree and so was Aleksandra. Germanas didn't object either. They sat down in the room haphazardly, they drank quite a bit, but they didn't feel any better or more relaxed. Then Lukšas went off and brought more whiskey. Only Germanas seemed to be sincerely enjoying himself, the other three were keeping him company reluctantly, to all appearances they were responding with wit, on time, and yet they were out of tune, they even roared with laughter, but each of them separately rather than all together. All in all, it was very reminiscent of a farewell to one of them, probably Germanas, seeing him off on a long journey. The people who are seeing him off are sad because they have to say good-bye to someone dear to them, but they don't want him to see their sadness, they don't want to spoil his mood, in the meantime, the one who is actually leaving is glad, thirsting for new scenes and a new life. It's as if he were standing on a threshold, one of his feet is already raised to go *somewhere else*, it already is somewhere else, but the other foot is still here, in a moment it too will be raised, for a long time, perhaps even forever. The one who is leaving has already prepared himself for the next life, is inclined toward new impressions, the ones remaining feel acutely the monotony of their daily existence, from which they are not destined to escape this time, and their future is beginning to seem meaningless. Lukšas in particular felt this and was jealous. The more he drank, the fiercer his gaze became, even though he tried to hide it. Finally the time came when they were all quite drunk, when that which was destined to happen was bound to happen. Secretly they were all awaiting this moment, they waited anxiously and fearfully, possibly Germanas was the only one who wasn't at all afraid. At some point Aleksandra became aware of Lukšas's voice:

"You'll give birth to my grandchild, Germanas. You ought to thank me for raising you a wife like Aleksandra."

She glanced at Germanas hopefully, expecting to read pain in his face, but his face was still bright as always, when he declared:

"I will thank you."

Germanas stood up, and Aleksandra could see that his step was not as steady as usual. He went over to Lukšas, bent down, and vomited all over his host's face and chest. Everyone froze for just an instant. Then everything happened quickly, as if they had just been waiting for a sign. Lukšas wiped the sticky substance from his eyes, jumped up from his chair, the hunchback jumped up too, and the two of them knocked Germanas down on the floor, then Lukšas kept kicking the cowering Germanas until the hunchback brought a wet rope. Aleksandra saw how strong the hunchback was as he was tying Germanas up. He secured the knots, and they dragged their prisoner into the yard and left him in the cold, dewy grass until morning. Aleksandra realized that Germanas was destined for the worst fate. She went outside and placed herself in the shadow of the house, hoping to see at least a shade of helplessness in Germanas's face now. At that point she . . . yes, at that point she would have set him free and not given a damn for Lukšas or the hunchback or their anger. She would have made up some excuse. But Germanas's face was calm like the face of a sleeping child. Perhaps he heard her footsteps, perhaps her breathing, instead he opened his eyes and without looking at her said:

"I know that you're here, Aleksandra."

She was silent.

More than likely Germanas had lost consciousness, because when he opened his eyes again, the sun was shining down from a white sky, and the heat had made the grass wilt and bend toward the earth. Germanas lay in the same prone position in the middle of the yard. He didn't feel the ropes, but as soon as he moved, swarms of sharp scissors began to cut his numb skin: he was still tied up. His mouth was dry, his face was beaten and swollen. How much longer would he have to lie there like a pig before the slaughter? The flies, crazed by the heat, were crawling over the blood clotted on his face and trying to get into his mouth. Suddenly he became aware of a stench, and it seemed to him that it was the sun that smelled like the yellow eye of a dog decaying by the roadside. Longingly, Germanas thought about the cool, minty fragrance of moonlight.

"You're up?" Lukšas was standing at Germanas's head, knife in hand. "How did you sleep?"

"He thinks he can do anything he wants," said the hunchback, opening the wide barn door. "He thinks he can do anything that comes into his head."

"He won't think that anymore," Lukšas vowed. "I guarantee you, my dear fellow, you're going to have to pay for this. You can't even imagine how much."

He bent down to Germanas and put the knife to his throat. Lukšas's eyes looked kind, as if he had bent down in his garden to pick some green onions for his supper. Germanas shut his eyes: he knew Lukšas only too well. Yesterday, too, he had known what he was doing, only he didn't think he'd drink too much and everything would turn out this way. He felt the blade of the knife touching his throat, and it felt as if he passed out again. Or maybe not. He couldn't say. Everything got mixed up. As if in a haze he thought he saw the slaughter of lambs, their skin being flayed, the sweetly sour smell of blood, spots of dried-up blood, the color of rust, retaining that smell, the smell of blood, the smell of steaming hot intestines, then, or perhaps it was before, the smell of morning mist, someone's words "Wait, your turn will come," gentle, pretty lambs, the agony of the animals was right here by his face, blood spurting into his eyes, someone's laughter, the smell of urine, finally a black sun, or maybe it was a black moon.

Then Germanas clearly heard these words:

"Thank God, I got you away from them."

He was lying on the cool grass by the river's edge, dragonflies were quivering in the air. Zakaras was wiping his face with a wet scarf.

"How do you feel?" asked Zakaras.

Germanas didn't answer, he just nodded his head.

"You're a fine mess, I'd say," Zakaras was saying. "I expected as much, when you started coming over here. You're going to have to leave."

"Leave? What for?" Germanas asked, but he wasn't sincere. He had already decided to leave yesterday, on his way to Lukšas's. And even though he didn't tell anyone, it was obvious to everyone yesterday.

The next morning, when Germanas, carrying a small knapsack that Zakaras had given him, turned into the road and paused to say good-bye to Zakaras, he inquired:

"How . . . how did you find out I needed help?"

"Aleksandra came running to tell me . . ."

"I'll write you," said Germanas, he pressed Zakaras's hand and walked away.

For six years there was no news of Germanas. Only Zakaras knew where he was. Lukšas tried several times to find out from Zakaras, but to no avail. The day after Germanas's disappearance Lukšas and the hunchback along with two other men forced their way into Zakaras's house at dawn and demanded that he surrender Germanas to them. They went through everything, searched all the corners, but they found neither hide nor hair of Germanas.

"What do you need him for?" asked Zakaras.

"We want to talk to him," said Lukšas. "After all, he's almost my son-in-law. Where is he?"

"He's not here," is all Zakaras would say, and they had to leave empty-handed.

Aleksandra also came to ask for news, about as regularly as if she had come to get the mail. Zakaras told her, too, that he didn't know anything because he didn't trust her. He spoke to Aleksandra very rudely, but in time he noticed that this caused mute suffering to appear on her face. So Zakaras relented: the torment she felt was too similar to the suffering of dumb animals. But even though he spoke to her more gently, he didn't reveal Germanas's whereabouts. Zakaras never ceased to be amazed at Aleksandra's humble demeanor and at her hope of finding something out from him. He had no doubt that Aleksandra was to blame for Germanas's exile and miseries, so now it was beyond his comprehension why she was acting as if Germanas had left her and betrayed her. Either this was a ruse to try to get information for Lukšas out of him, or she really did love Germanas.

"He has another woman there," said Zakaras once, but Aleksandra paid no attention.

"Is he coming back?" she asked. "Zakaras, can I expect him to return some day?"

"I don't know," said Zakaras. "You can hope. There's nothing I can tell you."

Three years slowly passed, and Zakaras became so used to her that he let her move into his house. She wanted to be at his side constantly so that she could talk about Germanas at any time. She wasn't interested in anything else and answered his questions reluctantly. She helped him treat the animals and do the housework, but Zakaras didn't trust her completely because several times he had observed a man's silhouette slipping off her windowsill into the darkness. He didn't really think she could be spying in his house, but one never knew . . . Her sight began to fail. Sometimes she bumped into things that she should have seen. Zakaras asked her about this.

"Oh, if only Germanas would come back," was all she would say.

And at that point Zakaras realized that she had been blinded by love.

"The god of the blind must be able to see," thought Zakaras to himself, "that is, if they have their own god. Just like the god of the seeing is all-seeing, able to see even more than just regular people. For Aleksandra, Germanas is becoming a god because he can see. She's praying to him, that's what it is."

Zakaras felt sorry for Aleksandra, he tried to cure her, but he was not successful. He managed to do only one thing for her:

wherever he was in the house, he tried to make a lot of noise. He threw things on the floor, he hummed, he dragged his feet as he walked or rapped his cane against the posts as he passed by the fence. "Noise," thought Zakaras, "which we who can see find so irritating day in and day out, must be a joy for the blind. For them all kinds of noise, from the silent falling of leaves and the clatter of sewing machines to the whine of airplanes and the whistle of trains, has to substitute for the world of color which constantly hovers before our eyes. The tones and half-tones of color have their equivalents in the universe of sound, in the realm of taste, smell, and touch, which we, being preoccupied with visible things, usually never enter, perhaps we only remember them when we feel lonely and unhappy, when we yearn for childhood, when we lie in the dark, smoking or motionlessly listening to the beating of our hearts and the dripping of rain from the roof. A man shoveling snow and picking at the ice, the rain, a whining dog, a pigeon ascending into the air, a crying woman, a horse munching on grass, a wine glass shattering—these are all sound. They're infinite, all different kinds, loud and quiet, clear and muffled. We might even envy the blind," thought Zakaras.

Aleksandra was aware of his efforts and felt grateful. Once, at the end of four years, Zakaras happened to mention to her that he had received a letter from Germanas. And even though he didn't tell her what was in the letter, she felt very happy. From that day on even her character changed in some indefinable way, she took to singing quietly. She sang blue and yellow songs of love, red songs of heartbreak, white and gray hymns of sadness and yearning, or she played lively, green melodies on the harmonica that Germanas had left behind. She herself realized that in four years she had become totally different.

Having taken leave of Zakaras, Germanas still didn't know what direction he was going to set off in. At first he wanted to settle in the land where people spoke the Latvian language, cold as ice. But later he realized that there he'd be too close and it would be too easy to find him. So then he set off for the south, he rode trains and cars, he was serene and incommunicative, he wore clean clothes that he washed in some stream every few days, no one mistrusted him, but then he gave no cause for trust either. The weather kept getting hotter and people's skin got darker. Germanas's face, neck, and arms became the color of polished walnut, he looked less and less like a person from the autumnal land of inclement weather. He became quite emaciated and felt constant hunger and thirst. Even though his jawbones of steel tempered in vinegar got enough to eat, he never felt satiated. Hunger and thirst were to remain the signs marking this period of his life, even when the day came that he felt satisfied. But that day was still far in the future, while for now Germanas made it to those parts where the sun heats up people's blood, his gaze became insolent, but the women there didn't take offense, they were sensitive to a man's hunger and thirst and allowed themselves to be made love to, they themselves desired to love and they did love. But they weren't able to satisfy Germanas's hunger, even though they did slow down the pace of his travels. Germanas came to realize that his hunger and thirst came not from the gut but that the hunger came from the heart and the thirst from the eyes. Hunger and thirst for memory. Germanas wanted to stop somewhere, but he couldn't; he wanted to settle down in one place but he couldn't carry it off. Each of his days was the day of the prodigal son, and the skin of his face became yellow like the skin of the sons of Lao-tzu. He sailed across the sea in a large steamship, he traveled hundreds of kilometers of hot paved roads on foot, he climbed over rocky mountains, sailed across one more sea, rode across a frozen white desert that you couldn't look at without squinting, and then he realized that traveling made no sense. No matter how far he went, the time would never come when the sight of the house swaying in the breeze and the creaking of the cables would cease to be the only content of his refreshing dreams. In the country where he came to rest the women pronounced words one way and the men another way.

He didn't care what he worked at because he didn't know how to do any work. Evenings and nights he labored in railroad stations, loading and unloading cement, fruit, coal, meat, logs, and fertilizer from the boxcars. Then he learned how to take photographs, and it became apparent that his sight was failing, and he got himself some glasses and a camera and went off to the steppes, where people worked hard and where their work had made their customs crude. Germanas now made his living at photography, and he fought his way into the midst of these crude people with his camera and took their pictures without asking, even though he knew that they might not want him to do this, and he knew that sometimes they definitely didn't want him to. He worked ceaselessly, not caring about himself, and so was able to avoid a multitude of those free moments when one can be besieged by memories with no warning. He learned to savor work, came to love his craft, despite the fact that he often had to suffer on account of it. Once someone broke Germanas's glasses, and it was hard for him to take pictures. The tears rolled down his cheeks, but he kept on taking pictures, weeping as he had once in childhood, taking pictures in order to record the moments when he was forced to suffer so much wrong.

Finally, the people among whom Germanas was living came to understand that he wasn't like they were, was not quite like them, that he was living there of his own free will, and slowly they started to pay attention to him and some even began to respect him. In the Asian steppes Germanas lived with a woman with narrow, wolflike eyes and broad cheekbones. He stayed with her more than three years, almost up to the moment when he resolved to return home. His wolf-eyed woman became disappointed with him and left him, or maybe she died, because it's hard to believe that she would leave him of her own accord. Perhaps some relatives, which Asians have by the dozen, appeared and took her away from him. Who knows. Later Germanas forgot all about it.

He lived in that alien land with a woman who, like everyone else there, didn't understand his native language. Longing made him sing and talk to himself in his own language, which sounded strange under the hot sun; he swore in that language and carried on, and the woman looked at him in amazement; unable to comprehend the reason for his words and his passions, she just barely felt the intoxicating, exotic breath of far-away countries. Somewhere in his own country—Germanas knew this—he would have been an ordinary person, he wouldn't have been different in any way. But here he was special, incomprehensible and mysterious. The locals couldn't distinguish his eruptions of real passion and emotion from unreal ones, they thought everything was real, they considered him to be a man of powerful temperament, he got in the habit of making use of this, but later he started to believe in it himself, he became such a man, and later, when he returned to his native land, no one recognized him, he was different from the way he had been before, he wasn't like the people there, he was lonely and peculiar, mysterious, a stranger to all, a citizen of some cosmic state, a gypsy.

But in spite of it all he was still Germanas. The changes that had befallen him were superficial ones, they didn't touch his heart. As he caressed his gentle-skinned and narrow-eyed woman, as he fondled her soft breasts and narrow hips in the hot air of night, he was only trying to convince himself that he loved her, that he would spend the rest of his days beside her. He was still hungry and thirsty. The woman's hair held no fragrance for him, her skin had no taste, her eyes could not soothe him, her hands didn't know how to put him to sleep or how to arouse him. Wounded by memories, his senses sought to experience real blessing in vain, the attempt to convince himself that he was happy was a substitute for happiness. Germanas desired something else. But what? He didn't know. It was as if he wanted release for his soul and body, a deep sleep, after which he would wake up different and somewhere else. Or perhaps even . . . No, he really didn't know.

The woman guarded Germanas jealously from the rest of the world, even from himself. On rainy mornings, when some damp little birds were chirping and the air smelled of snails and Germanas was beset by melancholy, he wouldn't say anything and would just sit with his gaze fixed on the window, smoking ceaselessly and slowly sipping strong brown tea; at those moments she felt that he was breaking away from her, he wasn't thinking of his love for her, his thoughts were simply wandering in hazy countries and his gaze was caressing the eyes, hands, and faces of strange women. Then her irritation would grow, her face would take on a look of humiliation, and Germanas would see this, he would force himself with great effort to break out of his melancholy, he would talk to her and play with her, but all the time she was aware that in reality he was by the window, with his tea and his cigarettes, that his heart had remained in those unknown lands, and she would become angry. Days like that brought discord and quarrels to their house.

Then one day Germanas up and left because there was no bond between him and the steppes and their people. He didn't even take anything with him, it seems, just his documents and his camera. But that's not so, a few months later his baggage in brown boxes, their sides marked in chalk, caught up with him. He left without explaining anything to anyone. He had no one to explain to. At that time his woman was no longer with him. Perhaps she was no longer on earth, perhaps she had never been at all. At that point Germanas was no longer thinking of her. He was only concerned about his return. Before he left, he sent Zakaras a letter in which he told him to wait for him.

One morning a few weeks later when Germanas knocked at Zakaras's door, Aleksandra opened it.

"I've waited six years for you, Germanas," she said.

"Six years . . . ," he mumbled, cowering from the morning mist.

Germanas wanted to embrace her, but he couldn't make himself do it. Not yet.

Zakaras heated up the sauna.

"Both of you go," said Zakaras. "Take her with you, Germanas."

Germanas took Aleksandra by the hand without saying a word. Zakaras looked at them holding hands like children as they walked over the meadow in the distance.

Germanas and Aleksandra spent four hours in the sauna. They washed so long, so patiently, so carefully that it seemed they weren't just washing their bodies but something more, they were even washing off their past, which in any case always hides in our bodies. This cleansing was like a ritual; when they had finished it, they could come together totally clean, having put all the evil behind them, everything that up till now they hadn't thought of as evil but that would have turned into evil in the future, a future that they had tacitly agreed they had in common. This was a cleansing of engagement, a sauna of marital union. Zakaras knew it when he went to heat the sauna. He knew this would be, that this had to be.

Zakaras helped them find a house to buy near the source of the river, thirty kilometers from his house. They settled there, among the maples that had been planted throughout the whole yard at some peculiar whim of the former occupants. Aleksandra's vision started to improve, she saw almost as well as before, and sometimes she saw the kinds of things she had never seen before. On warm nights Germanas would set up his lab equipment in the yard and take pictures there by the light of a red lantern, listening to the warm and cosy rumbling of thunder in the distance. Aleksandra would help him. Were they happy? Yes. Germanas no longer suffered from hunger and thirst. Did they need all those experiences and misfortunes in order to finally become happy anyway? Who knows? Were they in love? Yes. It was the stage of love when, looking at his beloved, he saw only her and thought only about her. Then came the day when, looking at his beloved, he saw only far-off lands and the people of those lands, a strange, alien sun and horrible rainstorms that lasted for months and months, the rolling of alien seas and the flight of unknown clouds across the expanse of sky. And all this was equal to the beloved and was equal to love. This was true love. Love that can't be sullied by memories of the material world, that can't be displaced by the darkness of the past or of habit, when you no longer love a person but the world and you can't change this world for another, nor can you betray it, because it's the only one there is. Love like this is very rare, it is almost impossible to find, but the love of Germanas and Aleksandra was just this kind of love.

One morning Aleksandra put her wash in a basket and went down to the river, leaving Germanas asleep. She was almost finished rinsing the clothes when she heard muffled voices in the fog. She grabbed her basket and hurriedly started to climb the hill toward home. At the end of the path she was almost running. In the yard stood Lukšas and some strange man. The door to the house was open. The hunchback came out the door, and a knife flashed in his hand.

"He didn't even wake up," said the hunchback.

Only now did the three men notice Aleksandra, standing a few steps away from them. For a moment they froze. Lukšas was the first to come to.

"Let's go home, daughter," he said. "There's nothing left for you to do here."

"No, I'm staying here," she replied, keeping her eyes fixed on the hunchback.

The latter waddled up to her, smiling, bent down, and wiped his bloody knife on her apron. Aleksandra smiled back at him. Then she walked them to the road.

"I'm your father, Aleksandra," Lukšas said by way of good-bye. "Don't forget that."

Aleksandra waved at them and wished them a good journey. And only when they had receded into the distance, she felt her heart breaking and a hot stream of blood spurting from it, a stream of lust for revenge filling her breast with blazing plasma. Staring at the men walking away, who had just taken Germanas from her, she tried to burn their images into her soul and into her brain so later, even in blind darkness, she would be able to distinguish them from thousands like them, and take vengeance. She touched her apron, wet with Germanas's blood, and felt the warmth of his spirit and body soaking into her, she smelled his blood, so that this smell would not permit her to relent later and would force her to keep searching . . .

In the east the red bridge appeared out of the mist. A second later the surface of the river, shining like steel, floated forth, then the log house that seemed to be suspended in the air. The sun had passed into the Fire solstice according to the new calendar.

1982
Translated by Violeta Kelertas

Juozas Aputis

The Point of Sticking It Out

He had it all down pat: when the truck drives into the shadow of the long building, depending on the season, of course, he has to start honking; let the people in their rooms hear it before he gets there and let them hurry down the stairs dragging their pails and packages and boxes. You can't honk all the time, sometimes you have to let up a bit, so you don't strain the city's peace and quiet too much; besides, they've made it illegal to lean on the horn all the time. Then you have to turn left, very carefully because there are a lot of cars in front of you here, there could be an accident. And while you let them pass, it's interesting to observe the beautiful rounded church steeples and imagine how calm everything inside becomes, when the evening sun shines in and gently mellows the angels and women, old people, and children who fill the church to overflowing.

Finally it's your turn, but now you have to honk again. Then honk even louder once you get to the yard, give it all you've got because people have called and written with complaints about not being able to hear the signal. You must understand, there are all kinds of people and plenty of them in this world who are hard of hearing. After you stop, your hand automatically presses the button, the rear of the truck starts to rattle and rumble, and all kinds of garbage and people's most secret belongings make their way into the bowels of the truck. Smashed together by the metal paws, they lose their shape. You can get your newspaper out now just as automatically; you could conceivably get some reading in, too, until the people run out of their entryways. But they've allowed for the mandatory waiting period at this point, so Tadeušas reads an article about life and literature that he began in the other yard. What can you say—Tadeušas liked to read books and everything that was written about books. His acquaintances could vouch for that. He especially enjoyed reading as a child, when he sprained his ankle on a hill and it went untreated, leaving him permanently lame. Forcibly knocked away from the feeding-trough of the life that he was accustomed to, he began to search for a niche among humble books and newspapers. Here we ought to mention that Tadeušas's mother also very much enjoyed books and—we point this out merely for the sake of accuracy—strong men. Tadeušas was the product of one of the latter, but that's not all that important. Nearly every day Tadeušas's mother would poke her nose into his room and say:

"Tadzio, why don't you go out somewhere or visit a friend, I'm going to have a kind of discussion here . . ."

Tadzio knew or could guess what sort of discussion it would be. Once, just like Clever Little Johnny in that story, he had suggested that they, his mother, whose name was Fele, or Felicija, and the guy, that is, take a walk and have their discussion, but he backed down and did as he was told. When he came home a good while later, he found Fele lying down, reading a book. Fele's outlook on life was interesting. She always said, "First you have to live your life, and then check it against what's down in black and white . . ." And black and white in most cases meant books.

Now back to business because we haven't got much time: the garbage truck's conveyor has stopped, having squeezed the possessions of various people, quite different in character, fate, etc., into one lump. Now Tadeušas has to climb out of the cabin and go to the rear of the truck to do a little work with a rather special pitchfork but—in heaven's name—nobody's brought out any garbage! Tadeušas remembered that there had been a lot of people at lunchtime, so maybe now they didn't have any more garbage, and he could stick his head in his paper again. In any case, by God, it was fun to be an ordinary mortal who had sucked in a vocation for reading everything written by and about writers with his mother's milk. Look here, it says: "Our writers must live at the very vortex of life, in the very center of people who work and create. A working person doesn't need some high-fallutin' intellectual gibberish; he needs to read about everyday life and the meaning of his daily labor." That's it, by God! Let some writer spend some time in Tadeušas's shoes for a while, and in the meantime Tadeušas would do some reading; let him live in Tadeušas's basement apartment for a while, let him watch the naked legs of the broads go by, that's all you can see from the basement, maybe then he'd write more like a human being. But now they're rolling in money, everyone kowtows to them, and they're just fighting amongst themselves like dogs. They're actually fighting over a bone and not over something else . . . And it's not an ordinary bone they're fighting over, it's ivory . . . Tadeušas begins to laugh. He's not angry at the poor writers or anything—it's just kind of comforting to know that someone makes fun of these so-called VIPs, just like they do of him, Tadeušas. A feeling of sweet solidarity comes over Tadeušas, so sweet that if some writer happened to pass by, Tadeušas might even kiss him or whisper some sweet nothings in his ear.

Almost deliberately, the one writer from the big building hasn't shown up either, he hasn't produced any garbage and, just like everybody else, hasn't brought anything out. Why are they always pressuring him and needling him in the newspapers and in books, when he's already miserable enough as it is—Tadeušas isn't half bad himself, he could probably have been a writer, if someone had just taught him where to put the commas. On the other hand, some bright acquaintance of Tadeušas who worked in a publishing house or a library had once told him that writers don't know where to put commas either, that it's the editors who put them in. Tadeušas can see from his garbage that things aren't going too well for his writer!

Oh, well, let's forget the writer for the time being; instead, let's talk about that graduate student, Ag . . . Why bother with his name—he's a grad student, that's all. He lives in the same building, always so damn energetic and eager in his striped suit, black hair, rosy cheeks, the nape of his neck is somehow . . . well, how shall we put it . . . well, trimmed in a token kind of way . . . Now we're talking nonsense like some woman! What does his hair have to do with anything? He gets it cut, just like everyone else, like everyone else upper class, that is . . . Let's talk about what he puts in his garbage can! Not necessarily him, it might be his wife or mother-in-law. Of course, it was nothing special, several times some typewritten pages just happened to catch Tadeušas's eye, all there was was one quotation after another, just one decree after another . . . And so what of it? Well, nothing, after all, there are young people writing dissertations, some who know how to write and some who know what needs to be written. Tadeušas can guarantee that it's that grad student Ag . . .'s dissertation. And anyhow, all of the student's garbage—God only knows where he gets it, all kinds of papers, and boxes, and rags, never ours, that is, they're ours, but they're not made here, they've always traveled here from overseas. And as for the student's shoes (Tadeušas notices them when the student brings out the garbage himself, and when he's not wearing his slippers because he hasn't had time to take off his shoes), they're so pointy, well-shined and gleaming. Domestic ones don't shine like that, no matter how hard you polish them. If at this point we might be permitted to mention the writer again, the one who, as we have said, also lives in this building, we'd be doing him an injustice if we failed to point out that his shoes are shiny too, he's not too lazy to polish them, but they don't shine like the student's do; in the terminology of a certain kind of criticism we could say that the smell of sweat is perceptible in the shine. The shine is lacking in playfulness, refinement, there are no levels of consciousness in it . . . And as for the writer's garbage! Potato peelings, a round can that once contained mackerel, some boxes with labels from the local shoe stores. But they keep poking fun at the writer. Why, he's one of us, if anyone is. It's not polite to speculate about such matters, but he's definitely more one of us than the grad student . . .

You know grad students! They even talk differently. The young dissertator (they say he's found himself a pretty cushy job, too) approaches the garbage truck relaxed somehow, energetic, the way one should approach a garbage truck; he looks ahead and waves to his young offspring staring out the window (recently some acquaintance or other brought the offspring a colorful little outfit all the way from Japan, and ever since then the grandmother has been taking the offspring outside a million times a day), then he greets Tadeušas very cheerfully, almost slapping him on the back:

"Hi! How's it going?"

"Not bad," Tadeušas used to say, "not bad. Same old story. There's plenty of garbage."

"What do you mean, not bad? That can't be right!" the student would object strenuously. "Why be so modest? Every day brings something new, every single day, my friend. Only we're not capable of noticing it. We rush around at such crazy speeds . . ."

"God knows . . . ," Tadeušas would mumble.

Life must be fun for the student! Tadeušas would just nod his head—how can you get into a heavy discussion at the back of the far-from-fragrant truck, but the student's words would still lift his spirits, or however you'd put it . . . Tadeušas had already read in books, in serious books, that is, that if you want to succeed at something, you have to use willpower. Or there was another way: to submit to someone else's will. But that's not much of a way out; that's not success, that's failure! And what kind of willpower does Tadeušas's writer have? All he can do is plod along, mumble good evening— mumble, mumble—you can hardly hear him, he seems to scrape his bits of garbage timidly somehow, all hunched over, sour-looking, wrinkled brow, God only knows what he's thinking about, then he drags himself back with downcast eyes, the seat of his pants patched up—sure, patches on the seat of your pants are now in style, especially for artistic types, but Tadeušas knows that in this case it's like in the old Italian movie—it's funnier than we think . . . The writer has just taken advantage of the prevailing fashion . . . Every cloud has a silver lining.

Hey! Tadeušas has been perched in the cab for seven minutes and no one's brought out even a scrap of garbage. There wasn't a soul at the other building, which was pretty big, too. They've all gone crazy! Tadeušas began to laugh, and at this point, gradually, modestly and restrainedly, we too can begin to laugh, because it really is funnier than our bookworm Tadeušas thinks. Engrossed in his article, Tadeušas did not find a single person at the second building, nor did he encounter anyone at the third. He didn't get a scrap of garbage at any of the buildings. He drove his truck to the dump very quickly, he was still enjoying himself, there was still a flicker of hope: his work would be easier if there were a significant decrease in the amount of garbage. It would make life easier, and he wouldn't have to let management know.

In the evening, when he returned to the basement apartment in which he lived alone—could it be that the books were to blame for this too? They've been known to ruin many a person's life—Tadeušas washed up, had a bite to eat, and fell into bed, then into the wee hours of the morning he read a book about a mad Japanese teacher, a bug collector, who lived for the longest time with some woman in a sandpit. Of all the . . . why a sandpit? Next thing you know someone will come up with a book about life in a garbage pit or on a trash heap!

Next morning it was back to work and it was the same thing all over again—those jerks in the apartment buildings did not bring out one scrap of garbage. When most of the truck drivers had come back to the garage, Tadeušas went around from one to the other, casually asking:

"So what's up?"

"What?"

"How'd it go?"

"You idiot, how else could it go? Has there ever been a shortage of that crap? The good things in life you have to search for, but that smelly stuff . . ."

"Yup, that's what I say . . . ," Tadeušas managed to stammer timidly, a little worm with its horrible teeth had started gnawing in the vicinity of his gut.

Tadeušas held out for a week, and that was only because he was a man of philosophical inclinations. On Monday, no sooner had he stopped the truck than he was already running up the stairs and ringing doorbells. It was strange, something so unheard of had happened, but no one got excited about it. When he rang a doorbell and was waiting for the door to open, he'd break into a sweat, expecting some sort of unusual, out-of-the-ordinary explanation; instead, clean-shaven men or fragrant, perfumed women would very calmly explain to him:

"Why are you making such a fuss? There just isn't any garbage, you know. And we're all doing our best . . . it's a unanimous effort to make less and less trash . . . Believe me, there has been less and less lately. We've begun to live more cleanly. As soon as we get some, then by all means, we'll . . . Don't lose heart, be patient, it'll turn up."

Now if we don't want Tadeušas to leave us, or at least not to abandon the garbage truck, let's think about what we, as modern producers of garbage, would do if we were in his shoes and wanted to keep some sense of balance in our lives. Would we litter enough for everybody else to maintain a proper equilibrium? But seriously, that would be impossible! Just try to litter enough for thousands of people! Try to come up with an artificial method for filling a naturally occurring gap! Perhaps, perhaps . . . Tadeušas's brain was no different from ours. Now he didn't drive into the city first thing in the morning, he drove beyond the city limits, to the dump, when none of his co-workers were there. The guard at the garage had already begun to curse Tadeušas for waking him so early every morning. One time he couldn't stand it any more and burst out: "You must have a good job on the side, Tadeušas . . . Just remember that without my permission you wouldn't be able to come and go here as you please!"

Tadeušas would back the rear of his truck into a convenient spot and scoop up all of life's complicated and intricate garbage with the transporter claws. He began to do everything backward. He would creep into the courtyards at dusk without honking the horn and carry bundles of garbage to the stairwells, and in the afternoon, whistling over the roar of the truck, he would push and shove the trash into the bowels of the truck with his pitchfork, swearing a little unnaturally from time to time:

"That's people for you! They dump everything in the doorways and then you're supposed to break your back picking it up! . . ."

He had no reason to grumble: he'd come up with a good solution, but he couldn't look into the future—in a week this respite too came to an end, one fine afternoon Tadeušas couldn't find any garbage! Not in any of the stairwells. You could go crazy trying to figure it out and still not be able to understand what happened, where the garbage went, but there just wasn't any. And there wasn't any peace of mind for Tadeušas, either. After he'd brought the trash in before dawn and parked the truck on some side street, he had to stand guard to see who dared to drag the garbage off somewhere. While he stood guard no one touched the garbage, but all he had to do was get back in his garbage truck and rub his eyes, red from insomnia, sleepily; as soon as, exhausted, he'd try to get a half hour's worth of shut eye, he'd go back and there wasn't a whiff of garbage to be found . . .

What the hell! Tadeušas isn't the only one who's curious about this and unnerved by it—we are, too. Where could the garbage be going? What should be done next? Drive around in an empty truck or stop doing a meaningless job altogether? Tadeušas drove around empty, waiting for things to get better, and in the evening and at night he'd bury himself in books even deeper, but the letters that were squeezed onto the pages yielded no answer. Where was the solution then, assuming all this was just an ordinary mystery and not something supernatural?

Tadeušas had one last card up his sleeve: one evening he rang the student's doorbell. He was in luck, for the student answered the door himself. He was very clean, the hall was gleaming, too.

"I've seen you somewhere before," the student said mechanically.

"Seen me! . . . Act normal and tell me what's happened, you're educated and you're up there at the controls, so to speak, I can't take it anymore . . . ," Tadeušas cried.

"What's wrong? We'll help you, please tell us . . . If there's anything we can do for you . . . I mean, we'll help. It's our duty . . . To us a human being is . . ."

"If there's anything you can do! . . . There's no more garbage!" Tadeušas was practically shouting. "I don't get any more garbage."

The student opened his eyes wide.

"Oh, it's you . . . I remember . . . So what of it? That's completely normal. And I'll tell you one more thing, there are times when it's downright necessary. The garbage has to decrease. Every day, every hour. How come you don't understand that?"

It's easy for him to say what has to happen, but how is Tadeušas supposed to survive when it's like this? When all of this has already happened?

The writer also met Tadeušas with open arms and the patch on his behind looked even newer and cleaner.

"There is no garbage, my dear writer!" Tadeušas burst out, without pausing to say hello.

"Hm," the writer replied. "There really isn't any garbage? Hm . . . It's got to be some kind of magic . . . What else would you call it. You see, if it's gone that far, then . . . If it's really disappearing, then, certainly we'll have to go into this matter more deeply, see the entire internal cross section, so to speak."

"There isn't any, I'm telling you, none! They're all rotting away in their cages and they don't understand anything at all . . . They can't even litter like regular human beings . . ."

Having received no answer, Tadeušas tried to dig still deeper into his books, but he couldn't take anything else in. One morning he rushed to the garage with his head wrapped in two wet towels. Of course, the dispatcher didn't let him go out on the job. Instead, he drove him to a pine forest outside the city, to a white house, and there they untied the towels and bound Tadeušas's arms and legs to a bed. We shouldn't be surprised, we would have done the same because, as soon as Tadeušas saw a full garbage can in the corridor, he fell on his knees, embraced it, shoved his head deep inside, and began to talk gleefully to the garbage.

Things are looking up for Tadeušas: he gets to read books again, he breezes right through the literary paper, too; he'll probably make a rapid and complete recovery, as he laughs quite normally when he reads about writers taking a beating, because he can enjoy life again seeing that fate punishes everyone equally.

We hope to God that in the end Tadeušas will get well; we've been sick ourselves and more than once (what's wrong with getting sick like any human being?), more than once we've tried to see, if not life itself, then at least its pale image, so let's try to answer two questions: (1) why did the garbage disappear so mysteriously; (2) what should Tadeušas have done to prevent such an unpleasant fate?

Undoubtedly, there could be any number of different answers, no one wants to force an opinion on anyone here, but why give up without trying to come up with a hypothesis? We were given two questions, and for our final conclusion we offer three assumptions, which may be of some help: (1) don't confuse literature with life; (2) once people get it into their heads to clean up, they will clean up; (3) once people have decided to clean up, at some point they'll decide to litter again.

So then, if you go and visit Tadeušas and want to say something nice to him, tell him: patience, more patience, and still more patience.

But, whatever you do, don't forget to stress that point of sticking it out.

1985

Translated by Rita Dapkus, Gregory M. Grazevich, and Violeta Kelertas

About the Authors

JUOZAS APUTIS (B. 1936)

Although he is an exponent of traditional Lithuanian village prose, Juozas Aputis moves away from naturalistic descriptions of daily life, thus avoiding the twin scourges of contemporary Soviet Lithuanian prose fiction—unimaginatively recursive realism and socialist realism, which lacks innovation by definition and design. Aputis writes of village life not only because that is what he is most familiar with but also from a sense that the wrongs he sees in the society created by the imposition of uniform Sovietization arise from an alienation from the old way of life, the loss of communal values, and severance from the soil. Aputis often verges on being a moralist; however, he has succeeded in relieving the poignancy and gloom of his subject by being especially inventive in his technique, experimenting with magical realism, humor, and elements of the surreal.

Aputis is a modern master of the short story. Like many of his predecessors in the early Lithuanian tradition he appears to pay less and less attention to narrative structure and lets the thread of his thought spin out its natural, meandering course, especially in his novellas. Thus, one of his major works, "The Autumn Grass," allows the insights and searchings of one of the main characters to dictate the transitions between loosely connected events and images. The reader is forced to follow the character's inner journey to make sense of the narrative.

Aputis is one of the most influential writers in Lithuania today, widely emulated by younger writers both for his attempts to renew the realist tradition, which had exhausted itself, and for his resistance to following the established canons of socialist realist writing. He earned the respect of his readers by consistently speaking of truth and goodness and of the individual's relationship to these values at a time when it was inconvenient and even dangerous to do so.

The critical success of his second short story collection, *Wild Boars Run on the Horizon* (1970), prompted an article in the American journal *Books Abroad*. This journal, now known as *World Literature Today*, regularly reviews

Baltic literature and is an excellent source for following the literary scene in Lithuania. During the pre-Gorbachev era, however, favorable attention in the American press (and even in the émigré press) made writers suspect to the regime. This raised their status among the covert dissident intellectuals, but often it could delay publication of their work for five years or more. Aputis's case typical. He was shunned by the state-run publishing house Vaga—a monopoly enterprise, of course—and his next collection, *Return over Evening-Darkened Fields*, did not appear until 1977. The author was able to make a living with his translations of Russian literature and waited out his period of official disfavor without compromising his work. Since the reforms in the Baltics in 1989 he has published two novellas: "The Organ's Voice in the Laundry" deals with the postwar years of guerrilla resistance from one of his favorite vantage points, that of a child, and epitomizes the terror and violence of the period; "An Ant Hill in Prussia" is his contribution "from the drawer"—that is, literature that could not be published during the Brezhnev era and had to wait for less oppressive times. Currently, he edits the major Lithuanian literary journal, *The Year* (Metai).

Birutė Baltrušaitytė (b. 1940)

The poet and prose writer Birutė Baltrušaitytė is the only female author in this anthology, which is indicative of the current sorry state of women's fiction writing in Lithuania (poetry by women is more abundant and of high quality). The hardships that Soviet life presents for women are usually cited as reasons for their lack of output in longer, more demanding literary forms. In Lithuania eighty percent of women are employed outside the home, most of the burden of housekeeping and standing in endless queues to shop falls to women, there are few household appliances, and there is no "room of one's own" in the small apartments. Although there have been some female proponents of the shorter forms of fiction, the first postwar novels by women began to appear only in 1980. On the whole, women have been thematically and technically less daring than their male counterparts.

Baltrušaitytė can be considered a regional writer. Although she has lived in the capital since her student days and teaches Russian literature at Vilnius University, she writes almost exclusively about the southwest corner of Lithuania, a bilingual territory close to what was formerly the German border. Her native region, with its mélange of people, languages, and traditions, has captured the author's imagination. Real figures from long ago appear in her works, and she often uses accurate historical backgrounds and information, splicing these into her texts. In one of her latest works, the author re-creates Morta Zauniūtė, a book-smuggler from the period when the tsar had banned Lithuanian books, using Zauniūtė's letters to her fiancé in the United States as creative inspiration.

Ričardas Gavelis (b. 1950)

Ričardas Gavelis is typical of the younger generation of Lithuanian prose writers in that he did not come from a rural background and did not study Lithuanian literature (this was the standard background for writers until recently). Instead, he studied physics and before becoming a full-time writer worked at the Physics Institute of the Academy of Science.

Early in his career as a writer Gavelis turned to forms of alternate realities, distinguishing himself in his long tale "Maybe" (Galbūt, 1982), in which he treats life as something other than a reflection of reality (the socialist realist cliché), demonstrating his firm convictions that reality itself is nothing but words and literature nothing but intertextuality, allusion, and play (in the images constructed by the narrator reality is neither "mirror" nor "ornament" but "kaleidoscope"). The two novellas included in this anthology, "Handless" and "Report on Ghosts," are *glasnost*-era works from his collection *The Punished* (Nubaustieji, 1987) and were perhaps the first to treat Stalinist themes in Soviet Lithuanian literature fairly overtly. Since then Gavelis administered shock therapy to conservative Lithuanian readers with his powerful postmodernist novel *The Vilnius Poker Game* (Vilniaus pokeris, 1989), which minces no words in castigating servile *Homo lituanicus* as an even more lowly form of the already degenerate *Homo sovieticus*. He reveals Vilnius under the Soviets to be a cesspool of paranoia and evil, naming the solitary remaining tower of its castle as "the short, blunt and helpless phallus" of this city of emasculated people; contrary to much Lithuanian writing, however, the author raises his insights about modern life to a universal level by making them a comment on the human condition. Whether we know it or not, we are ruled by "Them"—a multivalent symbol not only of the KGB or Stalinists but of the evil forces that control the world in general. In this respect we are all "Their" victims; anyone who tries to rip off "Their" masks is killed or transformed into lower level creatures; for example, the penultimate chapter of the story, "Vox canina," is narrated by one of the characters who tried to expose "Their" system and was turned into a dog. This novel is certainly the most arresting avant-garde work to have come out of Lithuania to date, and Gavelis is an author to watch.

ROMUALDAS GRANAUSKAS (B. 1939)

One of the authors following in the footsteps of Juozas Aputis, but marching to his own beat, is Romualdas Granauskas. He, too, is motivated by moral concerns and regret at the loss of the traditional rural life-style and values; from his earliest collections of stories, however, the author has been an innovator in form and style. He first attracted attention with his tale "The Offering of the Bull" (Jaučio aukojimas, 1975), which spans sixty-four pages and contains only three periods. The rarely used second-person narrative voice expresses the flow of consciousness, perceptions, and inner soliloquies of a pagan priest. After this tour de force, which was interpreted as being a veiled reference to the Russification policies of the Soviets, the author was silent for a decade.

Since then, Granauskas has continued to dazzle with his ever-deeper penetration into layers of consciousness and phenomenological perceptions. Every book has been an extension of his interests in a character's unique sensibility and a new experiment with form. In 1986, just as *glasnost* was beginning to be felt in literature, Granauskas brought up the havoc that collectivization of the farms has wreaked on the Lithuanian family in his controversial tale "Homestead under the Maple" ("Gyvenimas po klevu," published in book form in 1987). The story was received as direct criticism of the collective farm system and prompted a heated journalistic debate, attacks and recriminations, charges and cover-ups, in which writers, journalists, collective farm workers, and their bosses took part. In the atmosphere of liberalization the book was reissued in a huge edition of 90,000 copies in the Popular Library series.

Granauskas has also been writing scripts for the Lithuanian Film Studio, and this activity has influenced his literary work as well. The result has been a highly unusual novella, "A White Wreath for the Black Locomotive" (Baltas vainikas juodam garvežiui, 1987), which is an inquiry into how art influences reality and our perceptions of it. Notions of social progress, the relationship between individual paranoia and violence, the mythification of war—taboo subjects in an earlier Soviet context—are also questioned in the tale. Granauskas subverts many a literary and social cliché and chooses to renew various facets of prose writing that have become deautomatized and lost their force during the development of the genre. He may be perceived as complementing Aputis, rather than competing with him. Together, these writers have made modernist Lithuanian prose viable again.

EUGENIJUS IGNATAVIČIUS (B. 1935)

Eugenijus Ignatavičius originally intended to become an actor. Instead, he writes short stories, plays, and film scenarios while working as a theater and drama consultant. Although he, too, is concerned with the moral questions implicit in his society, his vision of life is calmer and less tragic than the dramatic collisions Juozas Aputis presents in his fiction. There is less rebelliousness and more tranquil resignation in Ignatavičius's work, perhaps because he was exiled to Siberia as a teenager and came to realize the value inherent in life itself. Notes of environmental concern resound in some of his stories. In others he experiments with writing from the point of view of birds and animals. *Glasnost* made him retrieve an earlier story from his "drawer"— "River to the North" (in *Chrizantemų autobuse*, 1988) describes the exile of a woman and her two young boys to Siberia and her desperate attempt to free them after seven years in the taiga. She stows them aboard a fishing vessel, hiding them in an empty herring barrel, and bravely takes the consequences of her action. She herself is then sent further north to the mines and certain death. Stylistically, Ignatavičius is one of the most complicated writers. He draws from a fund of rare words for the vocabulary of his stories and likes to use acoustical realism in his writing, exploiting the nuances of dialect and register. He thus harks back to the early tradition of Lithuanian prose fiction, before the written language was standardized, when writers wrote the way they spoke. The oral is always just under the surface of literary Lithuanian. "On the Chrysanthemum Bus" may be indicative of a new direction in Ignatavičius's work—away from the classical Lithuanian tradition and the rural, toward what I have been calling an "international style," Western influences, and the urban.

RAMŪNAS KLIMAS (B. 1945)

A graduate of the Kaunas Polytechnical Institute, Ramūnas Klimas comes from a scientific background and initially worked in a compressor factory in Panevėžys. He quickly turned to editorial work, however. He became a Communist Party member (the only author in this anthology to do so) in 1976. Ironically, this was to have a beneficial effect on his career as a writer and probably explains why he was allowed to be one of the first writers to treat the subject of the guerrilla war honestly, from the Lithuanian (and it must be added, the historically accurate) point of view, even if it was in an extremely coded and indirect way. Loyal Party membership conferred certain privileges, and this was one of them. It is doubtful that a non-Party member could have written "Gintė and Her Man" and had it published in 1981 (1979 in a literary journal). The novella may have passed censorship for other reasons as well. Local writers and critics like to say that perhaps the censor was sleeping and did not notice the implications of a certain work; at other times they make derogatory comments about the intelligence of the censor and say that the material was too deep for him. In the Soviet Union one rarely finds out for sure why some things are allowed and others are not; in the non-Russian republics, however, there were always ethnic reasons for allowing more freedom than in Moscow or Leningrad, and those reasons may well bear on the publication of the present tale. Literature was often used to let off some of the steam of the restless ethnic "nationalists," as they were perceived by the Soviet officials. Allowing a story like "Gintė and Her Man" to appear in Vilnius defused some of the hostility to the regime among the intelligentsia, and yet the story was obscure enough so that the general reader might miss some of its salient points. After all, it seemed to be about a disaffected history teacher and a naive, struggling writer who couldn't get a handle on his story. Not explosive stuff—not on the surface, anyway, and that was the level at which the censor read. As long as there was a logical explanation for the events (and Klimas had wisely included the first version of his draft that the censor was sure to like), then there was nothing to worry about. And so one of the more complex and significant prose works in postwar Lithuanian literature appeared.

Until the collection *Gintė and Her Man* Klimas had not distinguished himself much beyond some apt social criticism. This collection, however, established him as one of the contenders in the avant-garde movement. Some of his other stories used humor and irony (always in short supply in Lithuanian literature of all periods) and showed him to be a force to be reckoned with on the literary scene. His main subjects were corruption, the consumerism and middle-class values of the urban dwellers, and the shallowness and nihilism of the younger generation. The novella "Impromptu for a Stolen Guitar" (Ekspromptas vogtai gitarai) seemed to be aimed at the young people and was written with a heavy dose of slang and realistic first-person narrative and dialogue.

Recently, Klimas has written a historical novel, *Only the Fire Will Heal* (Tiktai ugnis išgydys, 1989); its reception has been rather lukewarm. Lithuanian writers are still struggling to develop a credible novel. In prose fiction the short story and novella are of high quality; the novel form, with a few exceptions, still eludes them. This may be due to the late development of urbanization (only since the 1960s) in Lithuania. The novel has always needed, and in fact arose in response to, a richly textured social life, which Vilnius and Kaunas are only now beginning to experience.

SAULIUS TOMAS KONDROTAS (B. 1953)

Saulius Tomas Kondrotas received attention from the critical establishment with the appearance of his first short stories and especially with his first novel, *The Serpent's Gaze* (Žalčio žvilgsnis, 1981), which treats the problem of evil. Kondrotas graduated in psychology and philosophy, taught Marxism-Leninism at the Art Institute in Vilnius, and at his debut was hailed as a much-needed philosophical writer. His style borders on the Baroque, his pace is relentlessly slow, and his allegories have mythical dimensions. Influences for his writing are to be sought in South American fiction, though perhaps Dostoyevski looms in the background as well. A close reading of his work also shows him to be reacting to Ramūnas Klimas's work, at times even carrying on a friendly dialogue with it. In 1986 he published a substantial second novel, *And the Faces of Those Glancing through the Window Will Darken* (Ir apsiniauks žvelgiantys pro langą). It can be read as a veiled allegory of the period of stagnation in Soviet life and how it developed. Hidden among the novel's complex layers of meaning is the myth of Cain and Abel. The novel appeared just as *glasnost* was getting under way in Lithuania, and a few months after the book's appearance Kondrotas went on his first trip to the West. He defected to West Germany on this trip and at this point in the age of *glasnost* was still soundly berated in the local papers for his decision and expelled from the Writers' Union. Thus, his last novel has never really had its political allusions deciphered, although today, even critics in Lithuania would be free to do so. Kondrotas has since declared that he had planned his defection for at least a decade and feels himself a citizen of the world, free to reside where he likes. So far he has lived in Los Angeles and Munich. In his interviews he has stated that he plans to start writing in English within seven years of his arrival in the West. So far, no new work has appeared by this talented writer, but then, the seven years are not yet up. Meanwhile, the author's first novel, *The Serpent's Gaze*, has been published in German and French.

SAULIUS ŠALTENIS (B. 1945)

One of the first writers to turn to irony, humor, and the grotesque, Saulius Šaltenis has had a successful career as a prose writer, dramatist, film writer, and musical comedy librettist. His plays and musicals especially have been enormously popular and have had runs stretching into years. Šaltenis has a talent for portraying the life of teenagers and young people and frequently draws on his childhood experiences of growing up in the Stalinist 1950s. He deftly avoids sentimentality, opting for grotesque juxtaposition or the fantastic perspective of the child. "The Ever-Green Maple" illustrates these tendencies. In the story the young female narrator speaks in her own voice; nevertheless, as Mikhail Bakhtin would have it, her monologue is dialogic—one can hear echoes of her parents' speech in it, their reactions to the lie propagated by the Soviets, which the child has internalized as her own speech. On the other hand, she perceives the duality in their thinking, and in her own way she critiques it, exposing the falsity at the center of their position. Thus, in Šaltenis's work the truth is always presented from a skewed, ironic perspective, imitating the mental contortions that the people had to perform to retain their dignity in this period. What we hear in her voice is the conflict between propaganda and truth. Using the vehicles of humor, fantasy, and hyperbole, Šaltenis was able to portray this conflict—no mean accomplishment against the background of what was current in the literature of the time.

Rimantas Šavelis (b. 1942)

Another writer who has yielded to the call of the world of film, Rimantas Šavelis has written short stories and a novel, as well as scenarios for television and film. Country life of the northeastern corner of Lithuania predominates in Šavelis's prose, especially in his novel *Lamb of God* (Dievo avinėlis, 1974) and the novella that makes up the major part of his latest book, *Eternal Light* (Amžinoji šviesa, 1987). The author's main preoccupation is the feelings of a young man who leaves his village and heads for the city. Taking his cue from an earlier generation, the hero feels that he has betrayed his roots. As a result, he poeticizes the native home. Even though Šavelis's prose has an epic texture, it is always filtered through lyrical expression. When the author writes of city people, his favorite ploy is to place them in a situation in which they return to the village and experience a spiritual shock. At the same time, if they are left in the city, they do not feel comfortable there. There is thus a distrust of the urban environment, yet the city people and their native surroundings have changed so much that reintegration is no longer possible.

Although Šavelis uses many poetic devices, his style can also have a rough edge to it, matching the colorful everyday speech of his coarse country cousin characters. "In the Autumn Rain," which is included in the present anthology, is characteristic of the author's attempts at fantasy and play in a lighter vein. This type of fiction, though rather rare in his general oeuvre, adds poignancy and humor to his writing while still retaining the serious, meaningful subtext.

Violeta Kelertas,

the editor of this collection, is an associate professor of Slavic and Baltic languages and literature at the University of Illinois–Chicago. Prof. Kelertas, who received her Ph.D. from the University of Wisconsin–Madison, has published numerous articles and reviews on Lithuanian literature.